Chinese Provincial Cooking

Chinese Provincial
Cooking

Kenneth Lo

Elm Tree Books
London

PLACE NAMES

At the beginning of 1979 the Chinese News Agency announced a new system for the spelling of Chinese place names and proper names in order to allow English-speaking readers to get closer to the actual pronunciation of Chinese. In this book readers will find that place names are given the more familiar old-style spelling

First published in Great Britain 1979
by Elm Tree Books/Hamish Hamilton Limited
Garden House, 57/59 Long Acre, London WC2E 9JZ

Copyright © 1979 by Kenneth Lo

British Library Cataloguing in Publication Data
Lo, Kenneth
Chinese provincial cookery.
1. Cookery, Chinese
I. Title
641.5'951   TX724.5.C5
ISBN 0-241-89764-5

Printed in Great Britain by
Bristol Typesetting Co. Ltd
Barton Manor, St Philips, Bristol

Contents

Introduction

To write about Chinese cooking—especially Chinese provincial cooking—is to write about China herself. The writer has to conjure up all the sights, sounds, fragrances and flavours of everyday meals, festival celebrations, family dinners which vary with the seasons and with all the different provinces and regions spread over this massive country. As the mind's eye sweeps across the Chinese landscape, it is constantly diverted by the memory of individual events, people and places. To remember the seasons—the piercing north wind in winter, the soft drizzly spring rain, the scorching summer, and brilliant windless sunshine in autumn—is to recall particular meals and dishes associated with them. Each place has its own evocative and inimitable flavours, from the food on display in shops and market stalls or served in government offices, schools, suburban eating-places, in sampans plied by boatmen and hovels frequented by rickshaw pullers and haulage labourers, to the dishes served in provincial inns, bath-houses and tea-houses, Buddhist monasteries or run-down country temples. Then there are the more refined and sophisticated specialities of the riverside restaurants frequented by the well-to-do of the neighbourhood and the famous delicacies of the *haute-cuisine* eating-houses in the big cities—the duck restaurants and crab restaurants in Peking; the Mongolian barbecue or hotpot restaurants in the famous East Market; the Szechuan and Cantonese eating places beside the busy thoroughfares of Shanghai; or the lacquered ducks cooked in wine-sediment paste by the Hung San Bridge beside the Min River. One remembers the houseboats specializing in shrimps on the West Lake, the frugal vegetarian meals of the temples in the Western Hills, or the much more elaborate vegetarian banquets served in the great monasteries built thousands of feet up on the Drum Mountain of Koo San . . .

One could hardly forget the first impact of the hot spiciness of indigenous west China dishes in wartime Chungking, and the meagre dishes served in Kunming in the far West when the uprooted South

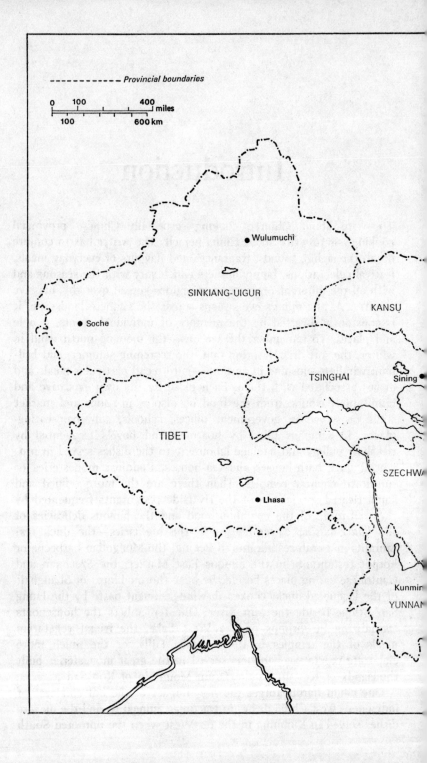

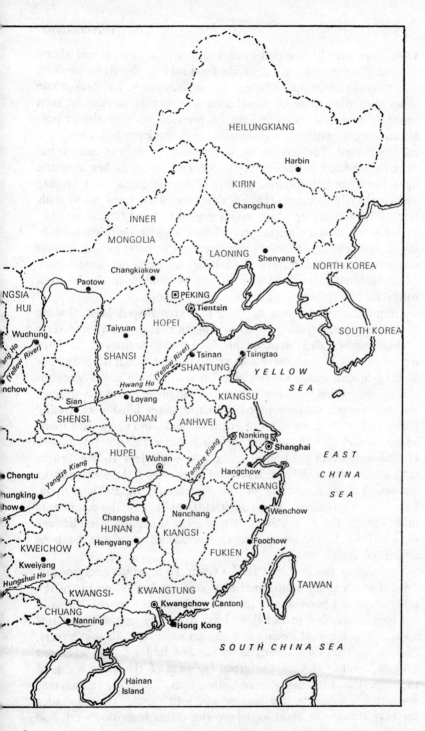

HEILUNGKIANG

Harbin

KIRIN

Changchun

INNER
MONGOLIA

LAONING

Shenyang

NORTH KOREA

Changkiakow

NGSIA

Paotow

HUI

PEKING

Tientsin

Wuchung

SOUTH KOREA

HOPEI

Taiyuan

nchow

Hwang Ho
(Yellow River)

SHANSI

Tsinan

Tsingtao

SHANTUNG

YELLOW

Sian

Loyang

SEA

Hwang Ho
(Yellow River)

KIANGSU

SHENSI

HONAN

ANHWEI

HUPEI

Nanking

Shanghai

EAST

Wuhan

Yangtze Kiang

CHINA

Chengtu

Yangtze Kiang

Hangchow

SEA

hungking

CHEKIANG

how

Changsha

Nanchang

Wenchow

HUNAN

KIANGSI

KWEICHOW

Hengyang

Foochow

Kweiyang

FUKIEN

Hungshui Ho

KWANGSI-

KWANGTUNG

TAIWAN

CHUANG

Nanning

Kwangchow (Canton)

Hong Kong

SOUTH CHINA SEA

Hainan
Island

A*

West University first settled in that city of high altitude and idyllic climate. No Chinese can forget the food sold by the street-vendors, who carried their mobile kitchens on shoulder yokes, and cooked one a hot dish of wontun or noodles on the spot in winter. As such instantly cooked dishes can have no pretensions, they always possessed certain qualities—absolutely fresh cooking and basic, unvarying flavour. The vendors along the coast sometimes cooked and served deep-fried oysters in batter, or soya meats in hot aromatic buns (an unforgettable combination of aromatic crust and savoury succulence). In summer the wayside was often lined with stalls stacked with gleaming white freshly peeled water-chestnuts, or half-peeled sugar canes, chopped to half-foot lengths, so thirst-quenching in the heat and excellent exercise for the jaws. In the autumn the vendors carried forests of 'kebabs' of many-flavoured olives, which children sucked and chewed just as children in the Western world these days chew gum and suck lollipops.

I remember the strings of firm, flat, coin-shaped buns (Kwang Bin) which people used to string together and throw over their shoulders when they went on picnics or long journeys. The buns were eaten with 'soya meat and gallatine' or chicken drumsticks—making incomparable sandwiches. Up north these cakes were replaced by steamed buns (for soaking up the juices in savoury dishes), and hot sesame-seed-encrusted aromatic cakes filled with freshly barbecued or stir-fried slices or strips of lamb, and eaten with leeks. There seemed to be a constant reek of garlic in this area! We often ate those buns in mud-hovel cafés (the equivalent to the British caff) as we dodged the warlords' gendarmes during the great student demonstrations, precursors of the Revolution, in 1930s' Peking. Otherwise we repaired to the safer surroundings of the restaurants in or around the East Market. The market was always resplendent with well-lit confectionery shops, stocked with Chinese bonbons and glacé fruits.

I remember my first visit to the Great Wall, which once roughly divided north China from Inner Mongolia. As I stood on top of the wall, what arid barrenness I saw stretching to the north! No wonder people who flew in to Peking from Russia, along the Ulan Bator route, often felt that Peking was like an oasis. But, to southerners, Peking, with its dust-storms in spring and late autumn, was itself a desert compared with the green lushness of the areas south of the river (the rich abundance of Chiang Nan, 'South of the Yangtze', was often extolled by the ancient poets to express their nostalgia for easy living). At Nankuo, where the trains from the south had to be pulled up on to the first stage of the Mongolian Plateau by two belching locomotives in double harness, the hotel rooms and floors were always covered with a thin layer of dust—dryness is a characteristic of the region. No doubt the same applies to Yenan, hundreds of miles inland to the west. All along this belt, the prevailing smells and tastes are of mutton, onion, garlic and leek. Still further west is Sinkiang; vast, open, horse and sheep country. Life is hard here, and there is little in its cuisine to recommend to the outsider. What *is* outstanding in the area is the Urumchi water-melon, a product of the oasis, which nowadays is widely available throughout China.

South of Sinkiang is Tibet, a region nearly as big as Sinkiang but entirely different in character. A friend who spent several years in Lhasa and opened a highly successful Chinese restaurant there, said that so far as cooking is concerned the whole region is 'under-developed'. Before Liberation the territory was ruled by a system which could only be described as feudal theocracy. Though there were elaborate eating rituals in the monasteries, the food served there was unspeakable—almost unchanged from the primitive foods served in China during the Hsia and Shang Dynasties a millennium or two BC, which was also characterized by rituals and sacrifices. The monks, 'the only Tibetans who could afford to eat,' were averse to killing poultry and did not fish, though they loved to eat them. Consequently the lakes and streams were alive with fish. A friend of mine went fishing at night with homemade nets and was soon drawing in fish by the hundredweight; and by cooking yak meat as mutton, and preparing chicken according to some of the scores of Chinese recipes, he soon filled his restaurant to overcrowding every day of the year. When the controls tightened after Liberation, he was suspected of running contraband and had to make his escape, which he achieved only by first submerging and hiding in a cesspool! The final verdict of this ex-thriving restaurateur from Lhasa on the region's cooking: 'Quite uneatable!'

The other great frontier region of China is the 'Great North Eastern Provinces', or Manchuria. The Manchurian cuisine should of course be reflected in the Court Dishes or Palace Cooking of the Forbidden City, for the last dynasty in China, the Ching Dynasty of 1644–1912, was Manchurian. When the first of the Manchurians galloped into Peking, they were rough-riders like the Mongolians before them, and it is unlikely that they carried much culinary technique or culture with them. It was perhaps out of exasperation that Emperor Chien-Lung (1736–96), when at the height of Manchu power, went on anonymous tours of the Yangtze region. Immediately after the trips, numerous more sophisticated dishes from the south began to blossom forth in the Imperial Kitchen!

For those interested in the culinary arts we should perhaps follow Emperor Chien-lung and retreat from the frontier regions, heading for the lusher regions of the Yangtze and the south. For, massive though they are, Sinkiang, Tibet, Manchuria and Mongolia are still small compared with China as a whole.

Before the days of trains, highways and airports the main travel routes were along the waterways—the Grand Canal was a thousand miles long. The poets and writers of the ancient dynasties in decline often depicted the carousing and eating orgies in the houseboats in Chiang-Nan (South of the Yangtze). Even in my young days much of our travelling was done by boat. Many of these boats and sampans had facilities for cooking in the shape of one or two charcoal-burning stoves, which could be quickly bellowed into a high blaze, set in the prow of the vessel. With traditional Chinese culinary dexterity, quite often a dozen courses could be cooked for a party dinner. But more often, hot snacks were cooked and served during short two- or three-hour voyages: usually noodles, complemented by a couple of stir-fried quick-cooked dishes.

One of my favourite trips in these small boats was to an aunt and uncle who lived on the south bank of the Min River in a high-walled house with many courtyards. My uncle's uncle also lived there: he was a calligrapher of great fame, and Imperial Tutor to the last Emperor. They lived as Chinese scholars and gentry of those days should live, in a classical manner. I used to sit by the riverside there and watch the endless procession of fishing boats with tall sails, heading out to sea to start the fishing season. The procession of many hundreds of boats, some of which would be spending months at sea, took several hours to pass by. The small local boats which went out for short runs would return the same evening and we would go down to the quays to buy crab claws—the claws which had been abandoned by the crabs when caught. To eat a dozen of them, plain-steamed and dipped in ginger and aromatic vinegar, was 'very heaven' to my teenage palate.

Most European visitors who travelled by sea to China in those days would remember how their liner would be surrounded by swarms of sampans as soon as it anchored. Some of the sampans would be plying food, of which one of the most popular delicacies was Soya Eggs—hard-boiled eggs cooked in soya sauce, and coloured a deep brown. When bitten into, the white of the egg and the yellow yolk would contrast sharply with the brown skin.

Most of the big eating occasions and dinner parties were held in houseboats, as they had been for centuries past. Many Chinese cities had their own 'West Lakes' (the most famous being the one in the Lake City of Hanchow in Chekiang, just south of Shanghai). These would be elaborate affairs with dozens of dishes prepared by famous chefs, and accompanied by superior rice wines like Hua Tiao or Shao Hsing. Such water-borne parties were usually held in the summer or early autumn when the harvest moon hung big in the sky, and were recorded in detail by their famous participants as long ago as the 'Three Kingdoms' (AD 300–400). Hence when we Chinese hold dinner parties today, we do so with a feeling for tradition. Through the essays and poems composed to commemorate these occasions, the vividness and flavour of those moonlit evenings survives the centuries as though they were only yesterday: the warm wine, brave sparkling words and the reflected moon all floating alive on the surface of the lake. The Puritan Confucians regarded these evenings as decadent, describing them as occasions of 'Flower and Wine' or Hua Chiu, the precursors of decline and defeat. They may not be turning points of history, but they were memorable moments in the life of the Chinese people.

Even in modern China, where the energy and life of the nation are bent on national reconstruction, and indulgence and leisure activities are strictly limited, there is bound eventually to be a natural swing towards eating and sport—the latter, being for the health and strength of the body (and therefore for the health and strength of the nation), is therefore a 'legitimate' activity; and as for eating, this is essential to life and with the steadily rising standard of living is bound to become a more officially legitimate diversion.

A survey of the recipes which have come out of China since the Cultural Revolution shows one concession to limiting unnecessary 'extravagance' to be the elimination of monosodium glutamate as a regular ingredient for Chinese cooking. This ingredient was originally introduced from Japan and has been much indulged in and abused by Chinese cooking abroad in recent decades. Wine, however, is still extensively used even in the remotest areas; for 'yellow wine' (the general term for rice wine), usually kept in large earthenware jars, is very much a traditional product of the people. Because of greatly improved communication and transport systems, the food served within each region is becoming less restricted than it once was. What were once local specialities are now much more widespread, and you are much more likely to find Moslem (Mongolian Sinkiang) and Pekingese dishes served in Canton, and Szechuan (west

China) dishes in Shanghai, or Cantonese dishes in Peking, than in days gone by. But in spite of the greater unity of China, the sheer vastness of the continent is enough to ensure that the regional differences and demarcations will remain. A study of the culinary differences between the various regions is tantamount to a study of their geographic, economic and historical backgrounds. A book on Chinese provincial cooking is therefore a massive undertaking and the author may justifiably feel awed by the prospect of writing a culinary *War and Peace!* Such a challenge can be fascinating to both writer and reader, and absorbing to all those who have a sense of history and geography and are interested in the ways people live and make the best uses of the resources available to them. To write about Chinese provincial cooking in English is to introduce the westerner to some of the basic realities of the country and the colour and flavour of Chinese life. What could be more of a privilege?

Perhaps even more than elsewhere, the quality of life and the quality of food in China are almost indivisible. Food and cooking persisted through all the exigencies of civil war and cultural revolution. We talk about shared cigarettes in times of war and stress; in Chinese history there must have been millions of moments of 'shared bowls of noodles' and 'spoonfuls of rice'. These moments were the daily, hourly, small expectations and satisfactions in the march of the life of the nation.

Having lived as a provincial Chinese for nearly two decades, and having experienced the rule of the warlords, civil war, revolution and foreign invasion at first hand, I hope to be sufficiently qualified to be able to recapture some of the characteristic flavour of these provinces as reflected in their food. China is still very much an agrarian country and the provincial lifestyle is therefore likely to be emphatically rustic; but this does not mean that it is primitive. Indeed, it is primitive only by comparison with the over-packaged and urbanized Western way of life. It is more accurate to say that Chinese provincial cooking is rustically civilized. Provincial cooking in every region remains closely anchored to the good earth, from which so much natural taste and texture, and the marked character of each region, derives. Compared with the average Western food of today, Chinese provincial cooking is much more directly reflective of the products and resources of the region concerned; and being rustic and thrifty, we make much more use of odds and ends, such as pig's trotters, duck's web, tripe, intestines, chicken blood, beef shin and hoof, ox's penis, fish heads, yams, turnips, cabbage and cauliflower roots and fungi of all types. In doing so we make no apology whatever; indeed, in making use of these 'crude' basic materials, the dishes produced often reach such standards of sophistication and refinement that they are classified as 'delicacies'. In these days of comparative affluence and processed foods the Western world has largely forgotten how to use these frugal materials and misses out on such delicacies.

In documenting this book I cannot, of course, rely entirely on memory for the recipes. I am fortunate in possessing a copy of the eleven-volume *Famous Dishes of China*, published in Peking in 1963 by the Financial and Economic Publication Bureau, and compiled and edited by the Ministry of Commerce Foods and Drinks Management Department. These volumes embrace the recipes of ten provinces of China, providing more than 1,200 recipes. A characteristic of technical books published in China today is their accuracy. Not only is every dish referred to the restaurant or catering establishment where it was cooked, but often the name of the chef is specified. In addition I have referred to another book, *Recipes and Dishes From The People's Dining Rooms*, published in Peking in 1966 by the Light Industries' Publication Department. The book contains 260 recipes drawn from the Public Dining Rooms of a dozen regions and main centres of China. As 1966 was the year of the First Cultural Revolution, the recipes strongly reflect the basic, no-frill approach to Chinese cooking. With these two invaluable sources of information, and over a dozen titles I have already written on the subject of Chinese food, plus twenty years of appreciative eating in China, I hope to give an adequate introduction to Chinese provincial cooking.

Finally, I should like to quote directly from the Foreword of the above-mentioned *Famous Dishes of China*:

Over the many thousands of years we as a nation have accumulated hosts of experience in cooking and food preparation, and in consequence we have developed a national cuisine which is characteristically our own. It is said that since the time of Spring and Autumn [about 600–800 BC] . . . because of the vastness of China, our abundance and variety of resources, together with the differing environments and customs in different localities, there have arisen different characteristic forms of cooking in different regions. According to inadequate statistics, there are over 5,000 well-known and well-defined Chinese dishes, each commanding its own distinctive colour, flavour, aroma and texture, which are appealing to the human palate. These have added to the physical and material health and welfare of the people, and have caused our cooking to enjoy a high international reputation. This fact is an attestation of the high degree of intelligence and cultural attainment always enjoyed by the working people of our country. Indeed, it is time that our cookery achievements are regarded as an integral part of the precious heritage which we have inherited from the history of our working people.

Not all the recipes in this book will be derived from the compendia just quoted. There are other sources—not least my contacts with other Chinese, born and bred in their respective provinces, some of whom are experienced practising restaurateurs. But one of my chief tasks in preparing this book is to adapt and abridge existing recipes, many of which were derived from catering establishments where the scale of measurements is far in excess of the requirements of a private kitchen, and which sometimes demand local spices and plants which would be difficult or impossible to obtain in the West. When writing for the Western kitchen I must keep my eyes on what is practicable and useful, and follow the dictum of Escoffier: *Faites simple!*

Kenneth Lo

Substitutes

Attempts should always be made to obtain the correct ingredients for each dish as substitutes do produce a slightly different result in flavour or texture. Where substitutes may be used they are given in the list of ingredients for each recipe. However, with the aid of the glossary and the list of suppliers on page 267, the reader should be able to buy the authentic foods required for the best results.

Flavour Powder

Monosodium glutamate is a flavour powder often used in Chinese cooking. As it is considered an optional ingredient it does not appear in any of the following recipes. It should be used sparingly if desired, according to the instructions on the packet (approx 2.5 ml/$\frac{1}{2}$ teaspoon to each 450 g/1 lb weight of combined ingredients). A chicken stock-cube may be used as a substitute.

Metrication

Metric measurements may vary from recipe to recipe, and it is essential to follow *either* imperial or metric measures throughout any one recipe.

US/UK Conversion Guide

Spoons
1 US teaspoon or tablespoon = 4/5 equivalent standard UK measure
16 US tablespoons = 1 US cup

Liquid Measures

	US	UK
1 cup	225 ml (8 fl oz)	300 ml (10 fl oz)
1 pint	450 ml (16 fl oz)	600 ml (20 fl oz)

In the US dry foods, such as flour, sugar and shortening, are usually measured by volume. If a recipe calls for ½ cup, pour the ingredient into a measuring cup up to the 4-oz mark, making sure that it is level.

In the UK dry foods are measured by weight. The following weights of common ingredients all equal 1 US cup.

Breadcrumbs	(fresh)	50 g (2 oz)
	(dried)	100 g (4 oz)
Butter		225 g (8 oz)
Dried Fruit	(generous cup)	175 g (6 oz)
Flour		100 g (4 oz)
Honey	(generous cup)	350 g (12 oz)
Rice	(uncooked)	200 g (7 oz)
Sugar	(granulated/castor)	225 g (8 oz)
	(confectioner's/icing)	100 g (4 oz)

Peking and North-China Cooking

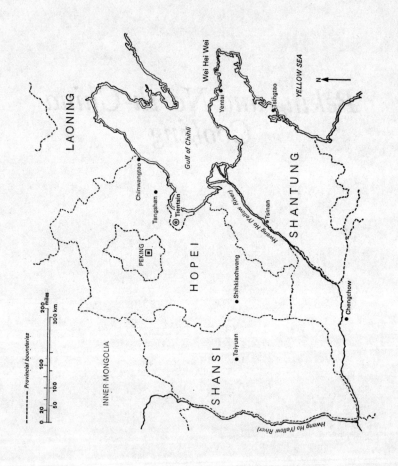

Peking and North-China Cooking

One of the most evocative impressions of Peking is the stillness of the air on an autumn day, with shafts of sunshine breaking through the bamboo grove in the courtyard, as you awake on one of its cloudless days of windless skies. There is coolness in the shade everywhere, but the autumn sun is still hot, and the air quite crystalline—clearer than I have seen anywhere else in the world. That, at any rate, is the indelible memory left by my first morning in Peking. Life was young, and the day was full of expectation. As the autumn deepened you first felt the coming of winter in the legs, through your thin summer trousers as you walked in the cool night air through the city under a dark, luminous sky. Up north in Peking the pattern of the stars is much more noticeable than in the south where the sky is frequently clouded over. The clear night skies of Peking are like the night skies of the desert; indeed, the Gobi is not far away.

When the winter arrives, it comes suddenly. After a day and night of freezing Kua Feng, the Chinese *mistral*, suddenly the ponds, lakes and canals would freeze over, and people would be walking and skating over the ice—a phenomenon which came as a great surprise to southerners. During the winter months the globe of the sun would rise orange on the horizon every morning at about 8–8.30. In the evening people would cluster around the iron stove, which was often fed until it became red-hot. King Winter takes a firm grip of the land in this part of China, and creates a world in which spring and summer become only a distant memory.

After months of pushing into the biting north wind there are signs that the grip of winter is being gradually slackened, witnessed by the light tremors and rumblings everywhere: icicles begin to fall off the trees and slip off drainpipes, and the sunshine looks less pale. As the thaw sets in properly, the ground becomes muddy and soggy—altogether the birth of spring is far from being a tidy process. It is only after a month or more, when the birds begin to sing louder and the willows start to turn green and grow heavy with foliage, that the new season finally seems to have arrived, and the tired memories of the hard winter and the previous year are ready to be buried.

As the earth slowly melts into life, you glimpse brightly through the passing of one more season the age of this ancient land, before being engulfed by the lushness of the northern spring. Summer in Peking is not half measure: the torrential rains and thunderstorms of July and August are subtropical. Towards the latter part of the season, every patch of ground is overgrown with vegetation. But if you have the chance to go to the coast—to such places as Pei-ta-Ho, Chingwangtao, Sanhaikwang, the coastline of the Gulf of Chihli which curves away to Manchuria or heads south to the Shantung Peninsula, to Wei-Hai-Wei, Yentai or Tsingtao—you would find idyllic seaside places, with great clean, hot, white beaches and blue sea.

But Peking is more strongly influenced by the vast hinterland beyond than by the sea on its eastern doorstep. Along the streets of Peking camels stride with slow, measured tread, and the eating habits of the Chinese Moslems from Central Asia are apparent on many restaurant menus; but the only reminder of the sea on the dining table is the fat, succulent prawns. It may be that the muddy waters of the Gulf of Chihli, where the Yellow River flows into the sea, provide more fattening nourishment for the crustaceans than the cleaner waters of the Pacific. Yet there is little variety in the fish which makes its way to the Peking dining table, compared with the abundant choice available to the people of the Yangtze or the southern coastal provinces. The Pekingese fish recipes are also limited: the fish are either deep-fried and served in a sweet and sour sauce, as in the famous Sweet and Sour Carp of the Yellow River, or deep-fried and braised in a thick soya-paste sauce. In this part of China, because of the muddiness of the water, unless the fish have been placed in a tank of clean water for several days to cleanse them, it is customary to deep-fry them initially to suppress any muddy taste and then to cover them with a strongly flavoured sauce.

But there is one Peking fish dish which all south-easterners appreciate, though few have the knack of cooking it. This is Chao Liu Yu-Pien, or Soft-fried Sliced Fish in Wine-lee Sauce. It consists of sliced fish fillets, first mildly poached in oil and drained, and then braised briefly in a sauce constituted of chicken stock, yellow wine, wine-lees and sugar. Jet black wood ear fungi are often used as a colour contrast to the whiteness of the slices of fish, which are usually coated in cornflour and egg-white. Southerners, even expert fish chefs, often fail with this dish, usually because they fry the fish slices in hot oil rather than poach them gently in oil which has been allowed to cool slightly, with the result that the fillets become crisp and stiff instead of remaining soft, smooth and tender as they should be. This dish restores Peking fish cookery to a semblance of respectability in the eyes of the south-easterners.

On the other hand, large prawns, measuring about 6.25–12.5cm (3–5 in) in length, are a regular feature of the Peking diet. These are usually cooked in their shells in a red garlicky sauce (the colour comes from the mixture of tomato sauce, soya paste, garlic, spring onion, wine and sugar), by a method sometimes described as 'dry-frying'. After an initial frying in a limited amount of oil, garlic and salt, the prawns are braised for a short time in the sauce, which is reduced and thickened until it is almost dry. The Chinese delight in shelling the prawns in the mouth, sucking at the highly savoury thick sauce as they do so. The piquant sauce enhances the juicy flesh of the prawns, which are in effect 'miniature lobsters'. These prawns are available most of the year round.

Whether the Sweet and Sour Sauce was originated in the north or south is unknown. The northern version, made from the simple blending of sugar with vinegar, without the intrusion of any fruit or tomato sauce, seems crude to the southerners. However, the Peking version of the Sweet and Sour Fillet of Pork, or Tan-Chu Li-Chi, should be appealing to the Western palate, for this recipe uses pork fillet instead of a fat cut such as belly of pork. The success of the dish depends largely upon the high temperature used in the frying, and the quality of the batter. The shock heat treatment reduces the time required in cooking and retains all the juices in the meat, giving them no time to evaporate. A similar method (high-heat frying) is applied to cooking plain-fried pork and chicken pieces in batter, which are served with piquant dips and small saucerfuls of Aromatic Salt and Pepper Mix set out on the table.

So far as meat is concerned, northern cooking is known for its marinated meats, or Chiang Rou, and for the plain-cooked dishes, where the meat is barbecued, roasted, plain boiled or 'scalded'. The meat cookery of Peking and north China is strongly influenced by Chinese Moslem and Mongolian methods. The Peking Duck prepared and exemplified by the two famous restaurants, Chuan Chu Te' (founded in 1873) and Pien I Fang (founded 1855) is a typical instance. Here, the ducks are 'hung roast' (Kua-lu Kao Ya) in a large kiln-like oven; no strong flavouring is added until the duck meat and crisp skin are rolled into a pancake, or served with steamed buns, when a plummy soya-paste sauce is liberally applied. Plain-cooked meat served with strong condiments is also the essence of the Scalded Lamb or Mongolian Hot Pot of the Cheng Yuan Lou and Tung Lai Suen restaurants, which introduced this cooking method to Peking around the turn of the century. Thin slices of lamb are cooked at the table over a charcoal burner, in a hot pot in which several pints of stock are kept at a rolling boil. The pieces of lamb are dipped into the stock for under a minute of 'scalding' before being retrieved and eaten with a variety of dips and garnishes.

In the case of barbecued lamb and beef, (specialities of Barbecue Wan and Barbecue Chi, the former restaurant having been established for over 200 years, and the latter for over 100 years), thin slices of meat are grilled at the table over a charcoal brazier. The meat is usually plain-cooked, and again the condiments are applied only as the meat is eaten. This method of cooking was introduced to Peking in the reign of Emperor Tung Chi of the Manchu Dynasty (1644–61), when a group of Mongolian dignitaries were on a prolonged visit to the capital, and has since become an established feature of its cuisine.

Deep-boiling is another form of plain-cooking, perfected by the Sa Kuo Chu or Home of the Earthen-Pot Casserole restaurant, which was established in Peking in 1741. Here pork is cooked slowly in a large earthenware pot, four feet in diameter. The pork becomes tender with long, slow simmering, then is cut into smaller chunks for deep-frying or braising. Alternatively, it is sliced into smaller pieces (White Cut Pork) and eaten with condiments, or cooked with noodles, thus putting to good use the rich stock, flavoured in limitless different ways by the addition of mushrooms, fresh vegetables, vinegar, wine, etc. A wide range of soup noodles are produced, outstanding for both their richness of flavour and their fresh natural ingredients. The tenderized pork is deep-fried for 5–8 minutes and then sliced into bite-sized pieces which are consumed with great relish, in much the same manner as Peking Duck or Barbecued Meats, often brushed with a piquant sauce and rolled in pancakes or sandwiched in steamed rolls, with a selection of shredded vegetables.

Peking has been called the Mutton City of China. Mutton or lamb is used so extensively that, as I remember it, almost every restaurant or eating-place seemed to reek with the smell, which makes it unbearable for many southerners who do not eat mutton.

It is perhaps to neutralize the strong smell and taste of this meat that a great deal of garlic and spring onion are used in north China cooking. The result is that instead of the strong smell and taste of mutton you have an even stronger smell and taste of garlic and onion cooking with mutton! In every little eating place in the north you are hit by this smell as soon as you poke your head through the door. It is especially strong in winter, when the doorway of most eating establishments is hung with a heavy padded curtain, weighed down with a wooden batten at the bottom, to keep the warm air in and fresh air out.

Another characteristic of Peking and northern cooking is the frequent, lavish use of soya paste (a thick form of soya sauce), usually to thicken sauces or as a marinating and seasoning ingredient. Meat and poultry keep well in the cold northern winters, but they are sometimes preserved by a method using soya paste. These preserved cold meats, including Chiang Rou, Chiang Ya, Chiang Chi, Soya-paste Seasoned Pork, Soya-paste Seasoned Duck and Soya-paste Seasoned Chicken, are a form of Chinese *charcuterie* and are a useful convenience food for Chinese housewives. The meat is first rubbed and heavily coated with a mixture of soya paste, soya sauce, wine, sugar, minced ginger and garlic, and left to season for a day or two. It is then fried for a few minutes and cooked slowly in a marinade or sauce of the same constituents. Meat prepared in this way will generally keep for a week in a cool place. It is served cold, sliced or chopped into bite-sized pieces, with hot rice. The jellified gravy from such a dish is exceptionally delicious with hot soft rice or Congee.

A popular style of northern cooking in which soya paste (Chiang) is the essential ingredient is the process called Chiang Pao which, literally translated, means Stir-fried and Exploded in Soya Paste. In effect the process consists of double stir-frying. The main ingredients, usually breast of chicken, fillet of pork, or kidney and liver, are diced into sugar-lump size cubes and quick-fried over a very high heat for a minute or less, then drained and removed. A small amount of lard is added to the pan, along with soya paste, ginger-water, sugar and wine. The mixture is stirred with the fat in the pan into a shiny paste and cooked slowly until the moisture has evaporated. At this point the fried meat cubes are returned to the pan and turned several times until thoroughly coated with the paste. The dish is then ready to serve. Since they are very partial to offal in the north, a favourite variation in this range is Pao San Yang, sometimes called the Three Delicious, which consists of the double-quick-frying together of diced lamb or pork cubes with pieces of liver and kidney; occasionally prawns and squid are also thrown into the double-quick-fry, resulting in an expanded dish called the Five Delicious! These dishes appeal to almost everyone, so long as only one or two cloves of garlic are thrown into the frying, instead of the ten or twelve sometimes added by northern cooks.

The most commonly eaten vegetable is the Tientsin White Cabbage. This is now becoming quite well known in both America and Britain, where is usually called Chinese cabbage or Bok Choi, which is the Cantonese version of white cabbage. In north China in winter, the height of the season for these cabbages, they are piled up like coal in the courtyards outside, or in cold corridors, where they keep well, but are often covered over with sand and dust. When washed under running water their pure, delicate appearance makes them look as if they were carved from jade. Chinese cabbage can be cooked with almost anything, and is frequently put into soups which are flavoured simply by adding a teaspoon or two of dried shrimps. Red-cooked Cabbage is slow-braised with soya sauce, meat-gravy and a tablespoon of fat or butter, and has a strangely meat-like quality. For White-cooked Cabbage the vegetable is cooked in a good meat or bone broth, flavoured by dried shrimps and 'glossed' with a small amount of lard. Red- and White-cooked Cabbage are the two staple vegetable dishes of north China, to be found on almost every dining table.

Fu-yung sauce is often used in Peking on vegetables. Fu-yung does not mean just egg (a frequent misnomer in Chinese restaurants abroad) but egg-white, beaten up with minced breast of chicken or fillet of white fish. This thick white savoury sauce is poured over vegetables such as cauliflower, broccoli, courgettes, or what have you, and often sprinkled with minced ham as a garnish. Crab meat is sometimes braised with the cabbage to make a more refined party dish.

Tomatoes are plentiful in Peking during the summer, and are often cooked with beef, or made into soups. Courgettes, cucumbers, marrows and aubergines are all widely used in season. Although it is the Chinese tradition to use dried mushrooms, several varieties are popular fresh. Mushrooms are ideal in shape and size for stir-frying and combine well with almost every other stir-fried food material, shrimps, prawns, and all diced cubes of meats, and other vegetables.

The greengrocers' stalls in the northern provinces are flooded with pears and persimmons in winter. The region is famous for the quality of its large, juicy pears. The orange and red persimmons look like large, burnished tomatoes and lend warmth to the freezing winter like small lanterns. They are sometimes placed outside the window overnight, where they freeze through, and next day the inside can be dug out with a spoon and eaten like ice-cream. In summer strawberries are sometimes available, though they are not widely cultivated. Grapes of all varieties are widely produced. Nowadays, they are made into a good range of grape-wines, some of which are exported. The Peking red and white wines are becoming quite well known, and there is even a variety of Chinese champagne but these are innovations and a contrast to the ordinary grain-based Chinese wines—such as the yellow wine. Crab-apples are usually made into sweets, and Chinese confectioners display an unimaginable range of native-made bonbons and glacé fruits which are bought in quantities to place on side tables at home on festive occasions, especially during the New Year holidays.

Historically Shantung, the province where Confucius and his disciple Mencius lived and died around 600–500 BC, has always been a cultural centre of China. Some of this culture must have rubbed off on its cooking during 25 centuries of uninterrupted cultural revolution. Certainly most of the best-known cooks in north China seem to come from Shantung. This could be due to the fact that the Ming Dynasty (the Dynasty before the Manchus) employed a succession of Shantung chefs for nearly two centuries, or because Shantung, being two to three hundred miles further south, is marginally milder in climate and the most productive province in the region. Bounded by the China Sea to the east, it is a great province for fruit (grapes, apples, pears, peaches, apricots, etc) and vegetables and cereals (corn, peanuts, maize wheat) which also help to make this ideal chicken-rearing country. Crisp, deep-fried whole *poulets* used to be sold through the train windows in the station at Tsinan (the capital of Shantung) on the way north or south. Boiled soya eggs are also sold as a snack.

The Shantung chefs are past masters in quick-fried chicken dishes such as Quick-fried Diced Chicken Cubes, Soft-fried Sliced Breast of Chicken with Mushrooms, Tossed-fried Diced Chicken Kidney and Liver, or Fu-yung of Chicken. The last is a great delicacy, made by blending finely minced chicken with egg-white, poaching spoonfuls of the mixture in oil until firm, and then simmering the cakes in a clear blended sauce.

During the last (Manchu) dynasty some 2,000 chefs and cooks were employed in the Palace Kitchens of the Forbidden City. The kitchens were divided into departments with such titles as the Picnic and Travelling Kitchen, Kitchen of Dawn and Dusk Sacrifice, Departments for Rice and Noodles, Department for Banquets, etc. However, the influence of Manchurian and court cooking on the food consumed in this region was relatively small, for there was little indigenous cuisine in Manchuria, which was chiefly populated by poor immigrants from Shantung. Apart from the Pheasant Hot Pot and a few mutton dishes there were few 'authentic' dishes, most recipes being duplicates of the better established Mongolian dishes. When Emperor Chien-Lung made his two famous anonymous journeys to the south he was struck by the quality and refinement of some of the dishes of Chiang-Nan (South of Yangtze), and on his return to Peking commanded that they be added to the Palace culinary repertoire. The Empress Dowager, who was an approximate contemporary of Queen Victoria, was the last powerful monarch of the Manchu Dynasty. She was a sweet-toothed woman, and she left behind a number of dishes incorporating copious sweet sauces. Soon after the establishment of the People's Republic in the early 1950s, a number of restaurants purporting to specialise in 'palace cuisine' were established in the capital and many of the elderly Imperial chefs were re-employed to pass on their expertise. But in spite of this, the impact of the Imperial cuisine has not been extensive, and a study of their recipes reveals little range or originality.

Meanwhile, many of the old established restaurants have continued to flourish. Many of these are of considerable proportions, with as many as fifty or more private rooms, each capable of seating ten to thirty people at up to three tables. These private rooms are gathered around inter-connecting courtyards, which are spread over a considerable area. Indeed, most of these grand old Peking restaurants do not look like restaurants at all to western eyes; they are more like residences, with all the bustle and activity taking place behind high walls, hidden from the passer-by. Even the fellow diners in the restaurant do not see much of one another, as the majority eat in private rooms, and only a basic menu of cheaper meals is served in the public dining room.

Because of the unique background and strong traditions of Peking, its food is markedly different from that of any other capital city in the world. It is undoubtedly well worth seeing and savouring, and there is little doubt that the road to Peking and north China is likely in the years to come to become wider and easier to traverse. Until that happens, perhaps the best thing to do is to experiment with some of the characteristic flavours of Peking and north China, using whatever materials you have to hand. The special ingredients which are necessary are comparatively few: with soya sauce and soya paste, which are now quite widely available, you can prepare most of the following recipes. I can assure you that the flavours you will create in your own kitchen will come very near to those of the Eternal City itself.

Soups

White Fish Soup with Croûtons
(Adapted from the U I-Sung Moslem Restaurant, Peking.)

225 g (½ lb) fillet of white fish
3 medium firm tomatoes
3 large Chinese dried mushrooms
1 egg-white
22 ml (1½ tablespoons) cornflour
1½ slices of bread
750 ml (1½ pints) stock (b)
2 slices root ginger

45 ml (3 tablespoons) green peas
15 ml (1 tablespoon) salt
1 chicken stock cube
30 ml (2 tablespoons) yellow wine or dry sherry
oil for deep- or semi-deep-frying (250 ml/½ pint)

Chop the fish finely. Pour boiling water over the tomatoes, remove the skin and chop each into a dozen regular pieces. Soak the mushrooms in hot water for 20 minutes, remove the stalks, and cut each cap into 8–10 regular pieces. Beat the egg-white with a fork for 10 seconds. Mix the cornflour with 60 ml (4 tablespoons) water until smoothly blended. Trim the crusts off the bread, and dice into small cubes.

Heat the stock and ginger in a saucepan. When it is about to boil, add the chopped fish and mushrooms. Stir, and when the mixture reboils, add the peas and tomatoes. Finally add the blended cornflour, stirring it into the soup to mix well. Add the salt and wine. Drip the egg-white slowly and evenly over the surface of the soup.

Meanwhile, heat a large bowl or soup tureen, and also the oil in the deep-fryer. When the latter is about to smoke, add the bread cubes. Fry them over a high heat for 2½ minutes. Remove with a perforated spoon, and drain any excess oil into the pan through a strainer.

Place the hot croûtons at the bottom of the well-heated tureen and pour the soup over them. The sizzling noise invites diners to commence.
Serves 6–10.

Minced Duck Soup with Croûtons
(Adapted from the U I-Sung Moslem Restaurant, Peking.)

225 g (½ lb) cooked duck meat
1½ slices bread
2 stalks spring onion
30 ml (2 tablespoons) cornflour
750 ml (1¼ pints) stock (b)
60 ml (4 tablespoons) green peas

10 ml (2 teaspoons) salt
1 chicken stock cube
45 ml (3 tablespoons) Chinese
   yellow wine or dry sherry
15 ml (1 tablespoon) chicken fat
oil for deep- or semi-deep-frying

Finely chop the duck meat. Trim the bread, removing the crust, and dice it into small cubes. Cut the spring onions into coarse shavings. Mix the cornflour in 90 ml (6 tablespoons) water until well blended.

Heat the stock in a saucepan. Add the duck meat, peas, salt, stock cube and yellow wine or sherry. Bring the contents to the boil, and stir in the cornflour mixture to thicken.

Meanwhile, heat the oil in the deep-fryer. When it is very hot, add the diced bread cubes to fry for 2½ minutes (stir them now and then so the frying is even) over a high heat. Remove and drain quickly. At the same time, warm a large bowl or tureen.

Place the freshly fried *croûtons* at the bottom of the soup bowl or tureen and pour the soup quickly over them. Sprinkle the surface with spring onion shavings and chicken fat.
Serves 6–10.

Sliced Fish, Pepper and Vinegar Soup

225 g (½ lb) filleted flat fish
5 ml (1 teaspoon) salt
15 ml (1 tablespoon) cornflour
1 egg-white
15 cm (6 in) section medium-
   sized cucumber
22 ml (1½ tablespoons) soya
   sauce
60 ml (4 tablespoons) vinegar
   (Chinkiang aromatic if available)

1–2.5 ml (¼–½ teaspoon) black
   pepper to taste, although this
   is meant to be a peppery soup
750 ml (1½ pints) stock (b)
2.5 ml (½ teaspoon) salt
1 chicken stock cube
15 ml (1 tablespoon) coriander
   leaves (or chopped spring-
   onion shavings)
15 ml (1 tablespoon) chicken fat

Cut fish into medium-sized pieces. Rub the pieces with salt and cornflour, and wet them with egg-white. Cut the cucumber into 3 sections. Cut each section vertically into triple-matchstick-thick strips (including skin). Mix the soya sauce, vinegar and pepper in a small bowl.

Heat the stock in a saucepan. Add the salt and stock cube. When the contents boil, add the fish piece by piece. Leave them to simmer in the stock for 2 minutes. Add the cucumber strips. On reboiling, stir in the soya-vinegar-pepper mixture. Simmer for a further 3 minutes.

Pour the soup into a large bowl or tureen. Sprinkle with coriander (or spring onion) and chicken fat and serve. This is a sharp, peppery soup, and the strong hot-and-sour effect on the palate is relieved by the cucumber strips and the smooth savouriness of the sliced fish. It is a soup suitable for a banquet, and is very popular in the winter.
Serves 6–8.

Duck's Liver Soup
(Adapted from the Feng Tse Yuan, the best-known Shantung restaurant in Peking.)

225–275 g (8–10 oz) duck livers
750 ml (1½ pints) good-quality broth
1 chicken stock cube
3 slices root ginger

15 ml (1 tablespoon) chicken fat
22 ml (1½ tablespoons) chopped spring-onion shavings (or coriander leaves)

Sauce

4 medium Chinese dried mushrooms
2 medium onions
22 ml (1½ tablespoons) vegetable oil
15 ml (1 tablespoon) brown bean paste

15 ml (1 tablespoon) tomato purée
15 ml (1 tablespoon) soya sauce
60 ml (4 tablespoons) dry sherry
125 ml (¼ pint) water
15 ml (1 tablespoon) cornflour blended in 45 ml (3 tablespoons) water

Soak the duck livers in water for 1½ hours. Drain and cut them into thin slices. Soak the mushrooms in hot water for 20 minutes, remove the stalks, and cut each cap into 4 pieces. Cut the onion into thin slices.

Heat the stock in a large saucepan. Add the stock cube and ginger, and leave to simmer while you prepare the sauce. Heat the oil in a small saucepan, and add the onion and mushrooms. Stir-fry them slowly over a medium heat for 5–6 minutes until the onions are quite soft. Add the bean paste, tomato purée and soya sauce.

Mix them all together, then pour in the water. Bring the contents of the pan to the boil, and simmer until the volume has been reduced to less than half. Add the sherry and cornflour, and stir for 1 minute, when the sauce should begin to thicken. Remove the pan from the heat.

Meanwhile, blanch the duck livers by dipping them in boiling water and removing immediately. Add them to the stock which is simmering in the large saucepan. As soon as the latter boils, pour in the sauce. Mix everything together in the pan. On reboiling, simmer the contents together for 3 minutes.

Add the chicken fat to the soup and pour it into a large bowl or tureen. Sprinkle with chopped spring onion or coriander. This is quite a substantial soup, suitable for winter.
Serves 6–8

Whole Duck with Shark's Fin Soup
(Adapted from Yu Hua Lou Restaurant, Peking.)

675 g (1½ lb) shark's fin
1.8–2.2 kg (4–5 lb) duck
2 medium onions
50 g (2 oz) winter bamboo shoots
8 medium Chinese dried mush-rooms
37 ml (2½ tablespoons) lard
4 slices root ginger
250 ml (½ pint) chicken stock (b)

60 ml (4 tablespoons) soya sauce
90 ml (6 tablespoons) Chinese yellow wine or dry sherry
10 ml (2 teaspoons) sugar
1.25 litres (2½ pints) water
22 ml (1½ tablespoons) corn-flour blended in 90 ml (6 tablespoons) water

Prepare the shark's fin by soaking in water overnight, then steaming for 3 hours. Dip it in boiling water to blanch for 3 minutes, wash under running water and drain. Clean the duck, parboil for 3 minutes, and drain. Cut the onions into thin slices and the bamboo shoots into thin slices; soak the mushrooms in hot water for 20 minutes and remove the stalks.

Heat 7 ml (½ tablespoon) lard in a frying pan. Add 15 ml (1 tablespoon) onion and ginger. Stir-fry for 2 minutes. Add the chicken stock, 30 ml (2 tablespoons) soya sauce, 45 ml (3 table-spoons) yellow wine or sherry, sugar and the shark's fin. Bring to the boil, and simmer for 15 minutes until the liquid in the pan has been reduced to a quarter, turning the fins over every 5 minutes.

Discard the onion and ginger. Stuff the shark's fin into the cavity of the duck, and sew to secure.

Place the duck on a flat bamboo or wooden frame in a large earthenware pot or casserole. Pour in just enough water to submerge the duck. Add the remainder of the onion, ginger and soya sauce. Bring the contents to the boil, and simmer gently for 2 hours. Skim off any impurities. Add the bamboo shoots and mushrooms and adjust for seasoning. Continue to simmer for 2 more hours. Remove and discard the onion and ginger.

Lift the duck out of the earthenware pot or casserole, and place it in the centre of a deep-sided dish. Bring the soup to the boil, add the cornflour and the balance of the lard. Stir over a high heat for 3–4 minutes. Pour the resulting soup over the duck in the dish and serve. The duck meat should now be so tender that it can be taken off the bones quite easily. This may be eaten in conjunction with the shark's fins which can easily be extracted from the cavity of the duck. The mushrooms and bamboo shoots are nibbled as 'extras'.

A banquet dish for 10 people.

Sweet Soup of Mixed Lotus-Root Shreds
(Adapted from Feng Shan Restaurant, North Sea Lake Park, Peking.)

450 g (1 lb) fresh lotus roots
225 g (½ lb) pears
100 g (¼ lb) dates
100 g (¼ lb) glacé fruit (in different colours)
3 egg-whites

45 ml (3 tablespoons) castor sugar
170 ml (⅓ pint) water
45 ml (3 tablespoons) cornflour blended in 375 ml (¾ pint) water and 45 ml (3 tablespoons) sugar

Cut the lotus roots and pears into triple-matchstick-sized shreds. Sprinkle and rub them with 22 ml (1½ tablespoons) castor sugar. Beat the egg-whites with the remaining castor sugar and 170 ml (⅓ pint) water. Chop the dates and glacé fruit into fine shreds. Mix the cornflour with the water and sugar until well blended.

Pour the egg-white and water mixture into a deep-sided, 30 cm (1 ft) long heatproof dish. Put the dish into a steamer and steam for 10 minutes, by which time the egg-white mixture should have set. Sprinkle with the remaining castor sugar, then with the lotus-root shreds and shredded pears. Over the shredded lotus roots and pears spread the coloured shreds of dates and glacé fruit, arranging them in

B

regular or symmetrical patterns. Stir and heat the cornflour-water-sugar mixture into a hot syrup.

Pour the syrup over the shredded fruits and put the dish into the refrigerator to chill for at least 2 hours. This dish of sweet soup is best served either at the end of a meal, or between savoury dishes in the middle of a multi-course dinner party.
Serves 6–8.

Chicken and Duck

Peking Duck
(From the Pien I Fang and Chuan Chu Te', Peking.)

Peking Duck is probably the best known of all Peking dishes. The two foremost restaurants in Peking which make it their speciality are the Pien I Fang (established 1855), and the Chuan Chu Te' (established 1864). With over a century's experience behind them they have developed the preparation of this duck dish into a fine art. The birds used are locally produced. During the last quarter of their life the ducks are artificially fed, and should be no older than 70 days when they are killed. The aim is for their lean meat to be interspersed with streaks of fat, so that when roasted the bird will achieve maximum tenderness and flavour. The male bird usually weighs 3–3.6 kg (7–8 lb), and the female 2.2–2.7 kg (5–6 lb). They need great care especially during the last stages of their rearing, when they appear to have little appetite or resistance to heat or cold, and are allowed hardly any exercise in order to prevent the meat from becoming sinewy. In effect these ducks are manufactured specially for the table. The same breed was first exported to Britain and the US in 1875, and to Japan in 1888, where they have assumed different names (the Aylesbury and Long Island duckling). In China they are called Peking Tien Ya, or the Peking Artificially Fed Duck.

In preparing the duck for the oven, great care has to be exercised in removing the feathers so that no damage is done to the skin, for this is paramount for the success of the dish. In rinsing or plunging the bird into hot water to remove the feathers, do not overheat the skin, which otherwise might start to ooze grease, thus making it difficult for the sugared water to be brushed on evenly afterwards. Hence each dousing must be kept short and quick. Prior to the first application of sugared water, the duck should be doused with boiling water (1 kettleful) and wiped dry immediately, then hung up in an airy spot overnight, or for at least half a day. In the winter in Peking it is the common practice to hang it up indoors for at least one full day, and occasionally for as long as 2–3 days. The sugared water to be brushed on to the duck, should be prepared in the proportion of approximately 15 ml (1 tablespoon) sugar to 120–150 ml (8–10 tablespoons) water. It should be applied twice; the second application after the first application has dried.

In the famous roast-duck restaurants in Peking, the ducks are hung up in dozens by the necks on long poles, and inserted into kiln-like ovens about the size of a small room to roast for varying lengths of time: the smaller ducks 1.35–1.5 kg (3–3½ lb) for no more than 30–35 minutes, and the larger birds 2.2–2.6 kg (5–6 lb) 40–50 minutes. In that comparatively short roasting, the ducks are rotated 3–4 times, to ensure an even roasting. The size of the oven, and the fact that the ducks are hung up, makes this possible. In such an oven, where the firing is done by coal or charcoal, the building of the fire often demands considerable skill. An essential requirement for such a large oven is that the fire heating it must be at a full blaze for three-quarters of an hour before any duck is inserted, so that the ducks will be roasted not only from the fire below but from the heated back and side walls of the oven as well. However, with an average Western domestic oven in which it is difficult or impracticable to hang ducks, it is best to lie the duck on a wire rack or roasting tier, with a roasting-pan half filled with water placed underneath to catch the drips. In our experience an average duck of 1.8–2.2 kg (4–5 lb) requires exactly 1 hour of roasting at 220°C (425°F)/Gas 7, and a larger duck of 2.2–3 kg (5–7 lb) will require 1 hour 10 minutes at the same temperature. When roasted for this length of time, the meat of the duck should be adequately cooked, and the skin well-crisped, but not over-dried or charred.

The processes carried out by the specialist caterers in Peking, which we have omitted, are (1) to blow air through an aperture in the skin of the neck so that the skin balloons up and loosens from the body, and (2) to fill the cavity of the duck about three-quarters full with boiling water, then sew up the aperture securely before roasting (in Peking's cold winters this is partly to ensure that all the ice inside the duck has melted, and that in the latter stages of cooking the duck will be boiled inside, and roasted outside). We feel that these two processes merely add complications and could mar the cooking rather than enhance it. Indeed, the prospect of the work involved might make the dish too forbidding to attempt; yet when cooked by the straightforward method, the recipe is comparatively simple.

The carving of the duck is usually done with a small but very sharp knife. The skin is first peeled off rather as one would peel an apple, in pieces about 5 x 2.5 cm (2 x 1 in). The pieces should be arranged neatly in one layer on a well-heated dish. The meat of the duck should be carved or peeled off in the same manner and arranged on a similar dish.

The crisp skin and meat are eaten either by sandwiching a piece or two of the skin with a piece of meat in a Hua Chuan or Steamed Flower Bun, or rolled up in a thin pancake made from just flour and water, with a light brushing of sesame oil (see below). The condiments served with Peking Duck are: shredded spring onion, shredded cucumber, and Peking Duck Sauce. The approximate proportion of ingredients for the sauce are: 30 ml (2 tablespoons) soya paste for each 15 ml (1 tablespoon) hoisin sauce, 30 ml (2 tablespoons) sugar, 30 ml vegetable oil, and 15 ml sesame oil. The mixture is stirred in a pan over a low heat for 3–3½ minutes until consistent, or until all the sugar has dissolved into the liquid ingredients. This makes a sharp piquant sauce, which adds to the already considerable character of the 'sandwich' or 'roll' in which the duck meat and crisp skin are eaten together with the fresh, crunchy vegetables. Few people have denied that to eat it is a gastronomic delight.

Serves 6–8.

Pancakes for Peking Duck

275 g (10 oz) flour   *225 ml (9 fl oz) boiling water*

Place the flour in a mixing bowl. Add the boiling water slowly, and mix into a dough with a wooden spoon. Knead for 5–6 minutes and let the dough stand for 15 minutes. Turn the dough on to a floured board and knead again for 5–6 minutes. Let it stand for another 15 minutes. Form the dough into a sausage-shaped roll, about 3.75 cm (1½ in) in diameter. Divide the dough into 18–20 equal sized pieces, either by cutting off discs with a knife, or breaking pieces off with the fingers. Pat and flatten the discs into round 'biscuits'. Brush the top of the biscuits with sesame oil. Stick the biscuits together in pairs, oiled sides inward, and roll out into a double pancake about 11.25–12.5 cm (4½–5 in) in diameter.

Put a dry frying pan over a low heat. When the pan is quite hot place one or two pancakes in it to dry-cook for 1–1½ minutes. Shake the pan slightly so that the heating is even. Turn the pancakes over and dry-cook the other side for the same length of time. Remove from the pan, and pull the double pancakes apart into single layers (because the sides which were pressed together were greased, they should come apart fairly readily). Pile the pancakes up one on top of the other (greased sides uppermost). When required, they should be placed in a steamer to heat through for 15–20 minutes. If not required they can be wrapped in tinfoil and stored in a refrigerator for a few days.

Deep-Fried Duck's Liver and Kidney

350 g (¾ lb) duck liver   *225 g (½ lb) duck kidney*

Dip

Aromatic Salt and Pepper Mix (page 68)

Clean and remove the membranes from the kidney and liver. Cut each piece of liver into equal wedge-shaped pieces. Place the Aromatic Salt and Pepper Mix in 2 saucer-sized dishes and place them strategically on the dining table for the diners to use as dips.

Parboil the liver and kidney pieces by putting them separately into two small pans of boiling water. Stir them in the boiling water for 30 seconds and drain. Heat about 250 ml (½ pint) vegetable oil in a medium-sized frying pan. When a crumb will sizzle when dropped into the oil, add the kidneys. Stir them in the oil for 1 minute, remove with a perforated spoon and drain.

Using the same pan and oil, heat the oil fiercely for 20 seconds until it is very hot. Add the liver pieces. Stir them in the hot oil for 1 minute. Remove with a perforated spoon and drain.

Finally, heat the oil again for 20 seconds. Return the liver and kidney to the pan. Stir them over a high heat for 30 seconds. Remove and drain well.

Serve immediately in a well-heated dish: it should be eaten hot, as soon as it is brought to the table. The liver and kidney should be crisp outside and juicy inside, and the texture should be firm and chewy. The Aromatic Salt and Pepper Mix gives it an added sharpness, making this simply produced dish a gastronomic delight—an excellent follow-on to Peking Duck (page 28), especially when served with Duck Carcase Soup which is usually accompanied by rice and one or two other simple dishes.

Serves 6–8.

Lotus-Leaf Wrapped Duck
(Adapted from the U I-Sung, Moslem Restaurant, Peking.)

1 medium duck (about 1.8–2.2 kg/4–5 lb)

2–3 lotus leaves (dried)

75–90 ml (5–6 tablespoons) coarsely ground rice

2 medium onions

4 slices root ginger

37 ml (2½ tablespoons) soya sauce

30 ml (2 tablespoons) hoisin sauce

45 ml (3 tablespoons) dry sherry

7 ml (½ tablespoon) sugar

10 ml (2 teaspoons) crushed peppercorns

75–90 ml (5–6 tablespoons) ground pudding rice

Chop the duck through the bone into approximately 24 pieces and place them in a basin. Soak the lotus leaves in water and cut them into 8 equal pieces. Heat the ground rice in a dry pan and stir over a medium heat until slightly aromatic (about 2½ minutes). Cut the onions and ginger into thin slices, then chop them coarsely. Put them in a bowl. Add the soya sauce, hoisin sauce, sherry, sugar, crushed peppercorns and pudding rice. Mix them together thoroughly and pour over the duck. Make sure the pieces of duck are well coated with the mixture, and leave to marinate for 1 hour.

Wrap 3 pieces of duck in each piece of lotus leaf, and secure with a wooden cocktail skewer. Arrange these lotus-leaf parcels on a heatproof dish, and put the latter in a steamer (see fig, page 199) to steam vigorously for 2 hours.

Bring the dish to the table. Each diner takes a parcel, which he unwraps to eat the contents along with the other items on the table. Serves 8.

Sliced Duck with Two Types of Dressing
(Adapted from the Chuan Chu Te' Restaurant, Peking.)

225–350 g (½–¾ lb) cooked duck meat

3 pairs of duck's wings

Dressing 1

37 ml (2½ tablespoons) Chinese yellow wine (or dry sherry)

15 ml (1 tablespoon) wine sediment paste (if available—or blend 15 ml (1 tablespoon)

hoisin sauce with 15 ml (1 tablespoon) brandy

7 ml (½ tablespoon) sugar

1 ml (¼ teaspoon) salt

Dressing 2

15 ml (3 teaspoons) mustard   15 ml (1 tablespoon) Chinese
   powder   aromatic vinegar
22 ml (1½ tablespoons) soya   22 ml (1½ tablespoons) sesame
   sauce   oil

Place the duck in a pan of boiling water to simmer for 15 minutes. Remove and drain. Carve off the meat into medium-sized thin slices. Place the duck's wings in a pan of boiling water, and simmer gently for ¾ hour. Drain and chop each wing into 3–4 pieces.

Blend the ingredients for the dressings in two bowls.

Arrange the wings at the centre of a dish and surround and partly cover them with pieces of sliced duck. Pour the two types of dressing evenly over them. This is a 'wine accompanying dish', which is also suitable as a starter for a multi-course dinner.
Serves 6–8.

Fu-Yung Poached Chicken Slices

(Adapted from the Chui Hua Lou, a well-known Shantung-style restaurant, in Peking.)

100 g (¼ lb) chicken breast   15 ml (1 tablespoon) water
   meat   10 ml (2 teaspoons) cornflour
100 g (¼ lb) filleted white fish   4 ml (¾ teaspoon) salt
3 egg-whites   oil for deep-frying

Sauce

3 slices root ginger   30 ml (2 tablespoons) white
2 stalks spring onion   wine
2.5 ml (½ teaspoon) salt   5 ml (1 teaspoon) sugar
15 ml (1 tablespoon) chicken   10 ml (2 teaspoons) cornflour
   fat   blended in 30 ml (2 table-
90 ml (6 tablespoons) chicken   spoons) water
   stock (a)

Chop the chicken breast meat and filleted fish finely. Beat the egg-whites with a fork for 30 seconds. Add them to the chopped chicken and fish. Beat them together with the water and cornflour mixture for 1 minute.

Heat the chicken fat in a small frying pan. Add all the other ingredients for the sauce. Stir until the liquid has slightly thickened. Remove from the heat and put aside.

Heat about 500 ml (1 pint) oil in a large frying pan. Stir the oil once or twice, remove the pan from the heat. Add the chicken, fish and egg-white mixture in tablespoonfuls, by sliding them in slowly one by one from the side of the pan, 3–4 spoonfuls at a time. On impact with the hot oil, the mixture immediately firms into slices. Turn the slices over with a perforated spoon, and, after about 10 seconds, remove them from the oil to drain. After reheating the oil over a medium heat for 15 seconds, repeat the procedure until all the mixture has been used up.

Heat the sauce in the smaller frying pan. Transfer the fried chicken-and-fish slices into the sauce. Bring to a gentle boil, pour the contents into a deep-sided dish and serve. This is a typical Pekingese dish, light and delicate in flavour, and generally served towards the start of a multi-course meal.
Serves 6–8.

Diced Chicken Cubes Quick-Fried in Bean Paste Sauce
(Adapted from the Chui Hua Lou Restaurant, Peking.)

225 g (½ lb) chicken breast meat   *blended in 22 ml (1½ table-*
1 egg-white   *spoons) water*
10 ml (2 teaspoons) cornflour   *125 ml (¼ pint) vegetable oil*

Sauce

30 ml (2 tablespoons) lard   *water (heat 2 slices ginger in*
15 ml (1 tablespoon) brown   *30 ml (2 tablespoons) water*
  bean paste   *until the water is reduced by*
7 ml (½ tablespoon) sugar   *half—use only the water)*
10 ml (2 teaspoons) ginger   *15 ml (1 tablespoon) dry sherry*

Cut the breast of chicken into small cubes. Beat the egg-white, blend the cornflour into it and beat with a fork for 30 seconds. Add it to the diced chicken. Work them together with the fingers until each chicken cube is evenly covered with the egg-white and cornflour mixture.

Heat the oil in a frying pan. Add the chicken cubes, and stir them quickly over a high heat (make sure that the pieces are not stuck together) for 1 minute. Remove with a perforated spoon, and drain immediately. Pour away excess oil or put it aside for other use.

Put the lard and soya paste into the same pan. Stir over a low heat for 15 seconds. Add the sugar, ginger water and sherry. Stir for about 30 seconds until the mixture has become a consistent

shiny, pasty texture. Return the fried chicken cubes to the pan.
Turn up the heat to high, and stir them with the sauce in the pan
for 1 minute. This is another very typical Pekingese dish, which
should be eaten immediately, while it is hot.
Serves 6–8.

Royal Concubines' Drunken Chicken
(Adapted from the Tung He Chu, a well-known Shantung
restaurant established in Peking in 1901.)

1 medium chicken (about 1.5–
  2 kg/3½–4½ lb)
10 ml (2 teaspoons) salt
30 ml (2 tablespoons) soya
  sauce
45 ml (3 tablespoons) Chinese
  yellow wine or dry sherry
oil for deep-frying

3 stalks spring onion
1.25 litres (2¼ pints) chicken
  stock (a)
3 slices root ginger
1 chicken stock cube
30 ml (2 tablespoons) soya sauce
250–375 ml (½–¾ pint) red
  (grape) wine

Clean the chicken thoroughly, remove head and claws and rub both
inside and out with the salt, soya sauce and yellow wine. Leave to
marinate for 3 hours. Heat the oil in the deep-fryer. Deep-fry the
chicken for 3–4 minutes and drain. Cut the spring onions into
medium-sized sections.

Heat the stock and root ginger in a large casserole. When they
start to boil, add the chicken. Cover the casserole and put it into a
preheated oven at 200°C (400°F)/Gas 6 for 2½ hours, turning the
chicken over after the first and second hour. Take the lid off the
casserole, add the stock cube, soya sauce, spring onion and red wine.
Stir them together, and leave to cook for another 20 minutes. Serve
in the casserole at the table. The aroma of the wine, the tenderness
of the chicken, and the richness of the soup make this Chinese
version of *coq au vin* very appealing.
Serves 8–10.

Quick-Fried Shredded Chicken with Shredded Vegetables
(Adapted from the Tung He Chu Restaurant, Peking.)

100 g (¼ lb) chicken breast meat
5 ml (1 teaspoon) salt
22 ml (1½ tablespoons) cornflour
  B*

1 egg-white
6 large Chinese dried mushrooms
½ green pepper
½ red pepper

3 golden needles (tiger lily   ½ chicken stock cube
buds)   22 ml (1½ tablespoons) dry
60 ml (4 tablespoons) vegetable   sherry
oil   15 ml (1 tablespoon) chicken
30 ml (2 tablespoons) soya   fat
sauce   7 ml (½ tablespoon) sesame oil

Cut the breast of the chicken into fine thread-like pieces. Mix and
rub these with the salt, cornflour and egg-white. Soak the mushrooms in water for 20 minutes, drain and remove the stalks. Cut the
mushroom caps and the other vegetables into similar thread-like
shreds. Soak the golden needles in water for 10 minutes, and drain
them.

Heat the oil in a frying pan; add the shredded chicken, and stir
quickly over a high heat for 1 minute. Remove and set aside.

Add the shredded vegetables to the frying pan along with the
chicken fat. Stir and quick-fry over a high heat for 3 minutes. Return the shredded chicken to the pan. Add the soya sauce, stock
cube, sherry and finally the sesame oil. Stir quickly for 45 seconds
and serve on a well-heated dish, to be eaten immediately.
Serves 6–8.

Tri-Coloured Chicken Soufflé
(Adapted from the Ngor Mei Café-Restaurant, East Peking.)

6 eggs   30 ml (2 tablespoons) white
225 g (½ lb) chicken breast meat   wine
2.5 ml (½ teaspoon) salt   45 ml (3 tablespoons) vegetable
pepper to taste   oil
15 ml (1 tablespoon) cornflour   30 ml (2 tablespoons) lard
45 ml (3 tablespoons) chicken   60 ml (4 tablespoons) tomato
stock (b)   purée

Separate the egg-whites from the yolks. Beat the yolks until well
mixed. Chop the breast of chicken finely. Beat it with the egg-whites
for 1 minute. Add the salt, pepper, cornflour, stock and white wine.
Beat again for 1 minute or until the mixture is consistent.

Heat the oil in a small frying pan. Add two-thirds of the egg-
white and chicken mixture, and stir and scramble it quickly over
a medium heat for 2½ minutes. Spoon just over half the mixture
from the pan into the middle of a well-heated oval dish. Add 12
ml (¾ tablespoon) lard and the yolks to the pan. Scramble this
quickly with the chicken and egg-white mixture in the pan for 1½

minutes. Spoon the yellow 'soufflé' on to one end of the oval dish. Heat the remaining lard in the pan. Add the remaining egg-white and chicken mixture, along with the tomato purée. Stir and scramble the ingredients together over a medium heat for 2 minutes, into a red 'soufflé'. Transfer this to the other end of the oval dish.

Many diners find this three-coloured dish both pleasing to the eye and appealing to the palate. It is meant for small meals, when a small amount of plain rice is eaten with each mouthful of 'soufflé'. *Serves 8.*

Peking Runny Scrambled Egg

6 eggs
30 ml (2 tablespoons) cornflour
10 ml (2 teaspoons) salt
1 crushed chicken stock cube
125 ml (¼ pint) stock (b)
60 ml (4 tablespoons) vegetable oil

30 ml (2 tablespoons) lard
30 ml (2 tablespoons) green peas
15 ml (1 tablespoon) chicken fat (or use butter)
30 ml (2 tablespoons) chopped ham

Beat the eggs with a rotary beater for 15 seconds. Add the cornflour, salt, crushed stock cube and stock. Beat for 30 seconds or until consistent.

Heat the oil and lard in a frying pan. Pour in the egg and stock mixture. Stir continually over a medium heat for about 5 minutes, when the egg becomes somewhat set. Add the peas and chicken fat. Stir once more, and transfer the contents into a dish. Sprinkle with the chopped ham.

The diners normally ladle spoonfuls of the egg mixture into their rice and eat them together. This is intended for big rice-eaters, unlike the previous recipe which is for more delicate helpings. *Serves 6.*

Stuffed Barbecued Duck
(Adapted from the Yu Hua Dining Room, Peking.)

6 stalks spring onion
1 sheet dried lotus leaf
90 ml (6 tablespoons) pudding rice
6 slices root ginger
22 ml (1½ tablespoons) peppercorns, lightly crushed

22 ml (1½ tablespoons) soya sauce
1 duck (1.8–2.5 kg/4–5½ lb)
15 ml (1 tablespoon) sugar blended in 90 ml (6 tablespoons) water

Cut the spring onion into short sections. Soak the lotus leaf in warm water for 5 minutes, and cut it into small pieces. Soak the rice in hot water for 15 minutes and drain it. Chop the ginger, each into thinner slices, and then quarter each piece. Mix all these ingredients together with the peppercorns and soya sauce in a basin, and stuff the mixture into the cavity of the duck. Sew or skewer to secure.

Douse the duck with 2 kettlefuls of boiling water. Dry it with absorbent paper or a towel. Hang it up to dry in an airy spot for 3–4 hours. Brush once with sugar water, and hang it up to dry for a further hour.

Place the duck on a revolving spit to barbecue for 1 hour 10 minutes under a medium heat. If the duck is barbecued over a charcoal fire, extra time and attention should be given to the sides and legs during the cooking, so that the heat penetrates the thickest part of the body, although the overall time required will be the same.

This duck should be carved and served in the same manner as Peking Duck: the skin and meat carved off separately, to be eaten sandwiched in Flower Rolls (Hua Chuan), brushed with Peking Duck Sauce (see page 30) and accompanied by chopped spring onion and shredded cucumber. The stuffings can be eaten after picking out and discarding some of the lotus leaf, ginger and peppercorns.
Serves 8–10.

Aromatic and Crispy Chicken Drumsticks
(Adapted from the Seng Lung Dining Rooms, Peking.)

4 slices root ginger
2 medium onions
5 ml (1 teaspoon) salt
45 ml (3 tablespoons) soya sauce
30 ml (2 tablespoons) sherry
22 ml (1½ tablespoons) five-spice (in pieces, not powder)
22 ml (1½ tablespoons) sugar
12 chicken drumsticks
30 ml (2 tablespoons) cornflour
6 lettuce leaves

Dip

45–60 ml (3–4 tablespoons) Aromatic Salt and Pepper mix

Chop the ginger and onion coarsely. Add them along with the salt, soya sauce, sherry, five-spice, and sugar to the drumsticks, and rub them in with the fingers. Leave to season for 3–5 hours in a heat-proof basin.

Cover the top of the basin with tinfoil, and put it into a steamer to steam for 1½ hours. Shake the drumsticks free of marinating ingredients. Sprinkle and rub the drumsticks with the cornflour. Shake off any excess of cornflour, place the drumsticks 6 at a time in a wire basket, and deep-fry them in hot oil for 5–6 minutes over a high heat. Drain them. Finally put all 12 drumsticks back in the basket, deep-fry them for another 1–2 minutes and drain again.

Spread the lettuce leaves over a large dish, and arrange the drumsticks neatly on top. Diners dip the drumsticks in the Salt and Pepper Mix and eat them with their fingers.
Serves 8–10.

Pork

Peking Lions' Heads with Tomatoes
(Adapted from Chef Wan Wu Ping, formerly of the Woo Fan Ch'ai Restaurant, Peking.)

550 g (1¼ lb) lean pork
10 ml (2 teaspoons) salt
30 ml (2 tablespoons) corn-flour
1 egg
30 ml (2 tablespoons) Chinese yellow wine or dry sherry
22 ml (1½ tablespoons) soya sauce
625 ml (1¼ pints) chicken stock (b)

7 ml (½ tablespoon) finely chopped root ginger
3 stalks spring onion
4 medium tomatoes
oil for deep-frying
4 slices root ginger
45 ml (3 tablespoons) vinegar
15 ml (1 tablespoon) sesame oil
15 ml (1 tablespoon) sugar

Chop the pork finely. Put it in a basin; add the salt, cornflour, beaten egg, wine or sherry, soya sauce, 30 ml (2 tablespoons) stock and the chopped ginger. Mix them together thoroughly with a wooden spoon for at least 3–4 minutes. Form the mixture into 4 meat balls. Cut the spring onions into medium-sized sections and each tomato into 5–6 thin slices.

Heat the oil in the deep-fryer. Lower 2 meat balls at a time to fry, totally immersed in the hot oil, for 6 minutes. Drain and place the meat balls in a casserole. Pour the rest of the chicken stock and vinegar over the meat balls and scatter the spring onion and ginger around them. Bring the contents to the boil, and skim off any impurities. Put the casserole into an oven preheated to 200°C (400°F)/ Gas 6 for 1¼ hours. Remove the onion and ginger with chopsticks or a perforated spoon. Sprinkle the stock and meat balls with sesame oil. Return the casserole to the oven to cook at the same temperature for a further 30 minutes.

Place the meat balls in a deep-sided dish (3 balls in a triangle and the last on top). Surround them with sliced tomatoes and sprinkle the tomatoes with sugar. Reduce the liquid in the casserole by a third over a high heat, and pour it over the meat balls. *Serves 6–8.*

Pork Crackling Sandwiches
(Adapted from the Fang Shan Palace Restaurant, North Sea Park, Peking.)

350 g (¾ lb) lean pork
3 stalks spring onion, finely chopped
4 slices root ginger, finely chopped
3 cloves garlic, finely chopped
22 ml (1½ tablespoons) soya sauce

15 ml (1 tablespoon) hoisin sauce (optional)
30 ml (2 tablespoons) sherry
5 ml (1 teaspoon) sugar
8 thin sheets of pork fat
oil for deep frying
2.5 ml (½ teaspoon) salt, pepper to taste

Batter

1 egg
37 ml (2½ tablespoons) corn-flour

37 ml (2½ tablespoons) flour
45 ml (3 tablespoons) water

Dip

45 ml (3 tablespoons) Aromatic Salt and Pepper Mix (page 68)

Cut the pork into thin slices. Place them in a basin. Add the spring onion, ginger, garlic, soya sauce, hoisin sauce, sherry, sugar, salt and pepper. Mix and rub them together with the fingers. Leave to season for 2–3 hours.

Mix the batter ingredients together in a separate bowl and dip the seasoned pork slices in the batter. Divide the pork slices into four lots. Arrange each batch, evenly spread out, between two sheets of pork fat, to form a 'sandwich'. Pile the 'sandwiches' one on top of the other. Place a plate on top to flatten and weigh them down.

Heat the oil in the deep-fryer. Lower two 'sandwiches' at a time in a wire basket to fry for 5–6 minutes until brown and crispy. Drain, and when all the 'sandwiches' have been fried, put them on a chopping board and chop each piece into four (16 pieces altogether). Arrange them neatly on a well-heated dish, and serve with Aromatic Salt and Pepper Mix.

Serves 6–8.

Quick-Fried Diced Pork Cubes in Peking Soya Paste

450 g (1 lb) leg of pork
22 ml (1½ tablespoons) cornflour

90–105 ml (6–7 tablespoons)
vegetable oil

Sauce

15 ml (1 tablespoon) soya
(yellow bean) paste
7 ml (½ tablespoon) hoisin sauce
(optional)
5 ml (1 teaspoon) sugar

22 ml (1½ tablespoons) ginger
water (boil 3 slices root
ginger in 45 ml (3 table-
spoons) water, until the water
is reduced to half, discard
ginger)

Dice the pork into small cubes. Sprinkle and rub them with corn-flour.

Heat the oil in a large frying pan. Add the pork cubes and spread them over the pan in a single layer. Stir-fry them over a high heat for 1½ minutes.

Remove and drain the pork and pour away the oil. Add all the sauce ingredients to the pan. Reduce the heat to low. Stir the ingredients together for about 30 seconds until they constitute a shiny, brownish paste. Return the once-fried pork cubes to the pan. Stir and mix them with the thick sauce in the pan, for about 45 seconds. Transfer them to a well-heated dish, and serve immediately.

Serves 6–8.

This is a popular and favourite Pekingese dish which, like its chicken counterpart (see page 34) is served in most Pekingese eating establishments. A variation is Quick-fried Three Delicious, in which half the pork is replaced by diced cubes of pig's kidney and liver. The cooking times are exactly the same as above, but quite often a couple of finely chopped cloves of garlic are fried in the remaining oil just before the sauce ingredients are added.

Deep-Fried Crispy Shredded Pork Served in Pancakes

675 g (1½ lb) lean and fat pork
15 ml (1 tablespoon) salted soya paste or yellow bean paste
15 ml (1 tablespoon) soya sauce
15 ml (1 tablespoon) hoisin sauce
3 cloves garlic, crushed and chopped

3 slices root ginger, shredded
30 ml (2 tablespoons) dry sherry
22 ml (1½ tablespoons) sugar
1 ml (¼ teaspoon) five-spice powder
3 stalks spring onion
oil for deep-frying

Batter

45 ml (3 tablespoons) flour
45 ml (3 tablespoons) cornflour

60 ml (4 tablespoons) water
1 egg

Cut the pork into strips 5 cm (2 in) long and the thickness of one chopstick and put them in a basin. Add the bean paste, soya sauce, hoisin sauce, garlic, ginger, sherry, sugar, five-spice powder and spring onion cut into shavings, and mix well. Leave them to season overnight. Place the pork, together with the seasonings, in a casserole.

Heat the casserole. When it is hot, put it into a preheated oven at 190°C (375°F)/Gas 5 for 1 hour. Break or loosen the pork into individual strips. Mix the batter ingredients together thoroughly, and dip the pork strips one by one into the batter to take on a coating.

Heat the oil in a deep-fryer. Place a quarter of the strips of pork in a wire basket, fry them for 3–3½ minutes and drain. When they have all been fried and drained, place the whole lot in the wire basket and give them a final frying of about 1½ minutes. Drain.

These crispy strips of pork are served in a pancake, supplemented with shredded spring onion and cucumber, and brushed with piquant Peking Duck Sauce (see page 30), in the same manner as Peking Duck. In fact, this popular north China dish can be described as the poor man's Peking Duck.
Serves 6–8.

Beef and Lamb

Barbecued Beef or Lamb

This recipe is adapted from the Peking restaurants called Barbecue Wan and Barbecue Chi, which are renowned for this type of cooking. The preparation and cooking of beef and lamb was first introduced into Peking from Mongolia during the reign of Emperor Sung Chi (1644–61) by visiting Mongolian dignitaries.

A principal feature of the Peking Barbecue of Beef and Lamb is that barbecuing is done on the dining table itself. The charcoal burner or brazier is a round fire-proof earthenware pot, about 60–75 cm (2–2½ ft) in diameter with an open top, which is covered with a close-meshed wire rack on which thinly sliced meats are cooked with extra-long (about 45 cm/1½ ft) chopsticks. Often such a meal is held outdoors in a courtyard or patio, where not infrequently the diners eat standing, one foot on the benches surrounding the table as they do their cooking. To start with the fire in the brazier should be built up to a considerable blaze, which helps to keep the diners warm as well as cook the meat. The calculation is for at least 450 g (1 lb) meat (4–5 platefuls, cut into paper-thin slices) per person; it is not infrequent for a person to consume as much as a dozen platefuls of meat. This is partly due to the fact that the slices of meat shrivel when cooked over a fierce heat, and because by this method of cooking the eating is spread over a good length of time.

Each diner is provided with several accompanying dishes. During the cooking the diner picks up a small bundle or large pinch of 'spring onion wool' (spring onions cut to thread-like shreds) and places it on the hot wire range. He then dips one or two slices of meat in the Mixed Dip, and places them on top of the spring onion to cook over the heat of the brazier. The Mixed Dip consists of ginger water, soya sauce, shrimp sauce and yellow wine or dry sherry, mixed by the diner himself in his own bowl. When the meat is cooked, generally in 1–1½ minutes, the diner picks it up with chopsticks, dips it quickly in a bowl of beaten egg, and consumes it by sandwiching it in a steamed Flower Bun (Hua Chuan) or, alternatively, in an Aromatic Hot Cake, with a garnish of coriander leaves and shredded cucumber and a thin spread of sesame paste as further accompaniments. These Barbecued Beef and Lamb meals

are among the most memorable features of Peking winter eating
(the only season when these barbecues are served).

Mongolian Hot Pot of Quick-Poached Lamb
(Adapted from the Tung Lai Shun Restaurant, East Market,
Peking.)

The Mongolian Hot Pot, with which many Westerners have now
become acquainted, is a circular brass construction about 30 cm
(1 ft) in diameter and 45 cm (18 in) in height. The central part of
the pot is the funnel-and-burner, which is packed with burning
charcoal and surrounded by a round 'moat' filled with stock or
water, in which the cooking is done. At the Tung Lai Shun, the best-
known establishment for this type of cooking, the hot pot used is
larger, with an additional 'extension' funnel which can be slotted on
to cause an additional 'draw' when the charcoal in the funnel is
first lit. Once the charcoal is in full blaze, and the liquid in the
'moat' starts boiling, the extension funnel is withdrawn. The meat
has to be cooked quickly, so the stock in the 'moat' has to be kept
at a rolling boil. Normally about 1 litre (2 pints) stock are used
when the meal starts. The stock has to be continually replenished,
especially during the latter part of the meal—for by this time one
of the best parts of the dish is the rich freshness of the soup. Often
noodles are served to accompany the soup at this stage. In winter
this meal is a most heat-generating exercise!

Rather less meat—not more than 450 g (1 lb) per person—is
allowed than in the barbecue described in the last recipe. This is
because meat shrinks less when poached than when grilled or barbecued, and there is plenty of soup, noodles and cabbage to go with
it. In orthodox Peking cuisine, the only meat used in the pot is
lamb, which is sliced paper-thin and placed on an array of small
plates on the table for the diners to help themselves. These they
pick up with chopsticks, and immerse in the boiling stock to cook
for not more than a minute. When retrieved, the meat is dipped in
a sauce concocted by the diners themselves from much the same
ingredients as the Mixed Dip used in the previous recipe, though
sometimes a little chilli sauce is added. The other accompaniments
to the hot pot are spinach, Chinese cabbage and transparent pea-
starch noodles. After the first few platefuls of sliced meat have been
eaten, the vegetables are gradually added into the 'moat' so that
the diner will be consuming a mixture of meat, noodles and veg-

etables. No buns or hot cakes are provided. After dozens of plates of thinly-sliced lamb have been cooked, not infrequently some par-boiled egg-noodles are added into the now very rich stock. The whole meal usually lasts for 1½ hours or more, as eating can pro-ceed no faster than the cooking. A person can hardly have been said to have tasted the food of Peking without having eaten this hot pot, which usually leaves the diner with a wonderful glow of health and warmth, since all the ingredients are of the finest quality and freshly cooked.

Deep-Fried Long-Cooked Mutton

(Adapted from the Lung Fu Ssi, Moslem Mutton Restaurant, East Peking.)

The original version of this dish is to cook a whole sheep in a vast cauldron, with the bones placed at the bottom and meaty parts built around the sides, whilst the innards and head of the sheep are arranged in the middle. The average weight of the carcase is about 22 kg (50 lb). Before the meat, cut into 2.7–3 kg (6–7 lb) pieces, is put into the cauldron, the chunks are first parboiled for 15 minutes, in order to eliminate any impurities.

The flavouring ingredients used are mostly either soya-based or herbs, plus water sufficient to cover the meat and bones. The con-tents are brought to a boil, then the heat is reduced to a gentle simmer which is maintained for 4–5 hours. The meat, which should now be very tender and flavoursome, is lifted out, cut into roughly 900 g (2 lb) pieces, and left to drain and dry.

When required, smaller cuts are lowered into boiling sesame oil to deep-fry for 8–9 minutes, drained, chopped into bite-sized pieces or easily manageable thin slices and eaten together with Aromatic Sesame Hot Cakes. These are sliced across the middle and pieces of meat, which should be crispy outside and tender inside, inserted into them sandwich-fashion. These 'sandwiches' should be eaten with the rich savoury stock, the product of the lengthy simmering. Alternatively, fresh noodles are often boiled in the stock, and pieces of the mutton placed on top of the noodles with some shredded fresh vegetables (cucumber, spring onion, celery, etc) as a garnish.

3–3.6 kg (7–8 lb) lamb
1.35–1.8 kg (3–4 lb) lamb bone
3.5–4 litres (7–8 pints) water

1 litre (2 pints) sesame oil (for deep-frying)

Stock

45–60 ml (3–4 tablespoons)
yellow bean paste

45–60 ml (3–4 tablespoons)
soya sauce

30 ml (2 tablespoons) black
bean paste

45 ml (3 tablespoons) five-spice
in pieces not powder

4 large onions

8 large slices root ginger

45 ml (3 tablespoons) rock
sugar

225 g (½ lb) Chinese dried
mushrooms (soaked first for
15 minutes and drained)

500 ml (1 pint) Chinese yellow
wine or dry sherry

15 ml (1 tablespoon) salt

After parboiling, the meat is cut into 4–5 pieces.

Place the bones at the bottom of a large casserole. Arrange the pieces of meat on top. Distribute the stock ingredients evenly around the meat. Pour in the water, and see that the solids are well covered. Bring the contents to the boil over the cooker, and insert the casserole into a preheated oven at 190°C (375°F)/Gas 5 for 1 hour. Reduce the heat to 170°C (325°F)/Gas 3, and continue to cook steadily for the next 3 hours.

Lift the meat out, drain and, when required, lower the pieces two at a time in a wire basket into the boiling sesame oil, to deep-fry for 7–8 minutes.

Bring the freshly deep-fried meats to the table, and cut them into slices or bite-sized pieces to eat in Aromatic Sesame Cakes accompanied by fresh shredded vegetables (cucumber, spring onions etc) and brushed with a plum sauce, such as Peking Duck Sauce (see page 30). Or, alternatively, the sauce from the cauldron could be used to parboil the noodles for a few minutes (250 ml/½ pint stock with 450 g/1 lb boiled noodles would be a suitable proportion); serve them garnished with pieces of lamb, accompanied by shredded vegetables. Serves 6–8.

Tung-Po Stewed Lamb

(Adapted from the U I-Yi Sung, Moslem Restaurant, Peking.)

675 g (1½ lb) leg of lamb

225 g (½ lb) carrots

225 g (½ lb) potatoes

2 medium onions

2 leeks

4 cloves garlic

oil for deep-frying

4 slices root ginger

5 ml (1 teaspoon) peppercorns,
lightly crushed

7 ml (½ tablespoon) salt

37 ml (2½ tablespoons) soya
sauce

10 ml (2 teaspoons) sugar

90 ml (6 tablespoons) Chinese
yellow wine or dry sherry

Cut the lamb into small, thin strips. Cut the carrots and potatoes into small, triangular wedge-shaped pieces. Cut the onion into thin slices, and the leeks slantwise into small sections. Crush the garlic.

Heat the oil in the deep-fryer. Deep-fry the lamb pieces for 5 minutes and drain them. Deep-fry the potatoes and carrots for 5 minutes and drain.

Place the lamb pieces in a casserole. Add the onions, ginger, peppercorns, salt, soya sauce, sugar and half the wine. Pour in water until the solids are covered by 1½ inches. Bring the contents to the boil, and insert the casserole, covered, into a preheated oven at 180°C (350°F)/Gas 4 for 2 hours, turning the contents twice. Now add the carrots, potatoes and leeks. Pour in the remainder of the wine. Turn the contents over a few times. Return the casserole to the oven to cook at 200°C (400°F)/Gas 6 for a further 20 minutes.

Bring the casserole to the table and serve with steamed buns (see page 63), or rice. The dish is named after Soo Tung-Po, a famous poet of the Sung Dynasty, but whether he actually invented the dish is not authenticated—though there is no doubt that he did cook some similar dishes.
Serves 6–8.

Long-Cooked Cow's Heel and Shin of Beef
(Adapted from the Ray Cheng Hou, Moslem Restaurant, Peking.)

900 g (2 lb) cow's heel
900 g (2 lb) shin of beef
oil for deep-frying
2 large onions
6 slices root ginger
22 ml (1½ tablespoons) five-spice (in pieces—not powder)

7 ml (½ tablespoon) salt
90–105 ml (6–7 tablespoons) soya sauce
60 ml (4 tablespoons) Chinese yellow wine or sherry
22 ml (1½ tablespoons) coriander leaves

Cut the cow's heel and beef into small cubes. Plunge them into a pan of boiling water to boil vigorously for 6–7 minutes and drain. Heat the oil in the deep-fryer. Lower half the cubes of meat into the hot oil to fry for 4 minutes and drain. Repeat with the rest of the meat. Cut the onions into thin slices.

Place the meat in a casserole. Add the ginger, onion, five-spice, salt, soya sauce. Pour in water to cover the solids by 2.5 cm (1 in). Bring to the boil, and place the casserole in a preheated oven at 180°C (350°F)/Gas 4. Leave to cook for 4 hours, turning the contents over every hour. Add the wine or sherry and chopped coriander. Stir and turn the contents. Cook for 15 minutes longer.

Serve in the casserole. The tough shin of beef should now be very tender, the cow's heel almost jelly-like and the gravy or soup rich and flavoursome. There is little more enticing to eat with hot rice or steamed buns after skating on the canals or lakes in the Peking winter.

Serves 8–10.

Braised Beef with Tomatoes
(Adapted from the Tientsin Municipal Catering Co.)

675 g (1½ lb) stewing beef
2 medium onions
2 leeks
6–8 medium tomatoes (must be firm)
22 ml (1½ tablespoons) sugar
4 slices root ginger
10 ml (2 teaspoons) salt
500 ml (1 pint) stock (b)

45 ml (3 tablespoons) lard
22 ml (1½ tablespoons) pepper-corns, crushed
4 cloves garlic
30 ml (2 tablespoons) soya sauce
15 ml (1 tablespoon) cornflour blended in 45 ml (3 table-spoons) water

Cut the beef into 3.75 cm (1½ in) cubes. Cut the onion into thin slices and the leeks into 2.5 cm (1 in) sections. Douse the tomatoes with boiling water. Remove the skins, cut into quarters, and sprinkle them with sugar.

Place the beef in a casserole. Add the onion, ginger, salt and stock. Bring to the boil, reduce the heat and simmer gently for 1 hour, turning the contents every 20 minutes. By this time the liquid in the casserole should have been reduced to a third or a quarter of its original volume. Remove from the heat and lift out the beef pieces with a perforated spoon.

Heat the lard in a large frying pan. When the fat is very hot, add the beef and peppercorns to stir-fry over a high heat for 2 minutes. Add the leeks, garlic and soya sauce and turn and stir with the beef for 2 minutes. Finally add the tomatoes; turn and stir with the other ingredients, still over a high heat, for 1 minute. Pour the blended cornflour into the sauce in the casserole and bring to the boil. Pour the thickened sauce into the frying pan. Mix it with the beef and tomatoes.

Bring to a high boil, and pour the contents into a deep-sided dish and serve. Another favourite for rice-eaters.

Serves 6–8.

Quick-Fried Lamb and Leeks

550 g (1¼ lb) leg of lamb
7 ml (½ tablespoon) soya sauce
7 ml (½ tablespoon) soya paste
3 cloves garlic
4 ml (¾ teaspoon) cornflour
45 ml (3 tablespoons) oil

4 young leeks
3 slices root ginger
45 ml (3 tablespoons) lard
30 ml (2 tablespoons) Chinese
 yellow wine or dry sherry
2.5 ml (½ teaspoon) salt

Cut the lamb into medium-sized thin slices. Mix and rub them with the soya sauce, soya paste, chopped garlic, cornflour and 15 ml (1 tablespoon) oil. Leave to season for 30 minutes. Clean and cut the leeks slantwise into small sections.

Heat the ginger in the remainder of the oil in a large frying pan. Add the lamb and spread the pieces out over the surface of the pan. Stir-fry quickly over a high heat for 1½ minutes; remove the lamb and set aside.

Melt the lard in the pan over a high heat. Add the leeks, sprinkle with the salt and stir them quickly for 1½ minutes. Return the lamb to the pan to turn and stir with the leeks. Sprinkle with the wine or sherry. Continue to stir and turn over a high heat for 1½ minutes, and serve. This is a quick and effective dish, which can be cooked when the meal has already started. It must be eaten immediately after the food leaves the pan.
Serves 5–6.

Quick-Fried Lamb's Kidney and Liver

225 g (½ lb) lamb's kidney
350 g (¾ lb) lamb's liver
7 ml (½ tablespoon) salt
15 ml (1 tablespoon) cornflour
45 ml (3 tablespoons) vegetable
 oil

1 green pepper
30 ml (2 tablespoons) wood
 ears tree fungi
30 ml (2 tablespoons) lard

Sauce

22 ml (1½ tablespoons) sugar
45 ml (3 tablespoons) wine
 vinegar
15 ml (1 tablespoon) soya sauce
15 ml (1 tablespoon) tomato
 purée

22 ml (1½ tablespoons) cornflour blended in 60 ml (4
 tablespoons) water
60 ml (4 tablespoons) cold stock

Remove the membrane from the kidney. Cut it and the liver into small, thin slices. Score each kidney piece with 6 criss-cross cuts. Sprinkle and rub them with the salt, cornflour and 15 ml (1 tablespoon) oil. Cut the pepper into small slices, soak the wood ears in water for 5 minutes, rinse clean and drain. Mix the sauce ingredients together until consistent.

Heat the remainder of the oil in a large frying pan. Add the kidney and liver, and stir them over a high heat for 2 minutes. Remove and put aside.

Melt the lard in the pan. Add the pepper and wood ears. Stir them over a high heat for 2 minutes. Return the kidney and liver to the pan. Stir the ingredients together for 1 minute. Pour the sauce mixture into the pan. Turn and mix with the solids in the pan. As soon as the sauce thickens and becomes transparent, pour it into a dish and serve. This is another dish which has to be eaten as soon as it leaves the pan. Its sweet and sour flavour makes a change from the stewed and other quick-fried dishes which are mostly soya-flavoured.

Serves 6–8.

Fish and Shellfish

Quick-Fried Sliced Fish in Classic Sauce

(Adapted from the Fan Shan Palace Restaurant, North Sea Park, Peking; recipe by ex-Palace Chef Wang Yu San.)

450 g (1 lb) fillet of white fish (sole, place, carp, halibut, etc)

7 ml (½ tablespoon) salt

30 ml (2 tablespoons) cornflour

oil for deep- or semi-deep frying (250 ml (½ pint) oil in a frying pan)

37 ml (2½ tablespoons) lard

Sauce

2 stalks spring onion

3 slices root ginger

30 ml (2 tablespoons) soya sauce

22 ml (1½ tablespoons) wine vinegar

10 ml (2 teaspoons) sugar

30 ml (2 tablespoons) Chinese yellow wine or sherry

30 ml (2 tablespoons) stock (b)

½ chicken stock cube, crushed

Cut the fish into small, thin slices. Sprinkle and rub them with the salt and cornflour (shake free of any excess). Blend the sauce ingredients in a bowl.

Heat the oil in a pan or deep-fryer. When it is very hot, remove from the heat for 30 seconds and lower the fish piece by piece gently into the oil. Return the pan over the heat to fry for 2 minutes, remove and drain.

Heat the lard in a frying pan. Pour in the sauce mixture and stir over a high heat for 1 minute. Add the pieces of fish, spreading them out over the pan. Turn and mix them with the sauce for 1¼ minutes. Remove with a perforated spoon and arrange them neatly on a well-heated dish. Pour the remaining sauce in the pan over the fish and serve. The dish should be eaten hot, as soon as it has left the pan.

Serves 6–8.

Deep-Fried Crispy Fish Sandwich
(Adapted from the Fan Shan Palace Restaurant, North Sea Park, Peking—recipe by Chef Wang Yu San.)

450 g (1 lb) fish fillet (carp, sole, salmon, halibut, etc)
6 large, very thin slices of bacon or pork fat
2 stalks spring onion
2 slices root ginger
30 ml (2 tablespoons) flour

22 ml (1½ tablespoons) cornflour
1 egg
2.5 ml (½ teaspoon) salt
15 ml (1 tablespoon) soya sauce
oil for deep-frying

Cut the fish into small, thin slices. Remove the rind from the bacon and trim it into equal rectangular pieces. Chop the spring onion and ginger finely. Mix them with the flour, cornflour, beaten egg, salt and soya sauce into a batter. Coat the slices of fish with the batter. Now place the fish between two slices of bacon, forming thick sandwiches (holding them firmly together by pinning or skewering them with wooden cocktail sticks at both ends).

Heat the oil in the deep-fryer. Lower the 'sandwiches' in a wire basket into the hot oil to fry for 2 minutes. Remove the pan from the heat so that the frying will continue in the remaining heat without burning for 1½ minutes. Return the pan over a high heat for 1½ minutes to make the bacon crisp.

Remove the 'sandwiches' from the wire basket, take out the cocktail sticks and, using a sharp chopper (Chinese chopper if avail-

able), cut each 'sandwich' into quarters. Serve immediately. An excellent dish to accompany wine.
Serves 6.

Sliced White Fish in Wine or Wine-Lee Sauce
(Adapted from the Chui Hua Lou, Shantung Restaurant, Peking.)

450 g (1 lb) filleted fish (carp,
  sole, halibut, haddock, etc)
7 ml (½ tablespoon) salt
30 ml (2 tablespoons) cornflour
1 egg-white

oil for deep-frying
37 ml (2½ tablespoons) lard
30 ml (2 tablespoons) wood ears
  (tree fungi)

Sauce

60 ml (4 tablespoons) chicken
  stock (b)
60 ml (4 tablespoons) white
  wine
2.5 ml (½ teaspoon) salt

7 ml (½ tablespoon) sugar
15 ml (1 tablespoon) cornflour
10 ml (2 teaspoons) wine-lee
  (if available)

Cut the fish into small, thin slices. Sprinkle and rub them with the salt and cornflour, and wet with beaten egg-white. Mix the sauce ingredients in a bowl until well blended.

Heat the oil in the deep-fryer. Remove from the heat for 1 minute. Lower the slices of fish one by one into the oil with a perforated spoon. Allow them to poach in the oil for 30 seconds, still off the heat. Remove and drain.

Heat the lard in a frying pan. Add the wood ears and stir them over a medium heat for 30 seconds. Pour in the sauce, and mix it with the wood ears. As soon as the sauce thickens and becomes translucent, add the slices of fish, and spread them over the pan in the sauce. Cook for 2 minutes over a medium heat, and pour the contents into a deep-sided dish. The whiteness of the sliced fish, contrasting with the jet-black wood ears, immersed in a translucent sauce, make this a very attractive dish.
Serves 6.

Braised Whole Fish
(Adapted from Yuan Chao Ling, a well-known chef of Tsinan, Shantung.)

1 carp (about 1.2–1.35 kg/2½–
  3 lb)

oil for deep-frying

Sauce

3 stalks spring onion
45 ml (3 tablespoons) lard
45 ml (3 tablespoons) soya
   sauce
22 ml (1½ tablespoons) hoisin
   sauce
3 slices root ginger

22 ml (1½ tablespoons) sweet
   soya paste
60 ml (4 tablespoons) Chinese
   yellow wine or sherry
125 ml (¼ pint) stock (b)
10 ml (2 teaspoons) sugar

After cleaning, gutting and scraping off the scales of the fish, score
the fish lengthways with small deep cuts. Cut and coarsely chop
the ginger and spring onion.

Heat the oil in the deep-fryer. When a crumb dropped in will
sizzle, lower the fish into the oil to fry for 6–7 minutes (either
totally immersed, or turned over gently a couple of times) over a
high heat. Remove and drain.

Heat the lard in a large frying pan. Add the onion and ginger,
and stir them in the fat for 15 seconds. Add all the other sauce
ingredients. Stir them together for 1 minute. Turn the fish in the
pan, and baste it with the sauce for 1 minute. Turn the fish over
and baste again for 1 minute. Reduce the heat to low, cook until
the sauce has been reduced to less than a quarter of the original.
Turn the fish over once more. Transfer the fish to a well-heated
oval dish. Pour the remainder of the sauce over the length of the fish.
Serves 6–8.

Dry-Fried Small Fish
(From the town of Tai An, Shantung.)

6 small fish (herring, large
   sardines, whiting, pilchards,
   etc)
12 ml (2½ teaspoons) salt
7 ml (½ tablespoon) peppercorns, lightly crushed

90 ml (6 tablespoons) Chinese
   yellow wine or dry sherry
45 ml (3 tablespoons) plain
   flour
oil for deep-frying

Clean the fish and remove the innards. Rub the cavity of each fish
with salt and pepper. Pour wine or sherry over the fish and put in a
wire basket to fry for 2 minutes. Reduce heat and continue to fry
at a slow simmer for 6–7 minutes, then increase the heat to fry
for 1 minute over a high heat. Remove and drain. Serve with
Aromatic Salt and Pepper Mix.
Serves 6.

Sweet and Sour Yellow River Carp
(Adapted from the Peking Municipal Catering Co.)

1 carp (about 900 g/2 lb)
10 ml (2 teaspoons) salt
22 ml (1½ tablespoons) plain flour

22 ml (1½ tablespoons) cornflour
oil for deep-frying

Sauce

30 ml (2 tablespoons) sugar
60 ml (4 tablespoons) vinegar
15 ml (1 tablespoon) soya sauce
30 ml (2 tablespoons) Chinese yellow wine or sherry

45 ml (3 tablespoons) water
15 ml (1 tablespoon) cornflour blended with 45 ml (3 tablespoons) water
30 ml (2 tablespoons) lard

Clean the carp and remove the scales and innards. Rub inside and out with the salt. Score on both sides with shallow cuts. Blend the flour and cornflour with 60 ml (5 tablespoons) water into a batter. Coat the fish with the batter.

Heat the oil in the deep-fryer. Lower the fish in a wire basket to fry over a medium heat for 7–8 minutes. Drain and keep hot.

Heat the lard in a saucepan. Add all the sauce ingredients. Stir them together over a medium heat for 2–3½ minutes until the sauce thickens and becomes translucent. Place the fish on a well-heated oval dish, and pour the sauce over the length of the fish.
Serves 6–7.

Sai Pan Hsia or the Rival of Crab
(Adapted from the Fan Shan Palace Kitchen Restaurant, North Sea Park, Peking.)

225 g (½ lb) white fish
7 ml (½ tablespoon) salt
4 eggs
2 egg yolks

15 ml (1 tablespoon) tomato purée
2 slices root ginger
2 stalks spring onion
45 ml (3 tablespoons) lard

Sauce

15 ml (1 tablespoon) cornflour
60 ml (4 tablespoons) chicken stock

15 ml (1 tablespoon) shrimp sauce
5 ml (1 teaspoon) salt
30 ml (2 tablespoons) dry sherry

Dice the fish into small cubes. Sprinkle and rub with the salt. Beat the eggs in a basin for 10 seconds. Beat the yolks with 15 ml (1 tablespoon) water, then beat a quarter of the yolks with a quarter of the purée for 10 seconds in a separate bowl. Blend the sauce ingredients. Chop the ginger and spring onions finely.

Heat the lard in a frying pan. Add the ginger and onion and stir them over a medium heat. Add the fish cubes, turn and stir them gently with the other ingredients for 30 seconds. Stir in the beaten eggs and mix them with the fish. When the eggs are about to set, sprinkle or drop a few drops of the purée, yolk and purée-and-yolk mixture over the contents of the pan. Allow the cooking to proceed gently for 1½ minutes until eggs are scrambled. Turn the contents over, and pour in the sauce mixture. Continue to turn and stir gently for 1½ minutes.

Transfer the mixture to a well-heated dish and serve. The dish was invented in the old Palace Kitchen when real crab was out of season. Over the years the dish gained a certain reputation, and has since been regarded as a delicacy in its own right.
Serves 6.

Phoenix Tail Prawns
(Adapted from the Li Choon Avenue Communal Dining Room,
Tsingtao, Shantung.)

12 *large Pacific prawns (with*
  shells)
10 *ml (2 teaspoons) salt*
30 *ml (2 tablespoons) Chinese*
  yellow wine or dry sherry

1 *egg*
45–60 *ml (3–4 tablespoons)*
  plain flour
oil for deep-frying

Dips

30 *ml (2 tablespoons) Aromatic*
  Salt and Pepper Mix (page
  68)
60 *ml (4 tablespoons) soya*

sauce mixed with 20 ml (4
teaspoons) chilli sauce (div-
ide between 2 saucer-sized
dishes)

Remove the shells from the prawns, except for the last little bit nearest the tail and the tail itself. Remove the dark veins from the back, and cut two shallow criss-cross cuts there to prevent the prawns from curving excessively when fried. Sprinkle and rub the prawns with the salt and wine. Leave to season for 15 minutes. Wet the prawn with the beaten egg, and coat with the flour.

Heat the oil in the deep-fryer. Drop the prawns in one by one and fry them over a low–medium heat for $3\frac{1}{2}$ minutes, or until the prawns are golden brown. Remove and drain. Serve immediately, using the chilli-soya mixture and the Aromatic Salt and Pepper Mix as dips.
Serves 8–10.

Quick Dry-Fried Prawns with their Shells
(Adapted from the Fourth High Street Dining Room, Tsingtao, Shantung.)

12 large Pacific prawns
3 slices root ginger
2 stalks spring onion
45 ml (3 tablespoons) lard
2 cloves garlic (chopped)
5 ml (1 teaspoon) salt
30 ml (2 tablespoons) soya sauce

30 ml (2 tablespoons) stock (b)
30 ml (2 tablespoons) Chinese yellow wine or sherry
7 ml ($\frac{1}{2}$ tablespoon) sugar
3 fresh lettuce leaves
15 ml (1 tablespoon) sesame oil

Clean and remove the feet and tails of the prawns. Rinse them under running water and pat dry. Chop the ginger and spring onions coarsely.

Heat the lard in a large frying pan. Add the ginger, garlic and spring onion. Stir them around a few times over a high heat and add the prawns; continue to stir for $1\frac{1}{2}$ minutes. Add the salt, soya sauce, stock, wine and sugar. Stir and turn the prawns with the seasoning ingredients. In $1\frac{1}{2}$–2 minutes, when the sauce in the pan is about to dry up, sprinkle the mixture with the sesame oil and stir once more.

Serve the prawns on a bed of lettuce leaves. To eat Chinese-style, the diner puts the whole prawn in his mouth; the prawn flesh is instantly stripped from the shell by action of the teeth and tongue, and the shell is spat or pulled out of the mouth. An important part of the flavour is the stripping!
Serves 6–8.

Seven Star Crab
(Adapted from the Chu Nien Te' Restaurant, Tsinan, Shantung.)

7 medium crabs
30 ml (2 tablespoons) chopped onion

15 ml (1 tablespoon) chopped ginger
5 ml (1 teaspoon) salt

30 ml (2 tablespoons) stock (b)
30 ml (2 tablespoons) Chinese
  yellow wine or sherry
22 ml (1½ tablespoons) soya
  sauce
3 cloves garlic, finely chopped

45 ml (3 tablespoons) green
  peas
37 ml (2 tablespoons) lard
2 eggs
30 ml (2 tablespoons) finely
  chopped ham

Clean the crabs and steam them for 30 minutes. Scrape all the meat and crab eggs from the shells into a basin. Add half the onion, ginger, salt, stock, wine, soya sauce, cornflour, garlic and peas. Stir everything together until well mixed.

Heat the lard in a frying pan. Add the remainder of the ginger and garlic. Stir them around a few times. Add the beaten eggs. When they are about to set, stir and scramble them together. Put the scrambled eggs into the basin containing the crab meat. Stir the egg with the crab until they are well blended.

Place the seven crab shells on a heatproof dish. Spoon the mixture into the upturned shells, and pack it firmly. Insert the dish containing the shells into a preheated oven at 200°C (400°F)/Gas 6 to bake for 15 minutes.

Arrange 6 of the shells upturned in one layer on a large dish, and place the last shell in the centre of the others. Sprinkle the contents of the shells with the chopped ham and serve. Each diner will take a shell. The extra is left for the greedy one who needs a second helping!
Serves 6.

Vegetables

Braised White-Cooked Chinese Cabbage
(Adapted from the Municipal Services Co, Peking.)

1 medium Chinese cabbage
  (about 900 g/2 lb)
1 medium onion
45 ml (3 tablespoons) lard
12 ml (2½ teaspoons) salt

250 ml (½ pint) stock (b)
½ chicken stock cube
15 ml (1 tablespoon) cornflour
  blended in 60 ml (4 tablespoons) milk

Clean and cut the cabbage into small, thin pieces. Cut the onion into thin slices.

Heat the lard in a large saucepan. Add the onion, stir and leave it to fry gently over a medium heat for 1½ minutes. Add the cabbage, stir and turn it with the onion and lard. Sprinkle with the salt, and leave to simmer for 3 minutes. Add the stock and crushed stock cube. Bring the contents to the boil. Leave to simmer again for 3–4 minutes. Add the blended cornflour. Turn it a few times with the cabbage and soup.

When the soup thickens, turn the contents round a few more times, sprinkle with freshly ground pepper and serve in a large deep-sided dish. Although this is an extremely simple dish it has a meat-like quality about it, and is often eaten with rice in the absence of meat dishes.
Serves 6–8.

Quick-Fried Tomatoes
(Adapted from the Municipal Services Co, Peking.)

10 firm, medium tomatoes
3 stalks spring onion
60 ml (4 tablespoons) lard
10 ml (2 teaspoons) sugar

7.5 ml (1½ teaspoons) salt
30 ml (2 tablespoons) soya sauce

Skin the tomatoes by pouring boiling water over them. Cut each into 6 wedge-shaped pieces. Cut the spring onions into small sections.

Heat the lard in a frying pan. Add the spring onions, and stir them a few times in the hot fat. Now put in the tomatoes, turn them a few times with the fat and spring onions, sprinkle with the sugar, salt and soya sauce and leave to cook for 1½ minutes. Stir them around once more and serve. Another simple dish, but very popular during the summer.
Serves 6–8.

Quick-Fried Shredded Eggplant (Aubergine) with Shredded Pork
(Adapted from the Municipal Services Co, Peking.)

225 g (½ lb) lean and fat pork
450 g (1 lb) aubergines
2 stalks spring onions
45 ml (3 tablespoons) lard
7 ml (½ tablespoon) pepper-corns, lightly crushed

7.5 ml (1½ teaspoons) salt
7 ml (½ tablespoon) sugar
30 ml (2 tablespoons) Chinese yellow wine or dry sherry
30 ml (2 tablespoons) soya sauce

Cut the pork and eggplant first into slices, and then into triple matchstick-sized shreds, and chop the spring onion coarsely.

Heat the lard in a frying pan. Add the spring onions and pepper-

corns. Stir them in the fat for 30 seconds over a high heat. Add the pork, stir once and add the aubergine shreds. Stir them together for 1½ minutes. Reduce the heat and leave to cook, covered, for 3 minutes. Sprinkle the contents with the salt, sugar, wine and soya sauce. Turn the heat to high. Stir and turn for 1½ minutes, and serve in a well-heated dish. Another good accompaniment to rice, popular for ordinary household meals.
Serves 6–8.

Splash-Fried Bean Sprouts
(Adapted from Chef Yuan Chao Ling of Tsinan, Shantung.)

3 cloves garlic
2 stalks spring onion
550 g (1¼ lb) fresh bean sprouts
oil for deep-frying

22 ml (1½ tablespoons) soya sauce
10 ml (2 teaspoons) salt
22 ml (1½ tablespoons) sesame oil

Crush the garlic and chop it coarsely. Cut the spring onion into small sections.

Place the bean sprouts in a close-meshed wire basket, and suspend this over a pan of boiling oil. Sprinkle the top of the sprouts with the spring onion and garlic. Using a large ladle, pour 8–10 ladlefuls of boiling oil slowly and evenly over the vegetables in the wire basket.

Shake the sprouts free of any excess oil over the oil pan and turn the basketful of sprouts on to a well-heated dish. Sprinkle the vegetables evenly with soya sauce, salt and sesame oil. Turn and toss them together, and this hot sprout salad is ready for eating.
Serves 6–8.

Stir-Fried Bean Curd (also called Bean Curd Sweetbread)
(Adapted from the Shantung Commercial Corporation Catering Department.)

4 cakes bean curd (about 450 g/1 lb)
15 ml (1 tablespoon) dried shrimps
37 ml (2½ tablespoons) lard

15 ml (1 tablespoon) pork fat diced in small cubes
15 ml (1 tablespoon) chopped onion
2–3 cloves garlic, finely chopped

C

15 ml (1 tablespoon) finely
chopped ginger
90 ml (6 tablespoons) stock (b)
blended with 15 ml (1 tablespoon) cornflour
½ chicken stock cube

15 ml (1 tablespoon) soya sauce
15 ml (3 teaspoons) soya paste
30 ml (2 tablespoons) Chinese
yellow wine or sherry
10 ml (2 teaspoons) chilli sauce

Steam the bean curd for 10 minutes, then cut it into small cubes.
Soak the shrimps in hot water for 20 minutes and drain them.

Heat the lard in a frying pan. Add the diced pork-fat cubes, and
shrimps. Stir them over a medium heat for 2 minutes. Add the
onion, garlic and ginger. Stir them round with the other ingredients
for 1 minute. Add the blended stock, stock cube, soya sauce, soya
paste and wine. As soon as the liquid thickens, add all the bean
curd. Turn and mix everything together over a medium heat for 3–4
minutes. Serve in a large bowl. This is another 'dish of the people',
very satisfying eaten with rice.
Serves 6–8.

Noodles and Steamed Buns

Cold-Tossed Noodles with Shredded Chicken
(Adapted from the Ngor Mei Dining Room, the former Tung-An
Market, Peking.)

675 g (1½ lb) thin Chinese
noodles (freshly made, if
available; otherwise use spaghetti)

30 ml (2 tablespoons) sesame
oil
225 g (½ lb) bean sprouts
225 g (½ lb) cooked chicken
meat

Sauce

37 ml (2½ tablespoons) soya
sauce
22 ml (1½ tablespoons) Chinese
yellow wine or sherry
22 ml (1½ tablespoons) vinegar
(Chinese aromatic, if available)
7 ml (½ tablespoon) chilli sauce

2.5 ml (½ teaspoon) freshly
ground pepper
12 ml (¾ tablespoon) sesame
paste
7 ml (½ tablespoon) sugar
3 cloves garlic
22 ml (1½ tablespoons) finely
chopped spring onion

Add the noodles to 2–2.5 litres (4–5 pints) vigorously boiling water to cook for 5–6 minutes (if freshly made), or if spaghetti for 15 minutes. Drain thoroughly, and spread the strands out to cool on a tray, after sprinkling them with 22 ml (1½ tablespoons) sesame oil. Parboil the bean sprouts for 30 seconds, sprinkle with sesame oil, and place them on top of the noodles in a large bowl.

Make the sauce by crushing and chopping the garlic finely and mixing it in a bowl with the other sauce ingredients.

Chop the cooked chicken meat into matchstick-sized shreds. Place the shredded chicken on top of the sprouts and noodles, and sprinkle them with the sauce.

Serves 5–6.

Cha Chiang Mein, or Hot-Tossed Noodles with Minced Meat Sauce and Shredded Vegetables

100 g (¼ lb) bean sprouts
45 ml (3 tablespoons) vegetable oil
350 g (¾ lb) minced pork
30 ml (2 tablespoons) bean paste sauce
22 ml (1½ tablespoons) soya sauce

7 ml (½ tablespoon) sugar
45 ml (3 tablespoons) stock (b)
15 ml (1 tablespoon) cornflour blended in 45 ml (3 tablespoons) water
675 g (1½ lb) noodles or spaghetti

Shredded Vegetables

3–4 stalks spring onion
2 large carrots
2 radishes

15 cm (6 in) sections of cucumber

Blanch the bean sprouts in boiling water for 30 seconds and drain. Cut the spring onions into medium-sized sections. Cut the carrots and radishes into matchstick-sized shreds.

Heat the oil in a frying pan. Add the minced meat, and stir over a high heat for 5–6 minutes. Add the bean paste, soya sauce and sugar, and continue to stir-fry for 2–3 minutes. Add the stock and blended cornflour, and continue to mix and stir for 2–3 more minutes. Boil the noodles for 6–7 minutes, or if spaghetti for 15 minutes, and drain.

Place the freshly boiled noodles in a large bowl. Pour the meat sauce over these and toss. Place the shredded vegetables and bean

sprouts in smaller bowls on the table, for the diners to mix them with the noodles to their own taste. A very popular and satisfying dish.
Serves 4–6.

Lu-Mein, or Boiled Noodles in Long-Cooked Meat Sauce with Eggs

0.9–1.2 kg (2–2½ lb) belly of pork
60–75 ml (4 tablespoons) soya sauce
5 ml (1 teaspoon) sugar
4 hard-boiled eggs
125 ml (¼ pint) stock (b)

900 g (2 lb) noodles or spaghetti
30 ml (2 tablespoons) cornflour blended in 105–120 ml (7–8 tablespoons) water
60 ml (4 tablespoons) Chinese yellow wine or dry sherry

Cut the pork into 4 pieces. Heat them in a small casserole with the soya sauce, sugar and 125 ml (¼ pint) water. Bring the contents to the boil, put an asbestos mat under the casserole, and simmer very gently for 1½ hours, turning the meat every 30 minutes. Add the hard-boiled eggs and stock, and adjust the seasoning with 15–30 ml (1–2 tablespoons) soya sauce. Turn the pork pieces around and simmer them together with the other ingredients for a further 30 minutes. Boil the noodles for 5–6 minutes, or if spaghetti for 15 minutes.

Drain and divide the noodles among as many bowls as there are people. Cut each egg and each piece of pork in half, and place a piece of each on top of each bowl of noodles. Heat the casserole over a high heat. Add the blended cornflour and yellow wine and stir into the gravy. As soon as the sauce thickens, pour an appropriate amount over each bowl of pork, egg and noodles and serve. Another popular and highly satisfying 'dish of the people'.
Serves 6–8.

Casserole of Noodles with Long-Simmered White-Cooked Pork
(Adapted from the Sha Kuo Chu Restaurant, Peking.)

8 medium Chinese dried mushrooms
225 g (½ lb) spinach or spring cabbage
100 g (¼ lb) bamboo shoots
1.35 kg (3 lb) belly of pork

1.75 litres (3½ pints) water
10 ml (2 teaspoons) salt
60 ml (4 tablespoons) dry sherry
675 g (1½ lb) noodles or spaghetti

Soak the mushrooms in hot water for 20 minutes; strain them, and discard the stalks. Cut the cabbage or spinach into medium-sized slices, and the bamboo shoots into thin slices.

Place the pork in the water in a large casserole. Bring to the boil and reduce the heat to a fast simmer for 20 minutes. Skim away any excess fat or impurities. Place an asbestos mat under the casserole, and reduce the heat to a very gentle simmer to cook as slowly as possible for the next 3 hours.

Cut the pork into as many pieces as there will be diners, and put the mushrooms, bamboo shoots, spinach, salt and sherry into the casserole. Bring the contents to the boil, and simmer gently for 15 minutes.

Boil the noodles for 6 minutes, or if spaghetti for 15 minutes. Drain and divide into as many bowls as there are diners. Divide the pork and other ingredients proportionally into the same bowls. Pour the soup from the casserole over the noodles and pork in the bowls. These filling soup and noodle casserole dishes make warming and satisfying winter fare.

Serves 5–6.

Man Tou or Plain Steamed Buns

Man Tou is the Chinese bread which is as common a food in north China as rice. It is used in every home meal to accompany savoury dishes—meat, poultry, fish and seafood—and to soak up gravy and sauces.

450 g (1 lb) plain flour	*4 ml (¾ teaspoon) active dry*
225 g (½ lb) self-raising flour	*yeast*
500 ml (1 pint) lukewarm water	*15 ml (1 tablespoon) sugar*

Strew the yeast on the lukewarm water. Mix the plain and self-raising flour and sugar together thoroughly in a bowl. Add the water gradually, and knead into a dough. Continue to knead on a board dusted with flour for 10 minutes, using extra flour if necessary to prevent the dough from sticking to the fingers or board. Let the dough stand for 15 minutes, and roll it into a 50 cm (20 in) long roll. Cut the roll into twenty discs. Form each disc into the shape of a haystack. Line the 'haystacks' in several rows, and leave them to rise for another 30 minutes. Place the pieces of dough at least 1.25 cm (½ in) apart on the tiers of a steamer and steam for 15 minutes, when the Man Tou should be ready to be eaten

with savoury dishes. They are particularly suitable for eating with
rich meat and poultry dishes, to soak up the sauces and gravies.
Makes 20.

Stuffed Steamed Buns or Paotzu

We Chinese regard the Man Tou or unstuffed steamed buns more or
less as the Westerner regards bread, while the stuffed steamed buns,
Pao Tzu, are akin to sandwiches, something to be eaten for snacks,
on a picnic, or while on a journey.

The dough for Paotzu or Stuffed Steamed Buns is made almost
exactly in the same manner as in the recipe on page 63 for Man
Tou, except that Paotzu are often made slightly sweeter by adding
an extra tablespoon of sugar to the other ingredients.

The dough, shaped into a long roll, is cut into 20 discs. Each of
the discs is then rolled into a larger disc about 7.5 cm (3 in) in
diameter. The stuffing, which can be savoury or sweet, is prepared
separately (see below).

When the filling is ready, place 22–30 ml (1½–2 tablespoons) at
the centre of a dough disc. Place the dough in your left hand and
gradually turn up the rim around the filling with the fingers of your
right hand, until only a small opening is left at the top. Pinch the
edges together to close the bun. Now place the Pao Tzu in a
steamer, and steam for 15–18 minutes.

Preparation of Stuffing

Although the stuffings can either be savoury or sweet, they are
much more often savoury. Savoury stuffings are usually made with
chicken or pork, stir-fried with vegetables; occasionally they may
be made entirely with vegetables.

Meat Stuffing

225–350 g (½–¾ lb) pork, lamb
or beef—raw, roasted or 'red-
cooked'
1 small onion
150 g (5 oz) young leeks
30 ml (2 tablespoons) vegetable
oil

7 ml (½ tablespoon) sugar
5 ml (1 teaspoon) salt
22 ml (1½ tablespoons) soya
sauce
12 ml (2½ teaspoons) sesame oil

Cut the pork into thin slices. Slice the onion very finely. Clean and cut the leeks into thin slices.

Heat the vegetable oil in a frying pan. Add the onion and stir-fry over a high heat for 1 minute. Add the meat and leeks, and stir-fry them all together for 2 minutes. Sprinkle the contents with sugar, salt and soya sauce, and continue to stir-fry for 2 minutes more. Add the sesame oil and stir-fry for a further 30 seconds. Leave to cool. The stuffing is ready for use as soon as it is cold.
Makes 20.

Vegetable Stuffings

Repeat the recipe on page 64, but substitute Chinese cabbage for the meat and courgettes or aubergines for the leeks. Otherwise use the same flavouring ingredients and cook for the same length of time.

Sweet Stuffing

100 g (¼ lb) pork fat
60–75 ml (4–5 tablespoons) sugar
30 ml (2 tablespoons) roasted sesame seeds

75–90 ml (5–6 tablespoons) chopped walnuts
20 melon-seed kernels
22 ml (1½ tablespoons) lard

Chop the pork into small cubes. Roast the sesame seeds by frying them in a dry pan over a low heat for 2 minutes. Finely grind the walnuts. Coarsely grind the melon kernels. Mix the ingredients together.
Makes 20.

Another favourite stuffing used in China is a sweetened purée of black beans, or Chinese red beans, with added sugar.

When both savoury and sweet Paotzu are made for the same occasion—often for a festival or holiday—the sweet Pao Tzus are usually marked with a red dot on top.

Stuffed Boiled or Steamed Dumplings or Chiaotzu

Chiaotzu (dumplings) differ from Paotzu (steamed buns) mainly in that they are much smaller, and the dough is made without the use of a raising agent. Chiaotzu may be boiled or steamed, and can be eaten a dozen at a time. In the north these boiled dumplings often comprise a meal: the diners dip the cooked Chiaotzu in soya sauce or vinegar, and accompany these with a bowl of 'soup' made from the starchy water in which the dumplings were boiled. An appreciation of this almost totally tasteless 'soup' is an acquired taste, probably partly derived from the contrast of its blandness with the soya sauce or vinegar in which the dumplings are dipped, and the savouriness of the filling. This is particularly apparent when the soup is drunk in the Chinese way, a sip at a time, after each mouthful of dumpling.

The dough-skin for 50–60 Chiaotzu is simply made by mixing 675 g (1½ lb) flour with 750 ml (1½ pints) water. These are kneaded into a dough, which is shaped into a long roll, and cut into 50–60 discs. Each piece of dough is then rolled into a 7.5–8.75 cm (3–2½ in) diameter round sheet or skin, about 0.4 cm (⅛ in) thick. Before wrapping the stuffing in the skin, fold the skin lightly in half (in a half-moon shape), and pucker the edge of half the skin by making about six short folds. This causes a hollow to form at the centre of the skin. About 10 ml (2 teaspoons) stuffing is then placed in this hollow, and the unpuckered half of the skin is brought over to wrap around the puckered edge, and they are pinched together. Thus the stuffing is firmly enclosed.

A large pan of water (preferably not less than 4 litres (1 gallon)) is used for boiling Chiaotzu. When the water comes to a rolling boil, add all the dumplings, which cool the water temporarily. When it resumes boiling, pour in 2 bowls or cups of cold water to reduce the heat. After the second reboiling pour in another 2 cups of cold water. On the third reboiling, the dumplings are ready, and should be removed with a perforated spoon.

As previously mentioned, Chiaotzu should be served with vinegar and soya sauce as dips, and perhaps supplemented with chopped pickles.

Stuffings

In contrast to the fillings used in Paotzu, which can be cooked meat, the minced or chopped meat used in Chiaotzu should be raw (normally lean and fat pork), and seasoned with salt and soya sauce, supplemented with chopped Chinese cabbage or celery and some leeks or spring onion.

675 g (1½ lb) pork	7 ml (½ tablespoon) salt
675 g (1½ lb) Chinese cabbage	45 ml (3 tablespoons) vegetable
3 young leeks or 4 spring onions	oil
60 ml (4 tablespoons) soya sauce	

Finely chop the pork. Squeeze some of the liquid out of the cabbage and discard it. Slice the vegetables thinly. Mix all the ingredients and use as stuffing in the dough skin as described above. Most Chinese children in north China would join the women folk in the family in making Chiaotzu, especially during the holidays or festival times.
Makes 50–60.

Kuo Tieh or Stuck-to-the-Pan Dumplings

Kuo Tieh is a characteristic Peking variation on the ordinary boiled or steamed Chiaotzu. The recipe starts in precisely the same way as the ordinary version, but in the finishing stages the dumplings are given a short period of shallow-frying on a flat pan. Only a small amount of oil is used: about 45–60 ml (3–4 tablespoons) for a medium-sized pan—be sure that the surface of the pan is evenly greased. The dumplings to be fried are placed in rows, spread out over the pan. Apart from an occasional shake to the pan to prevent the dumplings from sticking at the start, the frying should be a static one. These Kuo Tieh should be eaten in the same way as Chiaotzu—using the same dips.

Peking Horse's Hoof Toasted Hot Cake
(Adapted from the Palace Kitchen, North Sea Park, Peking.)

450 g (1 lb) plain flour
225 g (½ lb) self-raising flour
15 ml (1 tablespoon) sugar
5 ml (1 teaspoon) salt
10 ml (2 teaspoons) dry active yeast

300 ml (12 fl oz) lukewarm water
100 g (¼ lb) sesame seeds
15 ml (1 tablespoon) sesame oil

Mix the flours together with 10 ml (2 teaspoons) sugar and the salt. Dissolve the yeast in the water, and add gradually to the flour mixture. Knead well (use additional flour to prevent the dough from sticking). Add the sesame oil, and continue to knead for 5 minutes. Form the dough into a 3.75 cm (1½ in) diameter roll. Cut segments off at 3.75 cm (1½ in) intervals. Form each segment into a crescent-shaped cake, like a horse's shoe. Dissolve 5 ml (1 teaspoon) sugar in 100 ml (4 fl oz) water. Wet or brush one surface of each 'cake' with sugared water. Spread the sesame seeds evenly over the surface

c*

of a tray. Press the wet surface of each cake against the sesame seeds to take on a layer of seeds.

Heat the sesame oil in a large, dry, flat-bottomed frying pan over a medium heat. Place 2–3 cakes at a time, seed-side down, on the hot surface of the pan. Cook for about 3 minutes, moving the pan around to ensure that it is evenly heated. Use a fish-slice to turn the cakes over. Continue to heat in the same manner for 3–4 minutes. Turn the cakes over again twice, allowing each side 2 minutes over a low heat, when the surfaces will be brown and aromatic while the inside remains quite soft.

These Toasted Hot Cakes are particularly suitable for eating with roast and barbecued meats: a slice is cut horizontally through two-thirds of the cake, and the inside is brushed with a plummy soya-paste sauce (page 30) and stuffed with the meat together with shredded cucumber and spring onion. These cakes are in effect hot aromatic sandwiches with hot meat inserted inside, and are extremely appealing even to people tasting them for the first time. *Makes 12.*

Aromatic Salt and Pepper Mix

Place 30 ml (2 tablespoons) of salt (table or sea) in a small, dry frying pan. Add 10 ml (2 teaspoons) of freshly ground black pepper. Stir, over a low heat, for 3–4 minutes.

Canton and South-China Cooking

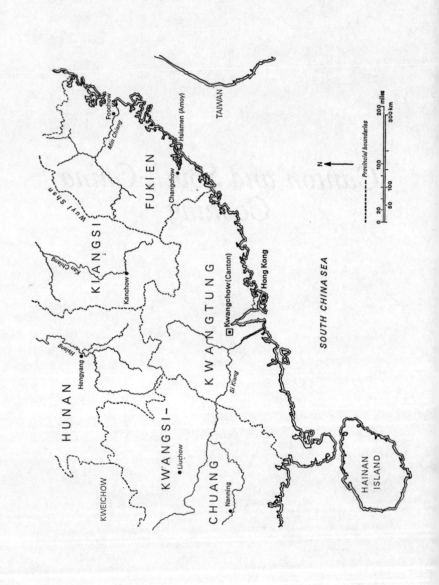

Canton and South-China Cooking

The Cantonese are the sybarites of China so far as food is concerned. Their indulgence has probably stemmed from the province's comparative prosperity and its mild, semi-tropical climate. As in southern Europe, the weather is warm enough for people to sit outside during much of the year. Many visitors to China have been struck by the contrast between the stark living conditions in the communes of the arid and wind-swept north-west and the lushness of the province of Kwangtung where, apart from being able to harvest two to three crops a year, the peasants often have time for subsidiary pursuits such as fish-farming in well-stocked lakes and reservoirs. A postcard I received recently from a member of a BBC television team visiting China succinctly described the magnificence of Cantonese restaurants thus: 'Infinitely larger than anywhere else, often combining lakes, miniature gardens or trees around which galleries are built.' In days gone by, in Kwangtung, of which Canton is the capital, there existed a sizeable middle class, not unlike the provincial French bourgeoisie, with the time and means to spend on preparing copious meals at home, or to sit in tea-houses and restaurants to eat and drink and gossip with friends and acquaintances. These habits may have been modified by the Revolution, but they have never been erased; indeed, they are still very much a part of life in these southern provinces of China. The bounty of nature is still there, and the inclination to eat well will undoubtedly reassert itself as greater production and orderliness bring increased prosperity to society.

Those who have time to think about food naturally become arbiters of its quality. Since it is not the Chinese practice to take afternoon siestas, even in the summer heat, we southern Chinese always had the use of three hours more per day than southern Europeans; and much of that extra time was given up to the consideration of food. Eating is at least as often the subject of conversation there as the weather is in England. When people meet in

China, they as often greet one another by saying, 'Have you eaten?' (literally, 'Have you had rice?') as 'Good morning', or 'How are you?'. When the opening sentence is about food the conversation naturally turns around the same subject. Any person of education or refinement should be able to converse knowledgeably about it, just as his counterparts in the West are able to talk about music, art or sports. Hence the comparative ease with which an average Chinese can be turned into a cook. And where food and eating are involved, what is true of the Chinese in general is doubly true of the Cantonese in particular.

So far as women are concerned, the majority are domestically occupied like women everywhere, with their time at home often taken up with experiments in the kitchen. Having grown up and lived for fifteen years in south China, my impression is that the recipes favoured by Chinese women are more likely to be slow-cooked steamed or simmered dishes, requiring infinite care and patience to perfect. Male practitioners of the art of cooking, on the other hand, seem to be more attracted to methods which demand a certain amount of showmanship, be they stir-fried dishes to be served in an instant, or large roasts or barbecues. As a whole, in my experience, the men talked more, and the women cooked more. When it came to the great performances it was usually the men who held the stage and drew the applause—but they had to go to their women for advice if they got stuck.

So life goes on in Kwangtung, with its hot summers and mild winters, and every day the people attend to and enjoy their food— the seafood hauled in from the thousand miles and more of coast-line, and the products brought in via the West River and the East River, the two great tributaries of the Pearl River which flows by Canton. The West River carries mountain foods from Kwangsi, the neighbouring province in the interior; while many of the East River or Tiuchow dishes are akin to or influenced by the characteristic cooking of Fukien, the adjacent coastal province. The capital of Fukien, Foochow, is famous for its soup (a Cantonese friend who went to a Fukien dinner was surprised to find that of the eight courses served no less than four were soups!), wrapped steamed foods, and the extensive use of red wine sediment paste. Amoy, the port further south, and the inland town of Changchow, are well-known for their pork dishes, one of the specialities being to prepare 108 dishes from one pig. But none of these local variations can compare with Cantonese cooking for indulgence, variety and range of repertoire. Incidentally, the Western belief that we Chinese eat dog meat is in fact true only of the more rarified Cantonese palate; elsewhere in China such dishes are unknown.

One of the most distinctive aspects of Cantonese food is its savoury quality. This is often achieved by the incorporation of seafood flavours into meat cookery; and not infrequently even into vegetable dishes. Oyster sauce, shrimp sauce and shrimp paste are more widely used here than anywhere else in China. Sliced Beef in Oyster Sauce (see page 105) is a favourite dish in any Cantonese restaurant, as are Broccoli in Oyster Sauce and Hearts of Greens in Oyster Sauce (see page 30). The seafood savouriness is even more pronounced when shrimp sauce and shrimp paste are added to non-seafood dishes. Shrimp shells and shrimp heads are frequently boiled in meat stock or chicken broth to achieve a special nuance of flavour in the preparation of Cantonese soups (the Wontun Soup (see page 80) served in the United States often lacks authenticity because the seafood element is omitted and only chicken stock is used). While in the north the Steamed Buns (see page 63) and dumplings are usually stuffed with meat, in Canton they are more often than not stuffed with seafood, such as shrimps and crab meat; or where meat is used as a filling, it may well be flavoured with oyster or shrimp sauce.

Not only are seafoods used to flavour meat and poultry; the reverse is also true—sometimes meat is introduced into dishes with a seafood base, to vary and expand their savoury quality. For instance, minced or shredded pork may be stir-fried with onions, garlic and ginger together with sections of crab and lobster, to which chicken stock and wine are added. This 'cross-frying' of meat with seafood over a high heat, with a little wine and chicken stock poured in at the critical moment, creates not only a minor physical explosion, but also a 'savoury explosion' on the palate. The highly savoury taste of Cantonese food is also obtained by the use of salted black beans, soaked in water and drained, then fried and mashed into the oil in which meat or seafood is cooked over a high heat.

To counteract the fishiness in seafoods, fresh minced or shredded ginger is used extensively in Cantonese cooking. It is a part of the Chinese culinary concert that ginger and other strong spices are used to suppress and neutralize that 'rawness' which is present in game and strong-flavoured meat, as well as the otherwise overpowering fishy taste of some seafoods.

The refined and sophisticated Cantonese palate is quick to detect that when food materials are of undoubted freshness—live shrimps, crabs or lobsters, freshly caught fish or newly killed poultry—they have a special sweet flavour which will be destroyed by overcooking. Hence, when really fresh products are available, this 'sweet savouriness' is preserved by a very short or mild form of cooking. One method is poaching in boiling water, then allowing the receding heat of the water to do the remainder of the cooking; alternatively, the food may be subjected to a brief but vigorous steaming. Two of the most appealing Cantonese dishes are Plain Poached Shrimps (see page 127) and Plain Poached Snails. Freshly killed spring chicken is often poached, then allowed to cook as it cools in the water, thus retaining all its fresh juiciness. Because the flavour of chicken cooked in this way is so pure, battery-reared chickens are unsuitable as their flat, chemical taste is not counteracted by any strong-tasting sauce in the cooking. For the average Westerner, this poached chicken would seem undercooked, for there is still a little blood near the bones when the bird is chopped up—but to the Cantonese it is cooked to a turn.

Another classical Cantonese dish is the Steamed Whole Fish (bream, bass, carp, etc, see page 113). Its excellence lies partly in the accurately timed steaming, usually 10–15 minutes, depending on size and thickness. The fresh flavour of the fish is enhanced by the thin but strong sauce—a hot 'cocktail' of soya sauce, chicken stock, ginger and wine—served with it. This is a simple dish, but incomparably delicious.

The Cantonese have developed the cooking method called Cha Shao Roasting often very loosely translated as 'barbecue roasting'. The method usually involves the roasting of thin strips of seasoned or marinated meat in a hot oven for a very short time; by cooking over high temperature, the outside of the marinated meat is sealed and even slightly charred, but the flesh immediately beneath the surface is still fresh and juicy. A typical dish of this genre is Cha Shao Roast Pork (see page 100). Strips of pork fillet are marinated in a mixture of soya sauce, soya-bean cheese, wine, sugar or honey and wine and/or wine sediment paste, often also with a little five-spice powder and monosodium glutamate. The strips are then placed on a wire rack and roasted in a hot oven for 12–15 minutes. When the pork is allowed to cool slightly and is cut in pieces across the strips, the slices will appear very fresh inside with a dark, slightly singed rim—a particularly delectable combination. This cooking method could easily be adopted in the Western world, since every modern kitchen is equipped with an oven, and the Cha Shao roasting method can be applied not only to meat but also to poultry and even fish.

Another typically Cantonese method of cooking pork and poultry specializes in making the skin crisp and crackling. Siu Yuk or Crispy Pork (see page 104) which is available in most Cantonese restaurants is an example of this. Many Westerners are deterred by the dish at first, because of its fatness: they forget that the emphasis is on the crackling which is superb when eaten with plain boiled rice. The crispness is usually produced by drying the skin overnight after dousing it with boiling water, wiping it dry and rubbing it with salt; before cooking (deep-frying or roasting), the skin is coated with a cornflour-and-egg batter. When ordering this dish in a restaurant it is probably best to mix it with Cha Shao Pork which, being fillet, is all lean, so that fat and pure lean meat are mixed.

The Cantonese also treat poultry (mainly chicken) simply by burying the whole bird in a sea-salt. East River Salt Buried Chicken (see page 90) is a typical dish of this genre. The salt absorbs all the moisture from the skin of the bird during the cooking, leaving the outside dry and crisp. The quantity of salt (2 kg; 4–5 lb) makes the bird less salty than one would imagine, and the flesh tastes particularly fresh.

A favourite banquet dish is Suckling Pig (see page 97), which is served not unlike Peking Duck, with the skin peeled off, cut into squares and served separately from the meat. The skin is brushed with a marinade before roasting, and the dish is another instance of the Chinese delight in contrasts in food; the dark, crisp, shiny skin, full of aroma, stands out against the tender and juicy white flesh. The Cantonese are also very fond of eating pigeon, which they also make into crisp dishes, by deep-frying either the whole bird or the shredded meat.

Other familiar items of crispy food in this area are the Fried Wontun or fried Crispy Pancake Rolls. One aspect of Cantonese Chow Mein which makes it different from the version cooked elsewhere is that in the Cantonese dish slightly more oil is used in the frying, and in the final phase the noodles are pressed down on the hot base of the pan to fry under pressure until crisp. They are then turned over and fried on the other side. The soft noodles in the middle are then sandwiched between the crisp ones on the outside. Noodles in this form make an excellent snack. Cantonese Chow Mein is not universally appreciated in China— northerners tend to regard it as unnecessarily fussy and greasy, although the western Chinese seem to take to it readily.

In the southern region, where fruit abounds, it is natural that elements of fruit tend to be used in savoury dishes. Apart from

Fukien, Kwangtung is the only area I know of in China where tangerine and lemon juice are used as dips on the table for roasts, barbecues or deep-fried dishes. Now and then shredded lemon or orange peel is combined with chopped spring onion to garnish dishes, or to wrap in pancakes with a shredded crisp meat. I was told by a leading Cantonese chef that in preparing the famous Sweet and Sour Pork (see page 103) almost any kind of fruit juice could be added to give extra flavour, so long as the sauce has a strong sugar and vinegar base. Plums and lichees are incorporated into many Cantonese dishes; and in Tiuchow (or Swatow) in eastern Kwangtung, sour plums are often used as sauce ingredients or as a stuffing for fish, as well as in cooking meat 'puddings'.

The Cantonese have many recipes for stuffed vegetables, and prawns and crab are frequently used in the filling. Even when chopped or minced meat is used instead, the stuffing is often capped with a prawn.

In domestic cookery the Cantonese are fond of preparing slow-cooked, long-simmered dishes in earthenware casseroles called 'po', among them Fish Head in Earthenware Pot, and Spiced Brisket or Shin of Beef in Earthenware Pot (see pages 115 and 106). Another favourite type of home-cooking is the range of soft rice or congee dishes. These seem to be more commonly eaten in Canton than anywhere else in China, as snacks during the day, or for midnight suppers. They are very light, savoury and easily digestible. Among them are the Sampan Congee (with seafood), Roast Duck and Chicken Congee, Mixed Meat Congee, Beef Ball Congee, and so on. The comfort and satisfaction derived from this domestic fare is equal to the splendours of the most elaborate Chinese banquet dish.

Anyone familiar with Cantonese cuisine will have seen something of their range of Dim Sums, or tea-house snacks, which are pushed around on heated trolleys in the vast restaurants of Hong Kong so that customers can select their choice. The following are among the most familiar:

Har Kao, steamed prawn-stuffed dumplings wrapped in thin dough-skin; Siu Mai, steamed open meat-stuffed dumplings; Cai Pao, chicken-stuffed steamed buns; Cha Shao Pao, steamed buns stuffed with Cha Shao roast pork; Fun Kao, steamed and shallow-fried dumplings stuffed with crab or chicken and prawn; Wo Kuk, miniature dishes of crisp deep-fried prawns on toast, steamed spare-ribs in black-bean sauce, steamed chicken skin wrapped in duck's web, deep-fried paper-wrapped prawns or chicken, and savoury rice wrapped in lotus leaves; Chuen Fun, steamed stuffings wrapped in rice-flour rolls with soya sauce.

Soups

After surveying several hundred recipes emanating from various restaurants and dining rooms in Canton, I was a little surprised that none of the catering establishments made a special feature of their soups. The inevitable conclusion is that there are no great or distinctive Cantonese soups in cooking, although the Cantonese are particular in preparing their Superior Broth. As a matter of fact they make this in much the same manner as it is produced elsewhere in China. One should, however, bear in mind that some of the best soups served at a Chinese dinner are often not classed as such. Whole Chicken or Duck Long-cooked in Clear Broth are in effect 'semi-soup' dishes, the solid ingredients of which are as important as the liquid. There are many semi-soup dishes in this category; they may contain large fish heads, pigs' trotters, lungs, pork sweetbreads and even snakes. Indeed, one of the most famous banquet soups of Canton in this category is called Great Assembly of Chicken with Five Varieties of Snake, which is exactly what it says. The choice of snakes in this dish is very important (if not crucial!), and since edible snakes of any species, let alone five varieties, are rarely seen in Western supermarkets, I shall not go into the detailed preparation of this famous 'semi-soup'.

The Fukienese specialize in highly refined broths for soups. In the initial stages they use much the same ingredients as they do elsewhere in China—chicken, lean pork, ham—though they always include knuckle of pork. When the Superior Broth is obtained after 5 hours of slow cooking, the soup is thoroughly skimmed, and all solids are filtered and removed. At this point the whole carcasses of one or two freshly killed chickens are cut through the bones into small pieces, or coarsely chopped, and added in to simmer for not more than 10 minutes. The solids are then removed by double-filtering. Soups or broths so obtained are said to possess greater freshness than the ordinary variety. The Fukienese are proud of their soups, the best-known of which are Swallow-Skin Soup, Swallow-Skin Meat Ball Soup (see page 132) and Clam and Abalone Mushroom Soup.

Sliced Pork Soup with Salted Pickles

225 g (½ lb) lean pork
salt and pepper to taste
15 ml (1 tablespoon) cornflour
½ egg-white

100 g (¼ lb) Cantonese salted
  pickles
1.25 litres (2½ pints) stock (b)

Cut the pork into very thin smallish slices. Rub these evenly with
the salt, cornflour and egg-white. Rinse the pickle under running
water, and cut it into thin slices.

Heat the stock in a saucepan. Add the pork and pickles and
simmer gently over a low heat for 25 minutes. Adjust the seasoning. Serve either in individual soup bowls or in a large tureen for
diners to help themselves.
Serves 5–6.

Beef and Watercress Soup

225 g (½ lb) stewing beef
1–2 bunches of watercress
750 ml (1½ pints) water

750 ml (1½ pints) stock (b)
salt and pepper to taste

Cut the beef into small cubes. Clean the watercress thoroughly, and
remove the roots.

Place the beef and water in a saucepan. Boil for 5 minutes and
skim away any impurities. Reduce the heat to very low, and simmer
very gently for 1½ hours. Add the watercress and stock. Simmer
gently for 5–6 minutes. Adjust the seasoning. Serve as in the previous recipe.
Serves 5–6.

Beef Ball Soup with Spinach

2 water chestnuts
1 small onion
225 g (½ lb) finely minced beef
¼ egg (beaten)
salt and pepper

225–350 g (½–¾ lb) fresh
  spinach (or lettuce)
1.25 litres (2½ pints) stock (b)
1 chicken or beef stock cube

Chop the water chestnuts and onion coarsely. Mix these into the
beef with the egg, salt and pepper; knead them together until they
are evenly mixed. Form them into 18–20 meat balls. Remove and

discard the tougher stalks of the spinach or lettuce and clean thoroughly. Tear the leaves into medium-sized pieces.

Heat the stock in a saucepan. Add the meat balls. Bring to the boil and simmer gently for 30 minutes. Add the vegetables and stock cube. Continue to simmer for 6–7 minutes. Adjust the salt and pepper seasoning. Serve as in the previous recipe.
Serves 5–6.

Fish Head and Bean Curd Soup

1 large fish head (675 g (1½ lb)   *22 ml (1½ tablespoons) lard*
   with part of body if available)   *2–3 slices root ginger*
1–2 rashers bacon   *1.25 litres (2½ pints) stock (a)*
2 leeks   *1 chicken stock cube*
2 cakes bean curd   *salt and pepper*

Rinse and clean the fish head thoroughly. Cut the bacon into strips, and the leeks slantwise into 1.25 cm (½ in) slices. Cut each cake of bean curd into a dozen pieces.

Heat the lard in a large saucepan or casserole. Add the bacon, and cook for 1 minute over a medium heat. Add the fish head and turn it in the hot fat to fry on either side for 1½ minutes. Add the ginger, pour in the stock and bring the contents to the boil. Reduce the heat to low to simmer for 30 minutes.

Add the leeks and bean curd pieces, and the stock cube. Bring to the boil for 1 minute, and simmer for 15 minutes. Adjust the salt and pepper seasoning.
Serves 5–6.

Minced Beef and Egg-White Soup with Green Peas, Spring Onions and Chopped Bacon (or Ham)

30 ml (2 tablespoons) cornflour   *1.25 litres (2½ pints) stock (b)*
1 egg-white   *225 g (½ lb) minced beef*
1–2 rashers bacon or slices of   *30 ml (2 tablespoons) green*
   ham   *peas (fresh or frozen)*
3 slices root ginger   *1 chicken or beef stock cube*
4–5 stalks spring onion   *salt and pepper*

Mix the cornflour with 125 ml (¼ pint) water until well blended. Beat the egg-white with 30 ml (2 tablespoons) water for 5 seconds with a fork. Coarsely chop the bacon or ham, ginger and spring onions.

Heat the stock in a large saucepan. Scatter the beef and ginger bit by bit into the soup. Bring the contents to the boil, and reduce the heat to low, to simmer for 15 minutes. Add the bacon or ham, peas, stock cube and spring onion. Stir and continue to simmer for 10 minutes. Add the cornflour mixture and stir well. Trail the egg-white mixture over the surface of the soup. Adjust the seasoning. Give the soup a final stir.
Serves 6.

Fish-Ball Soup

The important thing in making fish balls is to chop the fish flesh thoroughly with a pair of very sharp choppers, and then remove every bit of skin, membrane or fibre. During the chopping, scraping and rechopping process, for every 450 g (1 lb) of fish, add 45 ml (3 tablespoons) iced water, 15 ml (1 tablespoon) at a time. When the fish paste has been thoroughly worked on, and appears smooth and homogeneous, blend in the salt. Place the paste in the refrigerator for an hour until it stiffens. To make the fish balls, squeeze half a handful of fish paste through the hole formed by bringing together the tips of the thumb and index finger. As each ball of fish paste emerges, lop it off at the base with a spoon. Drop the fish balls into a large panful of iced water, chilled with ice-cubes. When a sufficient number of fish balls have been made—they should be about 1.8–2.5 cm ($\frac{3}{4}$ –1 in) in diameter—they are cooked simply by bringing the pan of water slowly to the boil. Simmer for 1 minute and turn off the heat and leave the fish balls to poach for 10 minutes. Remove them with a perforated spoon and allow to cool. Fish balls can be stored in a refrigerator for 2–3 days, and used for various dishes, including, in this case, for making soup:

675 g (1$\frac{1}{2}$ lb) filleted fish   1 chicken stock cube
7 ml ($\frac{1}{2}$ tablespoon) salt   salt and pepper
1 bunch watercress   4 stalks spring onion
1.25 litres (2$\frac{1}{2}$ pints) stock (b)

Prepare the fish balls as described above, allowing 4–5 per portion. Wash the watercress thoroughly.

Heat the stock in a saucepan. Add the fish balls, stock cube and

watercress. Bring to a gentle boil, and simmer for 10 minutes. Adjust the seasoning. Sprinkle with chopped spring onions and serve either in individual bowls, or from a large communal bowl set at the centre of the table.
Serves 6.

Wontun Soup

The term Wontun means 'swallowing the cloud'. This is presumably because the Wontun, which is a kind of thin-skinned ravioli, is made with one or two long skirt-like sides which float in the soup like 'trailing clouds'. The Wontun dough, made from flour, egg, and salt, can nowadays be bought quite easily from Chinese foodstores or supermarkets. In preparing this soup, the only slightly tricky process is the folding of the stuffing into the skin. Perhaps to emphasize the 'cloud' effect, the amount of filling wrapped into each Wontun is comparatively small—not more than 2.5–4 ml ($\frac{1}{2}$–$\frac{3}{4}$ teaspoon) of filling per Wontun, while the pasta casing consists of a square measuring not less than 7.5 x 10 cm (3 x 4 in). The Wontun should be wrapped as follows:

Folding a Wontun skin

Place 4 ml ($\frac{3}{4}$ teaspoon) of filling just below the middle of a square of Wontun dough, held in the palm of your left hand. Moisten the 2 left-side edges of the skin with beaten egg. Fold the moist edges together to make the square into a triangle and press to seal, at the same time pressing out any air-pockets around the filling. Brush the right corner of the 'triangle' with some beaten egg, and likewise the underside or the back of the left-hand corner. By twisting around the underneath of the left corner, bring the moist surface to press and seal against the moist surface of the right-hand corner. This leaves the third corner to trail as the 'skirt'.
5–6 Wontun skins per portion

Filling

100 g (¼ lb) chicken breast
30 ml (2 tablespoons) shelled
  shrimps
2 stalks spring onion
1 slice root ginger
10 ml (2 teaspoons) chopped
  parsley

15 ml (1 tablespoon) vegetable
  oil
10 ml (2 teaspoons) cornflour
2.5 ml (½ teaspoon) sugar
2.5 ml (½ teaspoon) salt
pinch pepper
10 ml (2 teaspoons) soya sauce

Mince the chicken, shrimps, spring onion and ginger, and mix them with the other ingredients until well blended. Fill and wrap the Wontun skins as described above, allowing 5–6 per portion.

Parboil the Wontuns by dropping them a few at a time into a pan of boiling salted water. Cook for 8–10 minutes or until they float up to the surface. Drain, and they are ready to add to the soup.

Soup

1.25 litres (2½ pints) stock (a)
15 ml (1 tablespoon) dried
  shrimps
60–75 ml (4–5 tablespoons)

shrimps' heads and tails
salt and pepper
watercress, spinach or lettuce
  leaves (optional)

Heat the stock in a saucepan. Add the dried shrimps and shrimp heads and tails, and simmer for 10 minutes. Add salt and pepper to taste. Strain off the solid ingredients. Add the Wontuns to the consommé and simmer for a further 5–6 minutes.

Wontun soup can be served in the usual manner, either in individual bowls, or in a large communal bowl for diners to help themselves. Watercress, spinach or shredded lettuce leaves may be added to the soup during the last 5–6 minutes of cooking to add colour. Serves 6.

Crab Meat Soup

2 eggs
3 spring onion stalks
2 lettuce leaves
1.25 litres (2½ pints) stock (b)
1 chicken stock cube
100 g (¼ lb) crab meat

30 ml (2 tablespoons) cornflour
  blended in 125 ml (¼ pint)
  water
salt and pepper
15–30 ml (1–2 tablespoons) dry
  sherry

Beat the eggs with a fork for 10 seconds. Coarsely chop the spring onions. Tear the lettuce leaves into small pieces.

Heat the stock in a saucepan. Add the stock cube and stir until it dissolves. Add the crab meat, and stir in the cornflour mixture until well dispersed throughout the soup. Sprinkle with spring onion and lettuce leaves. Bring the soup to the boil, adjust the seasoning, and sprinkle with sherry.
Serves 6.

Clam and Abalone Soup with Chinese Mushrooms

9–12 medium Chinese dried
 black mushrooms
12–18 fresh or tinned clams
50 g (2 oz) abalone
50–75 g (2–3 oz) flesh from
 chicken breast

6 water chestnuts
3 slices root ginger
1 litre (2½ pints) stock (b)
salt and pepper to taste
15–30 ml (1–2 tablespoons) dry
 sherry

Soak the mushrooms in water for 30 minutes. Remove the stalks and cut each mushroom into two. Parboil the clams and then shell them. Cut the abalone and chicken flesh into a dozen slices. Cut each water chestnut into 3–4 slices, the spring onions into small sections, and the ginger into shreds.

Heat the stock in a saucepan. Add the mushrooms, water chestnuts and ginger. Bring to the boil and simmer for 5 minutes. Add the clams, chicken and abalone. Bring the contents to the boil again. Reduce the heat and simmer gently for 5 minutes. Adjust the seasoning and sprinkle the soup with chopped spring onion and sherry.
Serves 6.

Chicken

The Cantonese tend to undercook quick-fried or poached chicken, and for these recipes it is essential that the bird is fresh and preferably free-range reared. In the following two recipes for chicken poached in a marinade, the cooking time is increased by 5 minutes in order to suit Western tastes and to reduce the traces of fresh blood in the meat around the bones.

Chicken Poached in Soya Marinade
(Adapted from the Heng Chien Restaurant, Canton.)

Marinade

1.5 litres (3 pints) water
15 ml (1 tablespoon) salt
250 ml (½ pint) dry sherry
8 slices root ginger
250 ml (½ pint) soya sauce

60 ml (4 tablespoons) sugar
45 ml (3 tablespoons) five-spice
(in pieces, not powder)
1 young free-range chicken
weighing about 1.35 kg (3 lb)

Heat the marinade ingredients together, and allow them to simmer for 1 hour. The five-spice pieces should be in a muslin bag.

Remove the giblets of a freshly killed plucked chicken. Clean the chicken thoroughly and remove its head and feet if still attached.

Bring the marinade to a gentle boil. Add the chicken and submerge it in the marinade. Simmer gently for 5–6 minutes. Turn the heat off, and allow the bird to poach in the receding heat for 30 minutes. Remove and drain the chicken.

Chop the chicken through the bones into large bite-sized pieces. Arrange these neatly on a serving dish.
Serves 6–10.

Chicken Poached in a White Marinade
(From the Ching Ling Restaurant, Canton; by Chef Tseng Ying.)

White Marinade

1.5 litres (3 pints) water
6–8 slices root ginger
3 medium onions, cut in half
30 ml (2 tablespoons) salt
45 ml (3 tablespoons) five-spice

(in pieces, not powder)
4 cloves garlic
1.35 kg (3 lb) fresh young
chicken

Prepare the marinade by heating all the ingredients and simmering them together for 1 hour. The five-spice pieces should be contained in a muslin bag. Remove the giblets of the chicken and clean the bird thoroughly.

Cook and serve as described in the previous recipe.
Serves 6–10.

Soya Chicken in Aromatic Oil
(Adapted from the Lien Wan Restaurant, Canton; by Chef
Tsai Chuan.)

1.35–1.5 kg (3–3½ lb) chicken
10 ml (2 teaspoons) peppercorns
3 cloves garlic
2 medium onions
37 ml (2½ tablespoons) lard
52 ml (3½ tablespoons) vegetable oil

3 slices root ginger
45 ml (3 tablespoons) star anise
125 ml (¼ pint) water
45 ml (3 tablespoons) soya
  sauce
15 ml (1 tablespoon) sugar
5 ml (1 teaspoon) salt

Clean the chicken and chop it through the bones into 18–20 pieces.
Pound the peppercorns lightly in a mortar. Crush and coarsely chop
the garlic. Cut the onions into thin slices.

Prepare the aromatic oil by heating the lard and oil in a small
saucepan or frying pan. Add the onion, ginger, peppercorns, anise,
and garlic. Stir over a medium heat for 4–5 minutes until the onion
begins to turn brown.

Pour the oil and fat mixture from the saucepan through a sieve
or filter into a large saucepan or casserole and place this over a
high heat. When the oil is hot, add the chicken. Turn the pieces in
the hot fat for 5–6 minutes. Add the water, soya sauce, sugar and
salt. Bring the liquid to the boil and turn the chicken pieces in the
hot sauce until the latter is reduced to less than half.

Arrange the pieces of chicken in a well-heated deep-sided dish
and pour the sauce over them, for the diners to help themselves.
Serves 8–10.

Crispy Deep-Fried Steamed Stuffed Chicken
(Adapted from the Canton Restaurant, Canton; by Chef Wu Ying.)

1.35 kg (3 lb) chicken

Stuffing

75 ml (5 tablespoons) glutinous
  rice
6 medium Chinese dried mushrooms
75 g (3 oz) lean pork
75 g (3 oz) fat pork
30 ml (2 tablespoons) lard
5 ml (1 teaspoon) salt

45 ml (3 tablespoons) soya
  sauce
15 ml (1 tablespoon) sugar
22 ml (1½ tablespoons) oyster
  sauce
1 egg
45 ml (3 tablespoons) cornflour
oil for deep-frying

Soak the rice in boiling water for 1 minute and then drain it. Soak the mushrooms in cold water for 20 minutes; remove and discard the stalks. Coarsely chop the mushroom caps and the lean and fat pork. Heat the lard in a small frying pan. Add the rice, chopped mushrooms, pork and salt, and stir-fry them together over a medium heat for 3–4 minutes. Leave to cool. Meanwhile, rub the outside of the chicken with 32 ml (2¼ tablespoons) soya sauce and the sugar which have been blended together. Fill the chicken cavity with stuffing and sew or skewer the opening. Rub the chicken again with the sugar and soya sauce mixture.

Put the chicken in a deep-sided heatproof dish and then into a steamer, and steam steadily for 2¼ hours. Remove from the steamer and place the chicken on a separate dish to drain. Pour the liquid which has collected during the steaming into a small saucepan. Add the oyster sauce and the rest of the soya sauce.

When the chicken has cooled slightly, rub it first with beaten egg and then thickly with cornflour. Heat the oil in the deep-fryer until a crumb dropped into it will sizzle.

Place the chicken in a wire basket and lower it into the hot oil to deep-fry for 8–10 minutes until quite brown. Remove and drain.

Place the chicken on a serving dish. Heat and stir the oyster sauce mixture in the small saucepan. As it boils, pour it over the chicken. Serve the chicken whole: the meat should be tender enough to be taken to pieces with chopsticks.

Serves 6–8.

Twice-Marinated Crispy Skin Splashed-Fried Chicken
(Adapted from the Ta Tung Restaurant, Canton.)

The two types of marinade used for this recipe are the same as those used in the recipes on page 84.

1.35–1.8 kg (3–4 lb) chicken   *2.5–3 litres (5–6 pints) Soya*
2.5–3 litres (5–6 pints) White   *Marinade*
   Marinade   *oil for deep-frying*

Clean the chicken thoroughly, and mix the marinades. Heat the White Marinade in a large saucepan or pot, bring it to the boil, and reduce the heat to a simmer. Add the chicken, and submerge it in the marinade to simmer for 20 minutes. Remove the pan from the heat and allow the chicken to cook in the remaining heat for 10 minutes. Remove the chicken from the marinade, and allow it to drain and dry completely.

Heat the Soya Marinade in a large saucepan or pot, bring it to the boil, and reduce the heat to a simmer. Add the chicken and submerge it in the marinade for 3 minutes. When the contents start to boil, remove the pan from the heat, and allow the chicken to cook in the remaining heat of the marinade for another 5 minutes. The skin of the chicken should now be quite brown from the marinades. Remove the bird from the marinade, and hang it up in an airy spot to dry for 4–5 hours.

Put the chicken in a wire basket. Heat the oil in a deep-fryer until a crumb dropped into it causes a mild sizzle (oil must not be too hot). Submerge the chicken in the hot oil and lift it up immediately to drain. During the next 15 minutes, hold the wire basket containing the chicken over the pan of hot oil and, using a large ladle, pour ladlefuls of oil all over the chicken. After 10 minutes the skin should have become quite crisp. Continue to ladle hot oil over the chicken for another 3–5 minutes.

Quickly chop the chicken with a sharp Chinese chopper into 24–36 pieces. Re-assemble these on a well-heated dish in the form of a chicken and serve. Small dishes containing Aromatic Salt and Pepper Mix, lemon juice, and plum sauce, are served as dips. *Serves 6–10.*

Hundred-Flower Chicken

(Adapted from the famous Pei Yuan Restaurant, in Siu San Park, Canton, whose courtyards, gardens, galleries, pavilions and ponds convey an inimitable ancient rustic scholarly atmosphere.)

1.45 kg (3 lb) chicken	*50 g (2 oz) pork fat*
350 g (¾ lb) extra chicken flesh	*5 ml (1 teaspoon) salt*
350 g (¾ lb) shelled prawns	*15 ml (1 tablespoon) cornflour*

Sauce

15 ml (1 tablespoon) lard	*blended in 60 ml (4 table-*
125 ml (½ pint) stock (b)	*spoons) water*
2.5 ml (½ teaspoon) salt	*5 ml (1 teaspoon) sesame oil*
30 ml (2 tablespoons) dry sherry	*pepper to taste*
15 ml (1 tablespoon) cornflour	

Garnish

30 ml (2 tablespoons) chopped smoked ham	*30 ml (2 tablespoons) crab meat*

Decoration
12 medium-size chrysanthemum flowers

Chop the chicken flesh, prawns and pork fat coarsely. Mix them in a basin with salt and cornflour until well blended. Make a cut in the chicken from head to tail. Remove the body and the bones, but keep the head and wings in the skin. Open the skin out on a large plate, and stuff it with the prawn, chicken and pork mixture from the basin. Place the stuffed chicken on a deep-sided heatproof dish.

Put the chicken on its dish into a steamer, and steam for 20 minutes. Remove from the steamer, and pour any liquid which may have accumulated into a small saucepan or frying pan. Add the lard, stock, salt and sherry. Bring to the boil, add the cornflour mixture, and stir continually. Finally add the sesame oil and pepper. Pour this sauce mixture over the stuffed chicken in the dish.

Garnish the top of the chicken with minced ham and crab meat. Surround it with chrysanthemum flowers and serve. A very colourful dish to serve at a banquet.

Serves 8–10.

Hand-Torn Fried Chicken

1.2–1.35 kg (2½–3 lb) young   45 ml (3 tablespoons) soya
 chicken   sauce
oil for semi-deep-frying   3–4 stalks spring onion

Dips

sweet soya paste   plum sauce
aromatic salt and pepper mix

Remove the legs and wings from the chicken with a sharp cleaver. Rub the chicken body, legs and wings thoroughly with soya sauce. Leave to season and dry for 1 hour. Coarsely chop the spring onions.

Heat 375 ml (¾ pint) oil in a deep-sided frying pan. Add the chicken liver and giblets first to fry for 4 minutes. Drain and cut each into 4–5 slices. Fry the wings for 4–5 minutes, and the drumsticks for 5–6 minutes, and drain.

Now fry the chicken in the hot oil for 6–7 minutes on either side, then on the breast and back, each for the same amount of time. Finally, turn the chicken over in the hot oil a few times, for about 2 minutes. Drain thoroughly and place on a serving dish, surrounding it with the legs, wings and giblets.

The different parts of the chicken should be eaten in the follow-

ing order: a) giblets, wings, drumsticks; b) the meat from the body; finally, c) the parson's nose. They should all be dipped into one of the selected dips, which should be strategically arranged on the table. The chicken pieces are eaten with the fingers.
Serves 6.

Shallow-Fried Chicken Breasts in Fruit Juice Sauce
(Adapted from the Pei Yuan Restaurant, Canton.)

350–450 g (¾–1 lb) chicken breast
5 ml (1 teaspoon) salt
22 ml (1½ tablespoons) corn-

flour
½ egg, beaten
75–90 ml (5–6 tablespoons) lard

Sauce

22 ml (1½ tablespoons) soya sauce
30 ml (2 tablespoons) tangerine juice
22 ml (1½ tablespoons) dry sherry

30 ml (2 tablespoons) tomato purée
30 ml (2 tablespoons) sugar-cane juice (or 15 ml (3 teaspoons) sugar)

Cut the chicken meat into small thin slices. Rub these with salt and cornflour and wet them with the beaten egg. Mix the ingredients for the sauce in a bowl until well blended.

Heat the lard in a frying pan over a high heat. Add the chicken slice by slice, spreading the pieces evenly over the pan. Turn them over after 1 minute, and shallow-fry for a further minute. Remove them with a perforated spoon. Pour away all excess fat from the pan. Add the sauce ingredients from the bowl, and return the pan to the heat. Stir the sauce until it starts to boil. Return the chicken to the pan. Stir-fry for 1 minute, and arrange on a well-heated dish to be eaten immediately.
Serves 6–8.

Chicken in Black-Bean Sauce
(Adapted from the Miao Chi Hsian Restaurant, Canton.)

350–450 g (¾–1 lb) chicken meat (breast and leg)

22 ml (1½ tablespoons) corn-flour
75–90 ml (5–6 tablespoons) lard

Sauce

15 ml (1 tablespoon) salted
   black beans
1 large onion
3 slices root ginger
1 chilli pepper
1 red pepper
3 cloves garlic (crushed)

30 ml (2 tablespoons) dry sherry
15 ml (1 tablespoon) cornflour
   (blended in 90 ml (6 tablespoons) stock) (b)
22 ml (1½ tablespoons) soya
   sauce
5 ml (1 teaspoon) sugar

Cut the chicken into medium-sized strips. Rub these with the corn-flour mixture. Soak the black beans in water for 20 minutes and drain them. Cut the onion into very thin slices and the ginger into shreds. Shred the peppers into similarly sized pieces, after removing the pips.

Heat the lard in a frying pan over a high heat. Add the chicken strips one by one and spread them over the surface of the pan. Stir-fry for 1 minute, and remove with a perforated spoon.

Pour away half of any excess fat in the pan. Add the black beans, onion and ginger and mash them together. Stir-fry over a high heat for 1 minute and add the crushed garlic. Stir and mix them well together in the pan. Return the chicken pieces to the pan and stir and turn them until well mixed with the other ingredients. Continue to stir-fry for 1½ minutes.

Place on a well-heated dish to be eaten immediately.
Serves 6–8.

East River Salt-Buried Chicken
(Adapted from the Pei Yuan Restaurant, Canton.)

1.35–1.8 kg (3–4 lb) chicken
22 ml (1½ tablespoons) Rose
   Dew (Mei Kwei Lu) Liqueur
22 ml (1½ tablespoons) soya
   sauce

4 slices root ginger
1 large onion
15 ml (1 tablespoon) five-spice
   (in pieces, not powder)
2.7–3.15 kg (6–7 lb) sea-salt

Dips

90–120 ml (6–8 tablespoons)
   stock (b)
4 slices root ginger

30 ml (2 tablespoons) dry
   sherry

Rub the chicken inside and out with a mixture of the Rose Dew liqueur and soya sauce. Shred the ginger, cut the onion into thin slices and mix them together with the five-spice pieces. Stuff the cavity of the chicken with the mixture and leave it in an airy spot to dry for 2–3 hours.

Place the chicken in a deep casserole. Pour in the sea salt to cover the whole of the chicken (there should also be a thin layer of salt under the chicken). Close the lid of the casserole, and place it over a medium heat for 10 minutes before putting it into a pre-heated oven at 180°C (350°F)/Gas 6. Bake for 2¼–2½ hours. Lift the chicken out of the casserole and shake it free of salt. Chop the chicken through the bones into 20–24 pieces, and serve on a well-heated dish.

Mix the stock with the shredded ginger and sherry. Divide this between 2 saucer-sized dishes for use as dips on the dining table. *Serves 6–8.*

Quick-Fried Chicken Slivers with Five Ingredients
(Adapted from the Shantung Dining Room, Canton, by Chef Lung Ying.)

350 g (¾ lb) chicken leg meat
5 ml (1 teaspoon) salt
22 ml (1½ tablespoons) corn-flour
½ egg
4 large Chinese dried mushrooms
100 g (¼ lb) fresh mushrooms

1 red pepper
1 green pepper
100 g (¼ lb) bamboo shoots
6–8 asparagus tips
125–250 ml (¼–½ pint) veg-etable oil

Sauce

1 dried chilli pepper
2 slices root ginger
3 cloves garlic
3 stalks spring onion
30 ml (2 tablespoons) lard
30 ml (2 tablespoons) soya sauce

30 ml (2 tablespoons) dry sherry
7 ml (½ tablespoon) sugar
15 ml (1 tablespoon) cornflour (blended in 75 ml (5 table-spoons stock) (b)
salt and pepper to taste

Cut the chicken flesh into medium-sized triple-matchstick-thick slivers. Rub these with the salt and cornflour, and wet them with beaten egg. Soak the dried mushrooms in water for 20 minutes, re-move the stalks and cut each cap into 6 strips. Cut the fresh mush-rooms and both types of sweet pepper and bamboo shoots into similar-sized slivers to the chicken. Pare the asparagus tips, removing all the tougher parts.

D

Shred the chilli pepper (discarding the pips) and the ginger. Crush the garlic and cut the spring onions into 5 cm (2 in) segments.

Heat the oil fiercely in a large frying pan. Add the bamboo shoots, asparagus and mushrooms and stir and turn them over a few times. Next add the chicken and the two sweet peppers. Turn and stir the ingredients in the hot oil, and leave them to cook over a high heat for 2 minutes. Remove from the heat and drain away all the oil, leaving the chicken and vegetables in the pan.

Heat the lard in a smaller pan. Add the chilli pepper, ginger and dried mushrooms. Stir-fry over a high heat for 1 minute. Add the garlic and all the other ingredients for the sauce. Stir until the sauce starts to boil. Pour the contents of the smaller pan into the large frying pan containing the chicken, asparagus, bamboo shoots, mushrooms, and peppers. Reheat the large frying pan over a high flame. Turn and toss the ingredients together for 1½ minutes. Serve on a large well-heated dish, to be eaten hot.

Serves 6–10

Cantonese Chicken in Aspic

1.35–1.8 kg (3–4 lb) young chicken
350 g (¾ lb) Yunnan ham (or smoked ham)
375 ml (¾ pint) chicken stock (b)
7 ml (1½ teaspoons) salt
1 packet gelatine powder (or jelly in one piece)

Heat one large pan (at least 3 litres/6 pints) of water. When it boils, add the chicken and the ham. Allow them to boil together for 30 minutes. Drain, and after leaving the meat to cool slightly, use a sharp knife to carve the chicken flesh into approximately thirty medium-sized pieces. Cut the ham into similar-sized slices. Heat the stock in a small saucepan. Stir in the salt and jelly until they have all dissolved.

Arrange the chicken and ham in three equal rows on a deep-sided dish, interleaving the slices in fish-scale fashion. Arrange a colourful selection of flower heads around the chicken and ham. Pour the jellied stock over them and put the dish into a refrigerator for 2 hours, or until the jelly sets. A useful dish to serve in the summer.

Serves 6.

Duck

Cantonese Roast Duck

Cantonese Roast Duck can be seen hanging in the windows of Chinese restaurants all over the world. The duck is filled with liquid and basted several times during roasting. The following quantities of ingredients are for an average 1.8–2.2 kg (4–5 lb) duck.

Mixture for Filling

45 ml (3 tablespoons) soya sauce

7 ml (½ tablespoon) sugar

2 slices root ginger, shredded

7 ml (½ tablespoon) peppercorns

3 cloves garlic, coarsely chopped

125 ml (¼ pint) stock (b) or water

7 ml (½ tablespoon) brown bean paste

2 stalks spring onion, chopped into 1.25 cm (½ in) segments

7 ml (½ tablespoon) star anise

15 ml (1 tablespoon) dried tangerine peel

Mixture for Basting

125 ml (¼ pint) boiling water

30 ml (2 tablespoons) soya sauce

30 ml (2 tablespoons) honey

30 ml (2 tablespoons) vinegar

Clean the duck and dry it thoroughly with absorbent paper. Rub it inside and out with 10 ml (2 teaspoons) salt, and hang it up to dry for 2–3 hours.

Tie the neck of the duck tightly to close it. Place the bird on a tray or in a bowl, and pour in the filling mixture. Sew the skin up securely so that there is no leakage.

In a Cantonese restaurant the ducks are normally hung up to roast, tail-side up. But if the oven is not big enough for the duck to hang vertically, the bird can be roasted on a wire rack over a drip pan containing a little water.

Pre-heat the oven to 200°C (400°F)/Gas 6. Brush the duck with the basting mixture, and roast it for 20 minutes. Brush it again with the basting mixture and roast it again at 180°C (350°F)/Gas 4 for the next 30 minutes. Brush it again with the basting mixture and roast it at 150°C (300°F)/Gas 2 for a further 30 minutes.

Place the duck in a large deep-sided dish or casserole. Cut the

strings so that the liquid filling drains into the dish. Strain the liquid and heat it in a small saucepan. Chop the duck through the bones into large bite-sized pieces. Re-assemble it on a serving dish and pour the hot filling liquid over the duck as a sauce. The duck can also be served cold, with sauce.
Serves 8–10.

Cantonese Crispy-Skin Duck

1.8–2.2 kg (4–5 lb) duck	15 ml (1 tablespoon) soya sauce
7 ml (½ tablespoon) salt	7 ml (½ tablespoon) malt sugar
15 ml (1 tablespoon) cornflour	45 ml (3 tablespoons) water

Pour a kettleful of boiling water slowly over the duck. Drain it and rub it dry with absorbent paper. Rub the skin and the inside of the duck with the salt, and hang it up to dry in an airy spot for 5 hours.

Place the duck on a spit and grill it under a moderate heat until slightly brown. Mix the cornflour with the soya sauce, malt sugar and water until well blended. Rub the mixture on the duck.

Put the duck on a wire rack in a preheated oven at 200°C (350°F)/ Gas 4 and roast for a further hour.

Chop the duck through the bones into large bite-sized pieces. Arrange, re-assembled on a serving dish in the form of a duck, and serve with Aromatic Salt and Pepper Mix (see page 68) as a dip.
Serves 8–10.

Family Onion and Ginger Duck
(Adapted from the Ting Hsian Restaurant, Canton.)

6 medium-sized onions	125 ml (¼ pint) oil for semi-deep frying
75–100 g (3–4 oz) roast pork	
6 slices root ginger	1 Chinese cabbage or 225 g (½ lb) celery
6 medium-sized Chinese dried mushrooms	
22 ml (1½ tablespoons) lard	15 ml (1 tablespoon) oyster sauce
45 ml (3 tablespoons) soya sauce	1.35–1.8 kg (3–4 lb) duck

Cut the onions into quarters, and the roast pork, across lean and fat, into small cubes. Shred the ginger, soak the mushrooms and cut the caps in quarters (discarding the stalks). Heat the lard in a small frying pan. Add the foregoing ingredients, stir-fry for $2\frac{1}{2}$ minutes, and stuff them into the cavity of the duck, after rubbing the inside with soya sauce. Skewer the duck to hold the stuffing inside.

Heat the oil in a frying pan. Turn the duck in the hot oil until slightly brown (about 5–6 minutes). Remove and drain the duck, and place it in a deep-sided heatproof dish. Put the dish into a steamer and steam vigorously for $1\frac{1}{2}$ hours. Tear the cabbage (or chop the celery) into individual leaves (or pieces), lay them under the duck, and steam for a further 15 minutes. Drain the liquid at the bottom of the dish into a small saucepan. Add the remaining soya sauce and oyster sauce and bring the mixture to the boil. Pour the sauce over the duck, and serve it in the heatproof dish. The duck should be tender enough to be taken to pieces with chopsticks.
Serves 6–10.

Steamed Deep-Fried Duck with Tangerine Peel Stuffed with Glutinous Rice and Almonds

1.35–1.8 kg (3–4 lb) duck	chopped
2 ducks' livers	5 ml (1 teaspoon) salt
50–75 g (2–3 oz) glutinous rice	30 ml (2 tablespoons) lard
50 g (2 oz) lean roast pork	15 ml (1 tablespoon) cornflour
30 ml (2 tablespoons) blanched	1 egg
almonds	15 ml (1 tablespoon) soya sauce
dried peel of 1 tangerine,	

Soak the glutinous rice in water for 1 hour, and drain it. Cut the ducks' livers and the roast pork into small, thin pieces. Heat the lard in a frying pan. Add the almonds and stir-fry for 1 minute. Add the rice, liver, pork and salt. Stir-fry for 2 minutes over a high heat. Fill the cavity of the duck with the mixture and use a skewer to close it. Mix the cornflour with the beaten egg and soya sauce until well blended.

Place the duck on a heatproof dish, cover it with the tangerine peel, put it into a steamer and steam it steadily for 2 hours. Remove the duck from the steamer, and when it has cooled rub the skin thoroughly with the cornflour-soya-egg mixture. Allow it to dry for 30 minutes, then truss the duck, place it in a wire basket, and deep-fry it in hot oil for 7–8 minutes.

Drain off the oil and serve the duck whole. It should be sufficiently tender to dismember at the table with chopsticks, or with the aid

of a knife. The diners eat the meat together with spoonfuls of the
highly savoury stuffings.
Serves 8–10.

Stir-Fried Roast Duck with Lichee and Pineapple

675–900 g (1½–2 lb) roast duck (ready chopped)

15 ml (1 tablespoon) cornflour (blended in 60 ml (4 table-spoons) water)

60–75 ml (4–5 tablespoons) lichee fruit

45 ml (3 tablespoons) lichee syrup

30 ml (2 tablespoons) pineapple rings, cut into cubes

45 ml (3 tablespoons) pineapple syrup

37 ml (2½ tablespoons) soya sauce

1 green pepper

30 ml (2 tablespoons) vegetable oil

Remove the bones from the pieces of roast duck. Cut the flesh into
medium-sized strips. Blend the cornflour mixture with the lichee and
pineapple syrups and 15 ml (1 tablespoon) soya sauce. Cut the
green pepper into small pieces.

Heat the oil in a large frying pan. Add the pepper and stir-fry it
in the oil for 30 seconds. Add the duck meat, sprinkle the pan
with soya sauce, and stir-fry together with the pepper over a high
heat for 2 minutes. Add the lichee and pineapple pieces. Stir and
turn them with the duck and other ingredients for 2 minutes. Pour
the cornflour mixed with the lichee and pineapple syrups evenly
over the pan. Stir until the sauce thickens. Turn them out on to a
dish and serve hot.
Serves 6.

Tiuchow Lemon Duck

(Adapted from the Assembly of Overseas Chinese Restaurant,
Tiuchow; proprietor, Huang Kuo Ching.)

3 slices root ginger

2 onions

2 lemons

1.35–1.8 kg (3–4 lb) duck

10 ml (2 teaspoons) salt

1 sheet pork skin (about 12.5 x

12.5 cm/5 x 5 in)

60 ml (4 tablespoons) soya sauce

250 ml (½ pint) water

45 ml (3 tablespoons) sherry

Shred the ginger, cut the onions into thin slices, prick 1 lemon a dozen times and slice the other lemon into 8 segments. Insert the punctured lemon into the cavity of the duck after having rubbed the duck inside and out with the salt. Place the duck in a deep-sided heatproof dish (or casserole), sprinkle it first with ginger and then with the remaining onion, and place the pork skin on top, which should help to keep the ginger and onion in place. Mix the soya sauce with the water and sherry, and pour this over the duck.

Cover the casserole firmly, place it in a steamer, and steam it steadily for 2½ hours; or cook in a tray half-filled with water in an oven at 180°C (350°F)/Gas 4 for 2½ hours.

Remove the pork skin, onion and ginger from the duck. Transfer the latter to a deep-sided serving dish and surround it with lemon segments. Skim the fat off the liquid in the dish in which the duck has cooked. Reduce the liquid by a third by rapid boiling. Pour half the liquid or sauce over the duck and serve. The duck should be tender enough to be taken to pieces with chopsticks; but a knife can be used if necessary.

Serves 8–10.

Pork

Although the most widely eaten meat in China, pork seems to be used mostly for domestic everyday dishes in Canton rather than the creation of elaborate banquet or restaurant dishes. But there are several outstanding pork dishes in the Cantonese repertoire.

Roast or Barbecued Suckling Pig
(Adapted from the Nam Yuan Restaurant, Canton.)

The average suckling pig used in China is about 4.2–6.6 kg (12–15 lb), too big to be barbecued on a spit under a domestic grill. Even the smaller suckling pigs sometimes obtainable in the West are best roasted in the oven.

15 ml (1 tablespoon) salt
7 ml (½ tablespoon) five-spice powder
1 suckling pig (about 3.6–4.4

kg/8–10 lb)
5 ml (1 teaspoon) malt sugar
15 ml (1 tablespoon) soya sauce
30 ml (2 tablespoons) water

Mix the salt with the five-spice powder. Rub the mixture thoroughly over the suckling pig, both inside and out, and leave to season for 2–3 hours. Pour a large kettleful of boiling water over the skin and the whole length of the carcase, and use another kettleful to rinse out the cavity. Wipe and dry thoroughly with a dry cloth or absorbent paper.

Mix the malt sugar with the soya sauce and water. Rub the mixture evenly over the cooled and dried skin of the pig.

Put the suckling pig on a wire rack into a preheated oven at 190°C (375°F)/Gas 5 for 45 minutes. Reduce the heat to 180°C (350°F)/Gas 4 and roast the pig for a further hour. Place a roasting pan half full of water at the bottom of the oven to catch the drips.

Peel off the skin of the suckling pig, which should now be deep brown, and serve cut to regular medium-sized rectangles on one or two well-heated dishes. Carve the flesh similarly. The crackling skin and tender pork should be consumed with small steamed Lotus Leaf Buns and pieces of spring onion, brushed with sweet soya-paste sauce, or plum sauce. A splendid starter to a banquet.
Serves 12–20.

Cantonese Soya-Braised Knuckle of Pork

*1 large cut of knuckle of pork
(about 1.35–1.8 kg/3–4 lb)*
30 ml (2 tablespoons) cornflour
*97 ml (6½ tablespoons) soya
sauce*
3 stalks leeks
oil for deep-frying

*52 ml (3½ tablespoons) oyster
sauce*
125 ml (¼ pint) water
10 ml (2 teaspoons) sugar
15 ml (1 tablespoon) star anise
3 lettuce leaves

Heat a large pan of water. Add the knuckle, bring the contents of the pan to the boil, and simmer for 15 minutes. Remove, drain, and rub the knuckle dry with a cloth. Rub the knuckle with the cornflour and 30 ml (2 tablespoons) soya sauce. Clean the leeks and cut them into short sections.

Heat the oil in the deep-fryer. When hot, place the knuckle in a wire basket, deep-fry it for 5 minutes and then drain it.

Mix the oyster sauce, 67 ml (4½ tablespoons) soya sauce and the water and sugar until well blended. Place the knuckle in a deep casserole and surround it with leek slices and star anise. Pour the oyster and soya sauce mixture over the knuckle.

Put the casserole into a preheated oven at 190°C (375°F)/Gas 5 for 1 hour, turning the knuckle over after 30 minutes. Reduce the heat to 180°C (350°F)/Gas 4 and cook for a further 1½ hours, turning the knuckle over every 30 minutes.

Tear the lettuce leaves in half, stuff them around the knuckle of pork, and bring the casserole to the table. The skin of the knuckle should be very succulent, and the pork meat very tender. An excellent dish to consume with rice at a domestic dinner.
Serves 6–10.

Quick-Fried Sliced Pork in Fruit Juice Sauce

350 g (¾ lb) leg of pork
2.5 ml (½ teaspoon) salt
15 ml (1 tablespoon) cornflour
½ egg
4 stalks leeks
1 medium onion
60–75 ml (4–5 tablespoons) vegetable oil
15 ml (1 tablespoon) lard

22 ml (1½ tablespoons) soya sauce
15 ml (1 tablespoon) dry sherry
22 ml (1½ tablespoons) tomato purée
5 ml (1 teaspoon) sugar
22 ml (1½ tablespoons) tangerine or orange juice

Cut the pork into medium-sized thin slices. Rub these with the salt, cornflour and beaten egg. Clean and cut the leeks slantwise into 2.5 cm (1 in) slices.

Heat the oil in a frying pan. Add the slices of pork, spread them out over the pan and stir-fry them for 1½ minutes over a high heat. Remove and drain them. Pour away all excess oil (retain for other use).

Melt the lard in the pan. Add the chopped onion and leeks. Stir them over a high heat for one minute. Push them to one side of the pan and add all the other ingredients. Stir these over a high heat until well blended. Return the pork slices to the pan and mix them with the sauce. Leave to cook for 1½ minutes. Serve on a well-heated dish with the pork in the middle, surrounded by the leeks and onion. Best eaten immediately.
Serves 6–8.

Pork Chop in Fruit Juice Sauce

Chinese pork chops are about a quarter of the size of Western pork chops (they should be cut to that size, with or without the bone).

D*

They can be cooked in precisely the same manner as the Quick-fried Sliced Pork on page 99, except that, being thicker, the chops should be given a couple of minutes more shallow-frying in an extra couple of tablespoons (30 ml) of oil. The final stir-frying in lard with all the other ingredients should also be prolonged by ½–1 minute. Otherwise all the other procedures are the same.

Pork Pudding with Red Southern Bean-Curd Cheese
(Adapted from the Northern Suburb Dining Room, Canton.)

675 g (1½ lb) belly of pork
oil for shallow-frying (about 125–250 ml/¼–½ pint)
675 g (1½ lb) sweet potato or yam (or plain potato)
15 ml (1 tablespoon) red bean-
curd cheese
22 ml (1½ tablespoons) soya sauce
30 ml (2 tablespoons) Chinese winter pickle
30 ml (2 tablespoons) sherry

Cut the pork through the skin into medium-sized pieces. Deep- or shallow-fry these in hot oil for 2 minutes and drain them. Cut the potatoes or yams into similar-sized pieces. Deep- or shallow-fry these for 1 minute and drain them. Mix the bean-curd cheese and soya sauce together and apply the mixture first to the pork, then to the potato, until every piece is well covered.

Arrange the pork skin-side-down in a heatproof basin, inter-leaving each piece of pork with a piece of yam or potato. Sprinkle the top with the pickles and sherry. Cover the top of the basin with tinfoil. Place the basin inside a saucepan, to stand 6.25–7.5 cm (2½–3 in) deep in boiling water. Simmer for 1½ hours. Turn the 'pudding' out on a dish to serve. A dish for the connoisseur of Chinese domestic cookery.
Serves 6–8.

Cantonese Cha Shao Roast Pork

Cha Shao roasting is a specialized Cantonese form of cooking which involves the long marinading and quick roasting over a high heat of strips or pieces of meat not more than 3.75 cm (1½ in) in thickness, so that they can be heated through in a matter of minutes.

675–900 g (1½–2 lb) fillet of pork

Marinade

30 ml (2 tablespoons) soya sauce

30 ml (2 tablespoons) sugar

10 ml (2 teaspoons) red bean-curd cheese

15 ml (1 tablespoon) vegetable oil

Trim the long strips of fillet of pork, so that no part of it is too thick. Mix the ingredients for the marinade in a large basin. Add the strips of pork, rub them with the marinade and leave them to season for 1 hour.

Lay the pork strips on a wire rack. Put them into a preheated oven at 220°C (425°F)/Gas 7 and place underneath it a roasting pan containing a little water to catch the drips. Roast at this high temperature for 8–9 minutes. Then turn the pork over (see that it is not burning or charred) and roast for a further 5 minutes.

Place the strips of pork on a chopping board, and cut across the fibre into very thin slices. Arrange them in 2 or 3 rows on a well-heated serving dish in fish-scale fashion. The marinade encrusted on the outside of the pork by the high-heat roasting frames every slice with a well-cooked rim which contrasts well with the fresh, lightly-cooked centre. This is the special feature of Cha Shao Roast Pork, which is a winner every time it is properly done.

Serves 8–10.

Pork and Ham Roll with Heart of Chicken Liver
(Adapted from the Northern Suburb Dining Room, Canton.)

1 thin sheet of fat pork (about 275 g/10 oz)

1 thin sheet of lean pork (slightly smaller)

75 g (3 oz) chicken liver

2 eggs

15 ml (1 tablespoon) cornflour

3 stalks spring onion

1 thin slice of ham (same dimensions as lean pork)

Marinade for Fat Pork

7 ml (½ tablespoon) salt

22 ml (1½ tablespoons) sherry

10 ml (2 teaspoons) sugar

Marinade for Lean Pork

15 ml (1 tablespoon) soya sauce   5 ml (1 teaspoon) sugar
15 ml (1 tablespoon) sherry

Mix the respective marinading ingredients together. Rub the fat pork with its marinade and leave it to season for 1 hour; rub the lean pork with its marinade and leave it to season for 15 minutes. Cut the chicken liver into equal-sized pieces. Beat the eggs with the cornflour into a batter. Mix half the batter with the chicken liver. Coarsely chop the spring onions.

Place the sheet of fat pork, opened out, on a large plate. Wet it and spread it with a small amount of batter. Sprinkle this evenly with spring onion. Place the sheet of lean pork on top. Spread the lean pork with half the remaining batter and place the slice of ham on top. Spread the chicken liver and batter mixture lengthwise across the centre of the ham. Roll up the fat, lean pork and ham with the liver inside into a sausage shape. Stuff the ends of the roll with the remaining batter, and tie a string around it to make it secure.

Cook the roll in a steamer for 30–35 minutes. Remove to drain and cool. Now place it in a wire basket and deep-fry it in hot oil for 5 minutes. Remove and drain again.

Cut the roll into slices about 1.25 cm (½ in) thick. Arrange these on a serving dish for the diners to help themselves.
Serves 6–8.

Quick-Fried Pork Liver with Chicken Slivers

(Adapted from the Western Suburb Dining Room, Canton.)

100–150 g (4–5 oz) pork liver
100–150 g (4–5 oz) breast of chicken
7 ml (½ tablespoon) salt
22 ml (1½ tablespoons) corn-flour
4 stalks spring onion
3 cloves garlic
75–90 ml (5–6 tablespoons)

vegetable oil
15 ml (1 tablespoon) lard
30 ml (2 tablespoons) soya sauce
7 ml (½ tablespoon) sugar
15 ml (1 tablespoon) vinegar
15 ml (1 tablespoon) sherry
30 ml (2 tablespoons) stock (b)

Cut the liver into slices, and the chicken into slivers. Rub these with the salt and cornflour. Cut the spring onions into short segments and crush the garlic.

Heat the oil in a frying pan over a high heat. Add the liver and chicken. Turn them in the hot oil to fry for 1½ minutes, then remove and drain them. Pour away all the oil (which may be kept for further use). Put the lard, spring onion and garlic into the pan. Toss them around 3–4 times over a high heat. Add the soya sauce, sugar, vinegar, sherry and stock. When the mixture boils, stir it a few times, and return the liver and chicken to the pan. Continue to stir-fry over a high heat for 1 minute. Serve immediately on a well-heated dish.

Serves 6–8.

Steamed Spare-Ribs with Plums
(Adapted from the Northern Suburb Dining Room, Canton.)

675–900 g (1½–2 lb) spare-ribs
12 ml (¾ tablespoon) black beans
6 medium plums
10 ml (2 teaspoons) sugar
15 ml (1 tablespoon) cornflour
30 ml (2 tablespoons) soya sauce
15 ml (1 tablespoon) vegetable oil

Chop the spare-ribs into short segments. Soak the black beans in water for 10 minutes, then drain them. Remove the stones from the plums and place them in a heatproof basin. Add all the remaining ingredients, and mix them together thoroughly. Cover the basin firmly with tinfoil, place it in a steamer, and steam vigorously for 1 hour. Serve either in the basin itself, or transferred to a well-heated dish.

Serves 6–8.

Sweet and Sour Pork
(Adapted from the Number Nine Restaurant, Canton.)

450 g (1 lb) belly pork (without skin)
7 ml (½ tablespoon) salt
45 ml (3 tablespoons) cornflour
1 egg
50–75 g (2–3 oz) bamboo shoots
½ red pepper
½ green pepper
1 medium onion

Sauce

30 ml (2 tablespoons) sugar
15 ml (1 tablespoon) soya sauce
30 ml (2 tablespoons) tomato sauce or purée
45 ml (3 tablespoons) vinegar
22 ml (1½ tablespoons) cornflour (blended in 90 ml (6 tablespoons) water)
30 ml (2 tablespoons) sherry
oil for deep- or shallow-frying

Cut the pork into small rectangular pieces. Rub these with the salt. Mix the cornflour with the beaten egg and coat the pieces of pork in the batter. Cut the bamboo shoots and peppers into large slices, and the onion into thin slices. Mix the ingredients for the sauce together.

Heat the oil in a deep-fryer, or 250 ml ($\frac{1}{2}$ pint) oil in a deep frying pan if shallow-frying. When the oil is hot enough for a crumb dropped in to sizzle, add the pieces of pork in batter one by one. Fry for $3\frac{1}{2}$ minutes, remove and drain.

If using a frying pan, pour away all the oil; if you used a deep-fryer, pour a little of the oil into a frying pan and heat. Add the bamboo shoots and onion to fry for 1 minute. Put in the peppers, stir them together for 15 seconds, pour in the sauce mixture and stir until the sauce thickens. Return the pork pieces to the pan. Turn them in the hot sauce. Reduce the heat and simmer for $1\frac{1}{2}$ minutes. Pour the pork and sauce into a deep-sided dish and serve immediately.
Serves 6–8.

Crispy-Skin Roast Pork

1.35–1.5 kg (3–3½ lb) belly of pork (with skin)
7 ml (½ tablespoon) salt
5 ml (1 teaspoon) brown sugar

15 ml (1 tablespoon) soya sauce
30 ml (2 tablespoons) water

Douse the skin side of the pork with a kettleful of boiling water. Drain, dry and rub the skin with salt. Leave it to dry, and score the skin in 2.5 cm (1 in) diamond patterns. Pierce the meat, not the skin, at regular intervals with a skewer. Leave to season for 1 hour. Grill the skin side of the pork until slightly brown. Mix the sugar with the soya sauce and water until well blended. Rub the mixture on the pork and pork skin.

Put the piece of pork on a wire rack and place it in a pre-heated oven at 170°C (325°F)/Gas 3 and roast for $1\frac{1}{4}$–$1\frac{1}{2}$ hours, turning over twice.

Cut the pork through meat and skin into medium-sized rectangular pieces, each with the skin, which should now be very crisp, attached. The crunching of the crispy skin together with the blandness of plain rice seems to release and enhance the quality of the dish.
Serves 6–8.

Beef

Quick-Fried Beef with Oyster Sauce

450 g (1 lb) beef steak
2.5 ml (½ teaspoon) salt
52 ml (3½ tablespoons) vegetable oil
15 ml (1 tablespoon) soya sauce
10 ml (2 teaspoons) cornflour
30 ml (2 tablespoons) water

30 ml (2 tablespoons) sherry
60 ml (4 tablespoons) stock (b)
2 slices root ginger
37 ml (2½ tablespoons) oyster sauce
4 ml (¾ teaspoon) sugar
pepper to taste

Cut the beef into small thin slices and rub these with the salt and 7 ml (½ tablespoon) oil. Mix the soya sauce, cornflour, water, sherry and stock in a bowl until well blended. Finely chop the ginger.

Heat the oil in a frying pan. When hot add the beef, spreading the pieces out, and stir-fry them over a high heat for 1 minute. Add the ginger, followed by the oyster sauce and sugar, and continue to stir-fry for 30 seconds. Pour in the sauce mixture from the bowl, and continue to stir-fry over a high heat for a further minute. Serve immediately on a well-heated dish. This mixture of seafood flavour with meat is a common Cantonese practice which most southerners enjoy, but which is not always accepted in central and north China.

Serves 6–8.

Beef Balls in Soup

(Adapted from the Ting Chang Restaurant, Canton.)

4–5 medium Chinese dried mushrooms
275 g (10 oz) lean beef
1 onion
5 ml (1 teaspoon) salt
15 ml (1 tablespoon) cornflour
½ egg

½ bunch of watercress
750 ml (1½ pints) stock (b)
15 ml (1 tablespoon) lard
50 g (2 oz) beef fat
15 ml (1 tablespoon) chopped spring onion

Soak the mushrooms for 30 minutes. Drain them, remove the stalks, and chop the caps coarsely. Chop the beef, beef fat and onion finely. Mix these ingredients in a basin with the salt, cornflour and beaten egg, and work the mixture with the fingers until thoroughly blended. Shape the mixture into small balls. Drop them into a bowl of iced water to cool for 15 minutes. Remove them and drain before cooking. Clean and remove the roots of the watercress.

Heat 1 litre (2 pints) water in a saucepan. When it starts to boil, drop the beef balls in one by one to parboil for 2 minutes. Remove and drain them.

Heat the stock in another saucepan. Add the beef balls. Bring them to the boil and simmer for 5 minutes. Add the watercress and lard. Bring to the boil again, and simmer for a further 3 minutes. Adjust seasoning, and serve, sprinkled with spring onion, in a large tureen for diners to help themselves throughout the meal. Being comparatively short-cooked, the beef balls should be juicy and fresh when bitten into.
Serves 6–8.

Braised Beef with Anise

75–90 ml (5–6 tablespoons) vegetable oil
900 g (2 lb) chuck or brisket of beef
2.5 ml (½ teaspoon) salt
7 ml (½ tablespoon) sugar
pepper to taste

52 ml (3½ tablespoons) soya sauce
60 ml (4 tablespoons) water
3 cloves star anise
45 ml (3 tablespoons) sherry
3 cloves garlic

Cut the beef into 4 pieces. Crush the garlic. Heat the oil in a frying pan. Turn the beef in the hot oil over a high heat for 2 minutes. Drain and place it in a double-boiler. Add the salt, sugar, pepper, soya sauce, water and anise. Turn the beef several times to mix with the ingredients. Bring the water in the double-boiler to the boil. Reduce the heat to a brisk simmer. Leave the beef to cook under cover for 4 hours, turning it once an hour. During the last 30 minutes' cooking, add the sherry and garlic.

Cut the beef into large bite-sized pieces. Place them in a deep-sided dish, and pour the sauce from the bottom of the double-boiler over them. This is an excellent dish to eat with rice.
Serves 6–8.

Braised Short Beef Ribs with Salted Black Beans

1.35 kg (3 lb) beef ribs
22 ml (1½ tablespoons) black beans

1 medium onion
3 cloves garlic
15 ml (1 tablespoon) soya sauce

30 ml (2 tablespoons) vegetable   30 ml (2 tablespoons) sherry
  oil   2 slices root ginger
165 ml (⅓ pint) water   pepper to taste

Chop the ribs with a sharp Chinese chopper into medium-sized
pieces. Soak the black beans in water for 10 minutes and drain
them. Chop the onion coarsely, shred the ginger and crush the
garlic. Mix and mash the black beans with the soya sauce and
onion.

Heat the oil in a frying pan with a lid. Add the beef ribs, and
stir-fry over a medium heat for 5 minutes. Add the black beans,
ginger, soya and onion mixture. Turn the beef with the mixture
for 3 minutes. Pour in the water and bring to the boil. Turn the
ribs several times. Reduce the heat to low, place a lid firmly over the
frying pan, and allow the contents to simmer gently together for 1
hour. Turn every 20 minutes. Add the sherry, garlic and pepper and
continue to simmer for 15 minutes. Serve in a deep-sided dish for
the diners to help themselves.
Serves 6–8.

Frogs and Pigeons

Deep-Fried Red-Cooked (Soya-Braised) Pigeon

2 fat pigeons   oil for deep-frying
125 ml (¼ pint) water   60 ml (4 tablespoons) soya
15 ml (1 tablespoon) five-spice   sauce
  (in pieces, not powder)   2 slices root ginger
15 ml (1 tablespoon) sugar   3–4 lettuce leaves

Chop the pigeons through the bone into quarters. Mix the other ingredients in a bowl, and bring them to the boil in a heavy pot or
casserole.

Put the pigeon pieces into the boiling sauce in the casserole.
Allow them to simmer gently for 30 minutes, turning them over
every 10 minutes. Remove them from the heat and leave them to
cool in the sauce for 30 minutes. Drain the pigeon pieces, and place
them in an airy spot to dry.

When the pigeon pieces are dry, place them in a wire basket
and deep-fry them in hot oil until brown.

Serve on a bed of lettuce leaves in a well-heated dish. To be consumed using Aromatic Salt and Pepper Mix and tomato ketchup as dips.

Serves 4.

Deep-Fried and Braised Pigeon in Fruit Juice Sauce
(Adapted from the Yu Yuan Restaurant, Canton.)

2 fat pigeons	*2 stalks spring onion*
1 stick celery	*oil for deep-frying*
3 firm tomatoes	*22 ml (1½ tablespoons) lard*
1 medium onion	

Sauce

30 ml (2 tablespoons) tangerine juice	*10 ml (2 teaspoons) lemon juice*
30 ml (2 tablespoons) soya sauce	*90 ml (6 tablespoons) stock (b)*
	7 ml (½ tablespoon) sugar

Chop the pigeons through the bone into quarters, cut the celery slantwise into small segments, the tomatoes into quarters (after pouring boiling water over them and removing the skins), the onion into thin slices, and the spring onions into small segments. Mix the other ingredients together into a cooking sauce.

Place the pigeon pieces in a wire basket and deep-fry them in hot oil until brown. Drain and put them aside.

Heat the lard in a frying pan with a lid. Add the chopped tomatoes, celery, and onions. Stir-fry them together for 3 minutes over a medium heat. Add the sauce. Stir the ingredients together, and leave to simmer over a low heat for 5 minutes. Add the pigeon pieces and turn them in the sauce until well covered. Place the lid over the pan firmly, and leave it to cook for 15 minutes over a low heat. Arrange the pieces of pigeon on a well-heated dish for the diners to help themselves.

Serves 4.

South of the River Crispy Pigeon and Shrimp Cakes
(Adapted from the Canton Restaurant, Canton.)

1 fat pigeon	*45 ml (3 tablespoons) lard*
37 g (1½ oz) pork fat	*½ egg*
175 g (6 oz) shelled shrimps	*45–60 ml (3–4 tablespoons)*
7 ml (½ tablespoon) salt	*flour*
15 ml (1 tablespoon) cornflour	*oil for deep-frying*

Chop the pigeon into quarters and cook them in a pan of boiling water for 7–8 minutes. Remove and drain them. Strip the meat from the bones, and chop it coarsely. Chop the pork fat and shelled shrimps in the same way. Mix them all in a basin, add the salt and cornflour, and mix again.

Heat the lard in a frying pan. Add the ingredients from the basin, and stir-fry them over a medium heat for 5–6 minutes. Allow them to cool somewhat before removing the mixture from the pan. Add the beaten egg, and mix well.

Shape the mixture into a dozen flat rectangular cakes. Coat each cake evenly with flour, and shake off any excess. Place the cakes 4 at a time in a wire basket, deep-fry them in the hot oil for 2½ minutes, and drain them. When all the cakes have been fried once, place them all in the wire basket, and deep-fry them together for 1 minute. Drain and serve on a well-heated dish. A good starter for a dinner party.

Serves 6–8.

Quick-Braised Soya Frog in Wine-Lee Sauce
(Adapted from a Tiuchow recipe.)

Frogs, which we in China call Tien Chi or 'chicken of the rice fields', are very similar to chicken in texture. They can in fact be cooked in as many ways as chicken.

675 g (1½ lb) fat frogs (about 3)
10 ml (2 teaspoons) salt
pepper to taste
15 ml (1 tablespoon) vegetable oil

3 slices root ginger
1 green pepper
100 g (¼ lb) bamboo shoots
6 large Chinese dried mushrooms
45 ml (3 tablespoons) lard

Sauce

22 ml (1½ tablespoons) soya sauce
30 ml (2 tablespoons) dry sherry
45 ml (3 tablespoons) chicken stock (a)
15 ml (1 tablespoon) tomato purée

15 ml (1 tablespoon) oyster sauce
30 ml (2 tablespoons) wine-sediment paste (occasionally available from Chinese food stores; otherwise mix equal amounts of brandy and soya paste)

Skin the frogs; remove the heads and innards. Clean each frog and chop it into 6 pieces. Rub the pieces with the salt, pepper, oil and shredded ginger. Leave them to season for 30 minutes.

Cut the green pepper into thin slices (discarding the seeds), and the bamboo shoots likewise. Soak the mushrooms for 20 minutes, and remove the stalks. Cut each into 4. Mix the ingredients for the sauce in a bowl.

Heat 30 ml (2 tablespoons) lard in a frying pan with a lid. Add the frog pieces, stir-fry over a high heat for 1½ minutes and push them to the sides. Add the remaining lard, the mushrooms, peppers and bamboo shoots to the centre of the pan. Stir-fry over a high heat for 1 minute. Return the frog-pieces to the centre of the pan to turn and stir together with the other ingredients. After 1 minute, add the cooking sauce, pouring it evenly over the contents of the pan. Turn and mix them together, still over a high heat. Reduce the heat to low, and place the lid firmly on the frying pan. Leave the contents to simmer for 5 minutes. Serve immediately on a well-heated dish.
Serves 4–6.

Quick-Braised Frogs' Legs in Oyster Sauce

1 dozen pairs of fat frogs' legs (about 675–900 g/1½–2 lb)

vegetable oil for shallow-frying (about 250 ml/½ pint)

30 ml (2 tablespoons) soya sauce

30 ml (2 tablespoons) oyster sauce

3 slices root ginger

30 ml (2 tablespoons) stock (b)

30 ml (2 tablespoons) cornflour

30 ml (2 tablespoons) sherry

1 small green pepper

5 ml (1 teaspoon) sugar

1 small red pepper

5 ml (1 teaspoon) chilli sauce

1 medium onion

15 ml (1 tablespoon) sesame oil

Disjoint the frogs' legs, and cut them in two if they are joined together. Rub them with the soya sauce and shredded ginger. Leave them to season for 30 minutes. Sprinkle the cornflour over them, rub it in and leave them to dry for 30 minutes. Cut the peppers in thin slices (discarding the pips) and cut the onion into even thinner slices.

Heat the oil in a large frying pan. Add half the frogs' legs, and turn them over on a high heat with a perforated spoon to fry for 2½ minutes, then remove them with the perforated spoon. Add the other half of the frogs' legs, fry them for a similar length of time, and drain them.

Pour away all except 15 ml (1 tablespoon) of the oil. Add the onion and peppers. Stir-fry them over a high heat for 1½ minutes. Return the frogs' legs to the pan. Stir and turn them with the other ingredients for 1½ minutes. Add the oyster sauce, stock, sherry, sugar, and chilli sauce. Continue to turn and stir them for 1 minute. Reduce the heat to low, and allow the contents to sauté for 4–5 minutes. Sprinkle them with the sesame oil, and serve immediately. *Serves 6–8.*

Tai Shih Frog Soup
(Adapted from the Pei Yuan Restaurant, Canton.)

Tai Shih is the classical term for the office of the Imperial Historian —in other words, a high-class soup for eminent diners.

3–4 frogs (about 675 g/1½ lb)
young bamboo shoots (like
* asparagus tips)*
½ medium cucumber
100 g (¼ lb) smoked ham
2 stalks spring onion
1 chicken stock cube

30 ml (2 tablespoons) veg-
* etable oil*
salt and pepper to taste
1 litre (2 pints) stock (b)
45 ml (3 tablespoons) dry
* sherry*

After skinning the frogs and removing the heads and innards, chop each one into 6–8 pieces. Cut the bamboo shoots slantwise into medium-sized segments, the cucumber into triple-matchstick-thick strips, the ham into similar-sized strips and the spring onions into small sections. Parboil the frog pieces in boiling water for 1½ minutes, and drain; then boil the bamboo shoots for 2 minutes, and drain them.

Heat the oil at the bottom of a casserole. Add the frogs, salt (7 ml/ ½ tablespoon) and bamboo shoots. Stir and turn this over a medium heat for 2 minutes and push to the sides. Put the cucumber strips in the middle of the casserole, spread them out and cover them with the frog pieces and bamboo shoots. Sprinkle the shredded ham over this. Mix the stock with the sherry and chicken stock cube. Season to taste. Pour this soup into the casserole. Bring the contents to the boil, and simmer gently for the next 30 minutes. Sprinkle with chopped spring onion and serve in the casserole. A soup to be consumed throughout the meal. *Serves 6.*

Fish and Shellfish

Cantonese fish dishes must undoubtedly rank among the top fish dishes in the world. Their quality is probably derived from the simplicity with which they are prepared. The Cantonese use of steaming as a principal method of cooking helps to achieve this. As in the treatment of chicken, great emphasis is laid on cooking fish exactly to a turn: not a minute too long, so that the flesh begins to turn tough and fibrous; nor a minute too short, so that it retains some raw fishiness. When it is just cooked and the heat withdrawn in the nick of time, and the fish is brought to the table and eaten immediately, the flesh should be possessed of that fresh juiciness and that characteristic 'sweet savouriness' which is associated only with truly fresh foods. Hence Chinese restaurants make quite a feature of keeping fish alive until they are ready for cooking, often in tanks where they can be seen swimming around.

Two or three other aspects of Cantonese cooking help to make their fish dishes doubly succulent and appealing. One is their use of a strong sauce: often a compound of soya sauce, wine, sugar, vinegar and ginger. The last two ingredients help to suppress any excessive fishy taste—especially in fish which has only been lightly cooked—and the first three ingredients seem to enhance the richness and savouriness of the flesh. Another common practice in Cantonese fish cookery is to use oil or fat—particularly bacon or pork fat—to assist in the steaming, which improves the succulence and smoothness of the dish. The flavour of the dish is sometimes further orchestrated by the introduction of a range of dried or salted foods (never fresh seafoods). These ingredients, which include dried mushrooms, dried prawns, dried tiger lily buds, sour plums, etc, impart a wealth of mellow yet strong tastes to the dish, imprinting a rich quality like vintage wine on the palate of the connoisseur.

Superficially it might seem that this 'orchestration' required in cooking a perfect Cantonese fish dish is a complicated process. But to the practised cooks, the addition of all these ingredients is easy and automatic; it can be done in a matter of a minute or two. The time required for the steaming has to be assessed and watched, but, to an experienced chef, the action required is honestly not much more than to boil an egg. If you are working in the right tradition, the whole complexity of the procedure becomes simplicity itself.

Steamed Whole Fish 1
(Adapted from the Li Ho Fook Restaurant, Canton.)

1.2–1.5 kg (2½-3½ lb) fish (carp, flounder, halibut, mackerel, perch, pike, salmon, rainbow trout, mullet, bass, sea bass, sea bream, turbot, etc)
7 ml (½ tablespoon) salt
7 ml (½ tablespoon) sugar
7 ml (½ tablespoon) sesame oil

22 ml (1½ tablespoons) soya sauce
4–5 stalks spring onion
4 slices root ginger
4–5 large Chinese dried mushrooms
2 rashers bacon (or lean and fat pork)

Garnish and dressing

2 stalks spring onion
15 ml (1 tablespoon) lard
15 ml (1 tablespoon) sherry

pepper to taste
15 ml (1 tablespoon) soya sauce

Rub the fish inside and out with the salt, sugar and sesame oil. Pour the soya sauce over it, and work it in with the fingers.

Cut the spring onions into large segments, and the ginger into shreds. Soak the mushrooms (discarding the stalks) and cut the caps into shreds. Cut the bacon or pork across lean and fat into double-matchstick-thick shreds. Shred the spring onion for garnishing.

Place half the chopped spring onion at the bottom of an oval heatproof dish. Lay the fish on top. Dress the fish with the ginger, mushrooms, and bacon. Put the fish in its dish into a steamer, and steam open and vigorously for 15 minutes.

Transfer the fish to a well-heated serving dish (preferably with deep sides). Pour any liquid which has collected (together with the other ingredients from the dish used for steaming) into a small pan. Add the dressing ingredients—lard, soya sauce, sherry and fresh spring onion shreds. Bring them to the boil, and pour the contents of the pan immediately over the length of the fish, arranging the solid ingredients in the sauce over the fish. Sprinkle generously with pepper.

Each piece of fish should be dipped before eating in the sauce, which should be sufficiently strong to bring out the freshness of the fish. The fat in the sauce should not only add greatly to the smooth texture of the fish, but also to the overall temperature of the food, which is a part of its appeal.
Serves 6–8.

Steamed Fish 2

It is not necessary to use a whole fish in the previous recipe; you can use a cut of a larger type of fish. The ingredients for the dressing can be varied to include dried prawns and tiger lily buds (golden needles). Chunks of fish often require longer cooking (an extra 3–4 minutes) than a whole fish of corresponding weight because of their thickness. For those who enjoy a sweet and sour flavour, add 12 ml (¾ tablespoon) sugar, 15 ml (1 tablespoon) Chinese aromatic vinegar or wine vinegar and a few cloves of crushed garlic to the final boiling of the sauce. When dried prawns are included, an extra minute of boiling or simmering helps to release some of their flavour into the sauce.

Clear Simmered Carp
(Adapted from the Pearl River Dining Room, Canton.)

1 carp (about 900 g–1.35 kg/ 2–3 lb)	for semi-deep-frying
7 ml (½ tablespoon) salt	22 ml (1½ tablespoons) lard
7 ml (½ tablespoon) sugar	15 ml (1 tablespoon) dried shrimps
30 ml (2 tablespoons) vegetable oil	500 ml (1 pint) stock (b) or water
4–5 slices root ginger	30 ml (2 tablespoons) sherry or Chinese yellow wine
4–5 stalks spring onion	salt and pepper to taste
250 ml (½ pint) vegetable oil	

Rub the fish with the salt, sugar and oil. Leave it to season for 30 minutes. Shred the ginger, and cut the spring onions into 5 cm (2 in) segments.

Heat 250 ml (½ pint) oil in a large frying pan. Lower the fish into hot oil to fry quickly for 2 minutes on either side. Remove and drain it.

Heat the lard in a casserole. Add the ginger, dried shrimps and spring onion. Turn and stir-fry them in the fat for 2 minutes. Pour in the stock, add the sherry and adjust the seasoning. Lower the fish in one piece into the casserole to submerge it in the stock. Bring the contents to the boil. Reduce the heat and simmer gently for 30 minutes. Serve in the casserole. For the connoisseur the soup in the dish, eaten with rice, is almost as satisfying as the fish. *Serves 6–8.*

Soya-Braised Fish

900 g (2 lb) fish (or piece of fish)
4 ml (¾ teaspoon) salt
15 ml (1 tablespoon) cornflour
7 ml (½ tablespoon) sesame oil

3–4 slices root ginger
3–4 stalks spring onion
125 ml (¼ pint) oil for shallow-frying

Sauce

60 ml (4 tablespoons) soya sauce
15 ml (1 tablespoon) vegetable oil

2.5 ml (½ teaspoon) salt
90 ml (6 tablespoons) stock (a)
5 ml (1 teaspoon) sugar
15 ml (1 tablespoon) sherry

Clean the fish and rub it with the salt, cornflour and sesame oil. Leave it to season for 30 minutes. Shred the ginger, and cut the spring onions into small segments. Mix them together in a bowl or basin with the sauce ingredients.

Heat 125 ml (¼ pint) oil in a frying pan. Lower the fish into the fat and fry it for 2 minutes on either side, turning it gently with a fish-slice. Pour away all excess oil.

Pour the ginger-soya-spring onion mixture over the fish. Bring the contents to the boil. Simmer this gently for 15 minutes, turning the fish over every 5 minutes. The reduced sauce should by then have become very tasty, and highly suitable for eating with rice, either hot or cold.

Serves 6–8.

Suburban Fish-Head Casserole
(Adapted from the Pei Yuan Restaurant, Canton.)

1 large fish head (about 900 g–1.2 kg/2–2½ lb)
7 ml (½ tablespoon) salt
15 ml (1 tablespoon) cornflour
6 large Chinese dried mushrooms
60 ml (5 tablespoons) Cha Shao roast pork (see page 100)
2 cakes bean curd
4 cloves garlic
3 slices root ginger

4 leeks
125 ml (¼ pint) vegetable oil for shallow-frying
500 ml (1 pint) stock (b)
salt and pepper to taste
22 ml (1½ tablespoons) lard or chicken fat
22 ml (1½ tablespoons) soya sauce
37 ml (2½ tablespoons) sherry

Clean and rub the fish head with salt and cornflour. Soak the mush-rooms for 20 minutes (discarding the stalks), and cut each cap into quarters. Shred the roast pork, and cut each bean curd cake into a dozen pieces. Crush the garlic, shred the ginger and slice the leeks slantwise into small segments.

Heat the oil in a deep frying pan. Add the fish head and fry over a medium heat for 6 minutes, turning over every 2 minutes. Remove the fish head and place it in a casserole. Add the bean curd, mush-rooms, ginger and roast pork. Pour in the stock. Bring the contents to the boil, reduce the heat and simmer gently for 20 minutes. Adjust the seasoning.

Meanwhile heat the lard in a small saucepan. Add the leek and garlic, stir-fry for 30 seconds, then pour in the soya sauce and sherry. Turn and stir this together, and then pour it over the con-tents of the casserole. Serve in the casserole. This is another favour-ite dish with rice-eaters.

Serves 6–8.

Casserole of Fish Head in Wine with Chicken Giblets and Pork Sweetbreads
(Adapted from the Sing Yuan Lai Restaurant, Canton.)

125 ml (¼ pint) vegetable oil for shallow-frying
1 large fish head (900 g–1.35 kg/2–3 lb)
5 ml (1 teaspoon) salt
15 ml (1 tablespoon) cornflour
100 g (¼ lb) chicken giblets
100–225 g (¼–½ lb) pork sweet-breads

2 medium onions
2 leeks
3 cloves garlic
3 slices root ginger
250 ml (½ pint) stock (b)
500 ml (1 pint) white wine or Chinese yellow wine
salt and pepper to taste

Heat the oil in a frying pan. Rub the fish head with salt and corn-flour and add it to the pan to fry for 6 minutes, 3 on either side. Drain and place the fish in a casserole. Parboil the giblets and sweetbreads for 2 minutes. Cut the giblets into small slices, and the sweetbreads into slightly larger pieces; chop the onion thinly and the leeks slantwise into thin segments. Crush the garlic.

Add all the ingredients to the casserole with the fish head. Bring to the boil and simmer gently, covered for 30 minutes. Adjust the seasoning, and bring the casserole to the table. The lid of the casserole should only be opened immediately before eating.

Serves 6–8.

Braised Eel with Roast Pork
(Adapted from Li Ho Fook Restaurant, Canton.)

1 eel (about 1.2 kg/2½ lb)
7 ml (½ tablespoon) salt
22 ml (1½ tablespoons) cornflour
4 large Chinese dried mushrooms
30 ml (2 tablespoons) dried
  tangerine peel
1 large onion
100 g (¼ lb) Cha Shao roast
  pork (see page 100)
3 young leeks
125 ml (¼ pint) vegetable oil
  for shallow-frying

3 slices root ginger
250 ml (½ pint) water or stock
  (a)
30 ml (2 tablespoons) soya
  sauce
45 ml (3 tablespoons) sherry
7 ml (½ tablespoon) sugar
15 ml (1 tablespoon) lard
15 ml (1 tablespoon) sesame oil
pepper to taste
12 ml (¾ tablespoon) Chinese
  aromatic vinegar

Parboil the eel for 30 seconds and drain it. Chop it through the bone into small segments. Rub it with the salt and cornflour, and leave it to season for 30 minutes.

Soak the mushrooms and tangerine peel for 15 minutes. Discard the mushroom stalks and cut the caps and tangerine peel into shreds. Cut the onion into thin slices and the ginger into shreds. Cut the pork into small slices, and the leeks into thin segments.

Heat the oil in a deep frying pan. When hot, add the pieces of eel. Shallow-fry these for 3 minutes (1½ minutes on either side). Drain away the oil. Add the mushroom, onion, ginger, tangerine peel, water, soya sauce, sherry and sugar. Bring the contents to the boil and simmer gently for 15 minutes, covered, turning the contents over once, very gently.

Heat the lard in a small frying pan. Add the leeks and pork. Fry these for 2 minutes, turning them over 2–3 times, and add them to the eel in the larger frying pan. Close the lid again, and continue to simmer gently for another 15 minutes.

Pick out the pieces of eel with a pair of chopsticks or tongs and arrange them neatly on a well-heated deep-sided dish, alternating pork slices with eel pieces. Raise the heat to high under the frying pan, stir, and reduce the liquid in the pan to half by rapid boiling. Pour the contents evenly over the eel and pork. Sprinkle them with sesame oil, pepper and aromatic vinegar and serve immediately.
Serves 6–8.

Quick-Fried Sliced Fillet of Fish
(Adapted from the Canton Restaurant, Canton.)

675 g (1½ lb) fillet of fish (sole, carp, bass, sea bream, halibut, cod, etc)
7 ml (½ tablespoon) salt
22 ml (1½ tablespoons) cornflour
½ egg-white
2 slices root ginger
2 stalks spring onion
22 ml (1½ tablespoons) wood ears

15 ml (1 tablespoon) cornflour
30 ml (2 tablespoons) white wine
60 ml (4 tablespoons) stock (b)
5 ml (1 teaspoon) sugar
chicken stock cube
salt and pepper to taste
125 ml (¼ pint) vegetable oil for shallow-frying
30 ml (2 tablespoons) lard

Cut the fish into medium-sized rectangular slices. Rub these with the salt and 22 ml (1½ tablespoons) cornflour, and wet them evenly with egg-white. Shred the ginger and cut the spring onions into small sections. Soak the wood ears for 15 minutes and drain and rinse them. Mix the cornflour in 45 ml (3 tablespoons) water, and blend the mixture with the wine, stock, sugar and chicken stock cube and adjust the seasoning with salt and pepper.

Heat the oil in a frying pan. Add the fish piece by piece. When they are all added, turn them over, remove the pan from the heat and leave the fish to 'poach' in the oil for 1½ minutes. Pour away all the oil, and remove the fish. Add the lard to the pan, and return it to the heat. Stir-fry the wood ears, ginger and spring onion in the hot fat for 1 minute. Pour in the sauce mixture and stir until the sauce thickens. As soon as it has done so, return the fish pieces carefully to the pan, distributing them evenly in the sauce. Bring to the boil, simmer for 30 seconds, pour the pan contents into a deep-sided dish and serve. To be eaten immediately.
Serves 6–8.

Deep-Fried Sesame Fish Fillets

550 g (1¼ lb) fish fillets
1 medium onion
3 slices root ginger
5 ml (1 teaspoon) sugar
30 ml (2 tablespoons) dry sherry
7 ml (½ tablespoon) salt

15 ml (1 tablespoon) flour
15 ml (1 tablespoon) cornflour
1 egg
75–90 ml (5–6 tablespoons) sesame seeds
vegetable oil for deep- or semi-deep-frying

Cut the fish into broad 'fingers'. Mince the onion and ginger, and mix them with the sugar and sherry. Rub the fish with salt, and then with the onion-ginger-sherry mixture. Leave this to season for 1 hour.

Mix the flour, cornflour and beaten egg into a batter. Dip the fish pieces in the batter and roll them in the sesame seeds until they are evenly coated.

Heat the oil in a frying pan or deep-fryer. Put in 5–6 pieces of coated fish to fry or deep-fry for 3–3½ minutes at a time. Drain, and arrange them on a well-heated serving dish; soya sauce, tomato sauce, Aromatic Salt and Pepper Mix can all be used as dips.
Serves 6–8.

Lobster and Crab Dishes

Cantonese Lobster and Cantonese Crab are two of the most interesting and appealing dishes served by better-class Chinese restaurants abroad. Few dishes in the world are as delicious as these; yet their basic preparation is comparatively simple if you have the right raw materials. Variations are often introduced, such as the addition of minced pork or beaten egg in the latter stages of the cooking (employed mainly to expand the dish); or the use of salted black beans, instead of just onion and ginger (to flavour the aromatic oil which is basic to the cooking). The use of flavoured oil is probably a more calculated procedure in Chinese cooking than in Western *haute cuisine*.

Cantonese Onion and Ginger Crab
(Adapted from the Pei Yuan Restaurant, Canton.)

3 large crabs (about 1.35–1.8 kg/3–4 lb in all)
4 slices root ginger
2 medium onions
3 cloves garlic
3 stalks spring onion
250 ml (½ pint) vegetable oil for shallow-frying
250 ml (½ pint) chicken stock (b)

5 ml (1 teaspoon) salt
37 ml (2½ tablespoons) soya sauce
45 ml (3 tablespoons) sherry
15 ml (1 tablespoon) cornflour (blended in 60 ml (4 tablespoons) water)
7 ml (½ tablespoon) sesame oil

Clean the crabs with a stiff brush. Remove all the feathery parts. Chop the shell of each crab into 2 pieces after lifting it off the body. Chop the body into 6–8 pieces, each with a leg attached. Crack the claws and chop each into 2 sections.

Shred the ginger, and cut the onions into thin slices. Crush and chop the garlic and cut the spring onions into small sections.

Heat the oil in a large, deep frying pan or wok. Add the onion and ginger and stir these in the hot oil for 1½ minutes to flavour it. Add the crab pieces and spread them out in the oil. Turn and fry them over a high heat for 2 minutes. Drain away all excess oil, and return the pan to the high heat. Add the stock, salt and soya sauce to the pan. Bring the contents to the boil immediately, place a lid over the pan and cook rapidly for 2½ minutes. Sprinkle the contents with the spring onion, garlic and sherry. Stir and turn a few times. Remove the crab pieces, and arrange them on a large deep-sided serving dish.

Return the pan to the heat. Stir the cornflour mixture into the liquid in the pan. Add the sesame oil and stir. Pour the resulting sauce over the crab pieces, and serve.

Serves 6.

Cantonese Lobster

Repeat the process described in the recipe on page 119, using a 1.35–1.8 kg (3–4 lb) lobster instead of crabs. After brushing and cleaning the lobster under running water, chop off the tail, claws and head, remove the tough sac near the eyes, and shear off the feelers. Cut the tail section into 2 pieces, the body into 6 pieces, and the thicker pieces again into halves.

After the onion and ginger have been fried in the oil, the frying of the lobster pieces is conducted in exactly the same way as the frying of the crabs (about 2 minutes). After the excess oil is drained away, the stock and other ingredients (garlic, onion, sherry, salt, soya sauce) are added, and brought to a rapid boil, to cook under a cover for 2½ minutes. The lobster pieces are then removed and arranged on the serving dish. The liquid in the pan is then returned to the high heat to be reduced rapidly and thickened by the addition of the cornflour mixture, with a few drops of sesame oil added to enhance the aromatic quality of the dish.

Serves 4–6.

Variations on Cantonese Crab and Cantonese Lobster

These two dishes are frequently varied by the addition of minced pork, or salted black beans, or both. When these are added, usually in quantities of 60–75 ml (4–5 tablespoons) pork, and 7–12 ml ($\frac{1}{2}$–$\frac{3}{4}$ tablespoon) black beans (which must first be soaked and drained) for each 1.35–1.8 kg (3–4 lb) lobster or crab, the crab or lobster pieces will have to be removed after the initial frying, when the excess oil is drained away. At this point the pork and/or black beans are added to stir-fry in the remaining oil in the pan for 1 minute and to mix and mash with the onions and ginger. It is only after this stir-frying that the stock and other ingredients are added, along with the crab and lobster, to mix and cook, covered, for $2\frac{1}{2}$ minutes of rapid boiling. From this point on the procedure is exactly the same as in the standard recipes. If and when beaten egg is used, it is dripped into the sauce by trailing it in a thin stream over the surface while the sauce is boiling, to obtain the 'cloud' or 'egg-flower' effect.

Baked or Steamed Crabs and Lobsters

Purists prefer their crabs and lobsters to be baked or steamed rather than fried. When cooked by these methods the crustaceans must first be brushed with or seasoned in marinades of soya sauce blended with chopped onion, ginger, garlic, and oil. Mashed black beans and chilli sauce may be added to the marinade for the sake of variation. Baking and steaming are fairly similar cooking processes: in the first, the heating is done by convection; in the latter, the heating is achieved by the circulation of hot steam. The time required for cooking is fairly similar in either process. The higher temperature to which an oven can be heated is compensated for in the steamer by the much speedier and more pervasive circulation of hot steam.

Steamed or Baked Lobster

1.35–1.8 kg (3–4 lb) lobster

Marinade

22 ml (1$\frac{1}{2}$ tablespoons) chopped spring onion

15 ml (1 tablespoon) finely chopped root ginger

2.5 ml ($\frac{1}{2}$ teaspoon) salt

15 ml (1 tablespoon) soya sauce

30 ml (2 tablespoons) sherry

30 ml (2 tablespoons) vegetable oil

Clean and chop the lobster as in the recipe on page 120. Prepare the marinade by mixing the ingredients in a bowl until well blended. After the lobster has been cleaned, chopped and dismembered, brush the pieces thickly with the marinade, and leave them to season for 1 hour.

Arrange the lobster pieces on a heatproof dish (pour any excess of marinade over them), and place the latter in a preheated oven at 200°C (400°F)/Gas 6, or in a preheated steamer, for 15 minutes, when it is ready to eat.
Serves 6.

Steamed or Baked Crab

Crab is generally considered a coarser version of lobster (although equally tasty). While lobster is usually cooked comparatively 'pure' —that is, without the intrusion of too many other ingredients— minced pork, mashed salted black beans, beaten egg and chilli are not infrequently added to the marinade for crab. The resultant mixture is not only brushed on to the chopped segments of the crab (especially on the exposed sections) but actually spread quite thickly over them. Crab prepared in this way usually require to be baked or steamed for an extra minute or two. Any excess of marinade can be poured or scraped into a small pan, and heated up for a minute or two with the addition of an extra 30 ml (2 tablespoons) of stock (b), 15 ml (1 tablespoon) sherry, 7 ml (½ tablespoon) soya sauce and 7 ml (½ tablespoon) sesame oil before being poured over the crab pieces.

Although the sauces from these crab and lobster dishes are extremely tasty, and excellent mixed with rice, the dishes are normally used as 'starters' before a meal.
Serves 6.

Stir-Fried Crab Meat with Pork and Young Leeks

350 g (¾ lb) crab meat (from 2–3 crabs)
100–350 g (¼–¾ lb) lean belly pork
2 slices root ginger
2 young leeks
3 cloves garlic
2 eggs

30 ml (2 tablespoons) sherry
30 ml (2 tablespoons) soya sauce
5 ml (1 teaspoon) sugar
2.5 ml (½ teaspoon) salt
2 stalks spring onion
7 ml (½ tablespoon) sesame oil

Pick over and shred the crab meat. Finely chop the pork and ginger. Cut the leeks into small shreds. Crush and chop the garlic and beat the eggs for 10 seconds with a fork. Combine the sherry with the soya sauce, sugar and salt. Cut the spring onions into fine shavings.

Heat the lard in a frying pan. Add the pork, leeks and ginger and stir-fry this over a high heat for 2 minutes. Add the crab meat, spread it out and trail the beaten egg evenly over the contents of the pan. Stir and turn a few times. Sprinkle the pan with the soya and sherry mixture. Stir and turn for 30 seconds. Add the sesame oil and spring onion. Stir and turn a few more times. Serve quickly on a well-heated dish. This recipe is considered excellent accompanied by wine. *Serves 6–8.*

Deep-Fried Crab Meat in Clam Shells

Use 2 dozen clam shells containing the same ingredients as in the recipe on page 134, except that only 1½ eggs are necessary, and these are blended with 22 ml (1½ tablespoons) of flour and 22 ml (1½ tablespoons) cornflour into a batter. The batter is used to close the clam shells after they have been stuffed with the mixed ingredients.

The stuffed clam shells are then deep-fried in three lots, 2½ minutes for each lot. Finally they are all placed together in a wire basket, and lowered into the hot oil to be deep-fried together for 1 minute and drained on absorbent paper. They are then arranged on a well-heated serving dish in a single layer, to be eaten immediately. Another excellent dish to accompany wine. *Serves 6–8.*

Deep-Fried Lobster

900 g–1.2 kg (2–2½ lb) lobster
2.5 ml (½ teaspoon) salt
1 egg
52 ml (3½ tablespoons) cornflour

30 ml (2 tablespoons) water
oil for deep-frying
3–4 selected lettuce leaves
pepper to taste

Clean and shell the lobster. Cut the flesh into small cubes. Sprinkle and rub these with salt. Mix the beaten egg with the cornflour and water into a batter. Coat the lobster cubes with this.

Heat the oil in a deep-fryer. When the oil is hot enough for crumbs to sizzle when dropped into it, add 6 lobster cubes at a time to fry for about 2–2½ minutes, or until golden brown. Drain them

E

on absorbent paper. Spread the lettuce leaves as a bed on an oval dish, arrange the lobster cubes on top, sprinkle with pepper and serve. *Serves 4–6.*

Deep-Fried Oysters

In China we never eat oysters raw, as in the West. Deep-frying is a popular Chinese way to cook them.

20–24 oysters
salt and pepper to taste
3 stalks spring onion
1 egg
60–75 ml (4–5 tablespoons) water

36 ml (2 heaped tablespoons) self-raising flour
36 ml (2 heaped tablespoons) cornflour
vegetable oil for deep-frying
½ lemon

Shell the oysters. Season them with salt and pepper. Clean and chop the spring onions. Beat the egg for 10 seconds. Add the water and beat for another 5 seconds. Add the two flours gradually and mix into a batter. Finally add the chopped spring onion, and blend well.

Dip the oysters into the batter and deep-fry them, 3–4 at a time, in hot fat until golden. Drain them on absorbent paper. When all the oysters have been fried and drained, place them on a well-heated dish. Sprinkle them with the balance of chopped spring onion, and lemon juice.
Serves 5–6.

Cantonese Quick-Fried Prawns in their Shells
(Adapted from the Canton Restaurant, Canton.)

675–800 g (1½–1¾ lb) large prawns (about 10–12)
15 ml (1 tablespoon) salt
2 slices root ginger
12 ml (¾ tablespoon) vegetable oil
2 stalks spring onion
60 ml (4 tablespoons) lard

2.5 ml (½ teaspoon) sugar
22 ml (1½ tablespoons) soya sauce
22 ml (1½ tablespoons) stock (b)
22 ml (1½ tablespoons) tangerine juice
30 ml (2 tablespoons) sherry

Clean and trim the prawns; remove the heads and entrails but leave tails and rest of shells attached. Rinse thoroughly and dry them. Cut each prawn into 2 sections. Rub them with salt, minced ginger and oil. Chop the spring onions.

Heat the lard in a frying pan. Add the prawns, turn and stir them a few times, and fry them for 1 minute. Stir and turn them once more, and leave them to fry again for a second minute.

Pour away excess fat, and remove the prawns from the pan. Add the sugar, soya sauce, stock and tangerine juice to the pan. Sprinkle them with the spring onion and mix them with the sauce for about 45 seconds. Pour on sauce and eat immediately.
Serves 5–6.

Quick-Fried Prawns without Shells
(Adapted from the Yu Yuan Restaurant, Canton.)

550 g (1¼ lb) prawns (shelled)
5 ml (1 teaspoon) salt
1 egg-white
22 ml (1½ tablespoons) corn-flour
22 ml (1½ tablespoons) self-raising flour

75–90 ml (5–6 tablespoons) vegetable oil
15 ml (1 tablespoon) lard
22 ml (1½ tablespoons) dry sherry
22 ml (1½ tablespoons) stock (b)

Rub the prawns with salt. Beat the egg-white for 10 seconds with a fork and add the cornflour and self-raising flour. Beat them together until well blended. Coat the prawns with the batter and place them in a refrigerator for 1 hour.

Heat the oil in a large frying pan. Add the prawns, stir and turn them a few times, and leave them to fry for 1½ minutes over a high heat. Stir and turn them again, leave to fry for a further 30 seconds, and remove them from the pan. Pour away any excess oil.

Add the lard and when it has all melted add the ginger, and then the spring onions. Stir them together a few times, add the sherry and stock, and return the prawns to the pan. Stir-fry over a high heat for 45 seconds. To be eaten immediately.
Serves 5–6.

Quick-Fried Prawns with Chicken Liver, Chinese Mushrooms and Peas

100 g (¼ lb) chicken livers
350–450 g (¾–1 lb) prawns (shelled)
5 ml (1 teaspoon) salt
4 large Chinese mushrooms
60 ml (4 tablespoons) vegetable oil

100 g (¼ lb) green peas
30 ml (2 tablespoons) lard
22 ml (1½ tablespoons) soya sauce
30 ml (2 tablespoons) sherry
30 ml (2 tablespoons) stock (b)
5 ml (1 teaspoon) sugar

Cut the chicken livers into equal-sized pieces. Sprinkle the prawns and chicken livers with the salt and rub it in evenly. Soak the mushrooms in water for 20 minutes, remove the stalks, and cut the caps into pieces the same size as the liver.

Heat the oil in a large frying pan. Add the mushrooms and stir them around, then add the prawns and liver. Stir them all together over a high heat for 1½ minutes. Add the peas. Mix and turn this together for another minute. Push the contents to one side of the pan. Put the remaining ingredients into the other side of the pan. Mix and blend them over a high heat. Bring over the prawns, peas and liver to mix with the sauce. Stir and mix them together for 1 minute. To be eaten immediately.

Serves 6–8.

Deep-Fried Stuffed Giant Prawns
(Adapted from the Ta Tung Restaurant, Canton.)

*675 g (about 1½ lb) large
    prawns (about 10–12)
22 ml (1½ tablespoons) cornflour
75–90 ml (5–6 tablespoons)*

*breadcrumbs
4 ml (¾ teaspoon) salt
2 eggs
oil for deep- or semi-deep-frying*

Stuffing

*4 large Chinese dried mushrooms
50 g (2 oz) ham
2 stalks spring onion*

*15 ml (1 tablespoon) snow
    pickle
7 ml (½ tablespoon) sherry*

Prepare the stuffing by soaking the mushrooms for 30 minutes. Discard the stalks and chop the caps finely. Chop the ham, spring onion and pickle. Combine all of these ingredients together in a basin with the sherry.

Slice lengthways through the bodies of the prawns, leaving the tails still uncut and linking the bodies. Rub the prawns with the salt. Mix half the egg with the cornflour until well blended. Spread the inside, and rub the outside, of the prawns with the batter. Fill the prawns with the stuffing mixture and close the two sides together. Place the stuffed prawns in a refrigerator for 1½ hours. When they are chilled and firm, wet the prawns with the remaining beaten egg and roll them in a coating of breadcrumbs.

Heat the oil in a deep-fryer (or semi-deep-fry by heating 250 ml (½ pint) oil in a deep frying pan). When the oil is hot enough to cause a crumb to sizzle when dropped into it, lower 3–4 stuffed

prawns at a time to fry for 3 minutes; then take them out and drain them. Finally put all the prawns in to fry at the same time for just 30 seconds. Drain them thoroughly on absorbent paper. Serve on a well-heated dish or on a bed of crisp lettuce leaves, accompanied by dips of tangerine juice, tomato sauce and Aromatic Salt and Pepper Mix (see page 68).
Serves 6–8.

Poached Shrimps

675–900 g (1½–2 lb) shrimps (must be very fresh)

2 large kettlefuls of boiling water
22 ml (1½ tablespoons) salt

Dips

tangerine juice
minced spring onion in soya

sauce
shredded root ginger in vinegar

Wash the shrimps, remove the legs and sprinkle and rub them with the salt. Leave them to season for 30 minutes.

Place the shrimps in a large basin. Pour in a kettleful of boiling water. Leave this to stand for 3 minutes and then drain away the water. Repeat with a second kettleful of water.

After draining the shrimps, place them in a bowl at the centre of the table for the diners to help themselves, with their fingers. One should remove the head of each shrimp first, and then shell two-thirds of the body by holding on to the tail. Now dip the shelled part of the shrimp in one of the dips, and eat. To extract the flesh from the shell, bite with the front teeth progressively from the tail forwards. Usually eaten as a starter before a multi-course meal.
Serves 6–8.

Stir-Fried Fresh Squid

675 g (1½ lb) fresh squid
2.5 ml (½ teaspoon) salt
7 ml (½ tablespoon) vegetable oil
1 green pepper
2 slices root ginger
2 stalks spring onion
45 ml (3 tablespoons) lard

22 ml (1½ tablespoons) soya sauce
2.5 ml (½ teaspoon) chilli sauce
22 ml (1½ tablespoons) shrimp sauce (or shrimp paste)
30 ml (2 tablespoons) stock (b)
30 ml (2 tablespoons) sherry

Cut the squid into medium-sized rectangular pieces, and score criss-cross cuts half-way through each piece of squid. Rub them with the salt and oil. Cut the pepper into similar-sized pieces to the squid. Finely chop the root ginger and spring onion.

Heat the lard in a large frying pan. When hot, add the squid, pepper, ginger and spring onion. Stir-fry over a high heat, and push them to one side of the pan. Pour the soya sauce, chilli sauce, shrimp sauce, stock and sherry into the other side of the pan. Mix them over a high heat until well blended. Bring the squid, pepper, etc, over to mix with the sauce. Stir-fry them together over a high heat for a further minute and serve on a well-heated dish to be eaten immediately.

Serves 6–8.

Chi Pow Tsi, or Great Assembly of Chicken, Abalone, and Shark's Fin

(An extravagant party piece to be eaten with other dishes—adapted from the Pei Yuan Restaurant, Canton.)

900 g (2 lb) dried shark's fin   1 medium onion
   (in large sheet pieces)   2 chickens (1 young chicken and
3 litres (6 pints) stock (a)   1 boiling fowl)
12 slices root ginger   1 litre (2 pints) stock (c)
900 g (2 lb) lean pork   275 g (10 oz) abalone
900 g (2 lb) pig's trotters   30 ml (2 tablespoons) soya
225 g (½ lb) ham   sauce

Prepare the fins by soaking them in water overnight, and brushing away any sand or extraneous matter. Place the fins in an enamel or earthenware pot and add 1 litre (2 pints) stock and 4 slices root ginger. Bring to the boil, and simmer very gently for 2½ hours. Change the stock and ginger, repeating the operation twice, making the cooking time 7½ hours in all.

Cut the pork, trotters, ham, onion and boiling fowl into quarters. Parboil them for 2 minutes, drain away any impurities, and add them into the pot with the shark's fin. Pour in the best stock. Bring to a gentle boil (put an asbestos sheet under the pot) and simmer very gently for 4 hours. Remove the pork, trotters, ham, onion and chicken and put them aside for other uses. Trim the fins into regular-sized pieces with a pair of scissors. Remove the head and feet of the young chicken, chop and quarter the body, parboil it for 5 minutes and put it in the pot to simmer together with the fins for 30 minutes. Add abalone and soya sauce and simmer for 5 minutes. Remove the chicken and abalone. Cut the abalone and chicken flesh into regular-sized medium-sized thin slices, and arrange them, overlapping, at the bottom of a deep-sided, ceramic, heatproof dish. Strain the liquid in the pot, skim away any excess fat and return it to the pot to simmer with the fins for a further 30 minutes to reduce further.

Pick the pieces of shark's fin out of the pot with a pair of chopsticks or tongs and arrange them on top of the chicken and abalone spread out in the serving dish. Pour some of the sauce, which has been thickened through prolonged cooking, over the pile of fins, sliced chicken and abalone, without drowning them. Insert the dish, firmly covered with tinfoil, into a steamer to steam for 5 minutes and serve.

Shark's fins are consumed for their texture, and for the richness of the orchestrated flavour. This is a party dish which is very time-consuming to prepare, rewarding only for those who have time to spare, and for the connoisseur's palate.
Serves 8–10.

Vegetables

Steamed Broccoli with Chinese Mushrooms
(Adapted from the Chai Kang Restaurant.)

8 large Chinese dried mushrooms
4–6 water chestnuts
450 g (1 lb) selected broccoli
5 ml (1 teaspoon) salt
15 ml (1 tablespoon) vegetable oil
375 ml ($\frac{3}{4}$ pint) stock (b)
salt and pepper to taste
7 ml ($\frac{1}{2}$ tablespoon) Rose Dew Liqueur (Mei Kwei Lu)

Soak the mushrooms in water for 30 minutes and remove the stalks. Cut each water chestnut into 6 slices. Break the broccoli into individual branches. Parboil the broccoli and mushrooms for 1 minute and drain them. Sprinkle and rub them with salt and oil.

Arrange the vegetables neatly in a deep-sided heatproof dish. Pour in the stock and adjust the seasoning. Cover the dish firmly with tinfoil, put in into a steamer, and steam steadily for 30 minutes. Remove the tinfoil, sprinkle with Rose Dew, and serve. This dish is known as Perfumed Broccoli and Mushrooms in the Chai Kang

restaurant, which is well known in Canton for its vegetable and vegetarian dishes.
Serves 6–8.

Stir-Fried Spring Greens in Oyster Sauce

675 g (1½ lb) spring greens (or spring cabbage)
45 ml (3 tablespoons) vegetable oil
5 ml (1 teaspoon) salt

15 ml (1 tablespoon) soya sauce
30 ml (2 tablespoons) stock (b)
15 ml (1 tablespoon) oyster sauce
15 ml (1 tablespoon) lard

Eliminate the tough and discoloured leaves and roots of the spring greens and cut the remaining leaves into medium-sized slices. Heat the oil in a very large saucepan or frying pan, tilting the pan so that the oil covers the whole surface. Add the spring greens, sprinkle with salt, and turn in the oil over a medium heat. Stir-fry them for 2 minutes. Add the lard and other ingredients, turn the vegetables in the melting fat and sauce until all the leaves are glossy (1½ minutes).

Serve on a well-heated dish. Excellent with meat dishes, the green of the vegetable contrasts well with the rich brown of the meat.
Serves 6–8.

Braised Chinese White Cabbage with Dried Shrimps and White Bean-Curd Cheese

550 g (1¼ lb) Chinese cabbage
45 ml (3 tablespoons) vegetable oil
10 ml (2 teaspoons) dried

shrimps
125 ml (¼ pint) stock (b)
22 ml (1½ tablespoons) white bean-curd cheese

Cut the cabbage into 6.25 cm (2½ in) slices. Heat the oil in a deep frying pan. Add the cabbage and turn it in the oil until most leaves are well coated. Add the dried shrimps and stock. Bring to the boil, and simmer for 2 minutes. Add the bean-curd cheese and mix it with the cabbage. Reduce the heat, and leave the contents to simmer for 15 minutes, then pour them into a deep-sided bowl and serve. Another good dish to accompany meat at a family meal.
Serves 6.

Steamed Stuffed Eggplant (Aubergine) (or sweet peppers)

6 medium eggplants (aubergines), or small peppers
30 ml (2 tablespoons) lard
125 ml (¼ pint) stock (b)

30 ml (2 tablespoons) soya
sauce
2.5 ml (½ teaspoon) sugar
22 ml (1½ tablespoons) finely
chopped spring onion

Stuffing

1 slice root ginger
225 g (½ lb) minced pork
½ egg
2.5 ml (½ teaspoon) sugar

60–75 ml (4–5 tablespoons)
crab meat (or crab eggs)
4 ml (¾ teaspoon) salt
30 ml (2 tablespoons) sherry
pepper to taste

Mince the root ginger and mix it with the other ingredients for the stuffing in a basin until well blended. Slice the peppers or eggplants in half, horizontally. Scoop out the insides and fill the cavity with the stuffing mixture.

Heat the lard in a large frying pan with a lid. Place the stuffed eggplants or peppers, stuffed side down, in the pan, well spaced out, to shallow-fry over a low-medium heat for 3 minutes. Turn the stuffed vegetables over with the aid of a fish-slice. Mix the stock with the soya sauce and sugar and pour the mixture into the pan. Sprinkle the stuffed vegetables with the spring onion. Bring the contents to the boil. Cover the pan, and simmer gently for 7–8 minutes. Transfer the stuffed eggplants or peppers to a deep-sided dish and pour the remaining liquid in the pan over the stuffed vegetables. Serves 6.

Four Fukien Specialities

Two of the most distinctive characteristics of Fukien cooking are the use of Swallow Skin (a thin dough-skin with a high meat content) as a wrapping for food which is then steamed or cooked in soups; and the use of Red Wine Sediment Paste in the preparation of meat and poultry dishes. The highly distinctive flavour of wine sediment paste is extremely versatile in the cooking of meat and savoury dishes, and imparts an inimitable quality and appeal. This 'paste' is not yet easily available in Chinese foodstores in the West

E*

but should become more easily available in due course. An imitation (though a poor one) can be made by compounding soya paste with tomato purée, sugar and brandy.

The difference between Fukien (or more precisely Foochow) soups and any other soups lies in the broth used as the base. Although initially prepared in very much the same manner as elsewhere in China, in preparing Fukien broth, the carcase of a fresh chicken is chopped into fine pieces—into a kind of 'minced bones'—and added to the broth, along with some fresh shrimp heads and a small amount of dried shrimps, to simmer together for about 15 minutes over a low heat, before the solids are strained away. The clear broth which results seems to have a fresher taste about it than any other.

Fukien Shredded Swallow-Skin Meat-Ball Soup

7 ml (½ tablespoon) dried shrimps
10–12 sheets swallow skin
350 g (¾ lb) lean and 100 g (¼ lb) fat pork
1 slice root ginger
3 water chestnuts
5 ml (1 teaspoon) salt
30 ml (2 tablespoons) cornflour
pepper to taste

15 ml (1 tablespoon) dry sherry
½ egg (beaten)
1 litre (2 pints) Fukien Broth (see page 131)
15 ml (1 tablespoon) coarsely chopped spring onion
10 ml (2 teaspoons) sesame oil
30 ml (2 tablespoons) vegetable oil

Soak the dried shrimps in water for 1 hour. Lay the sheets of swallow skin one on top of the other in a pile, and use a sharp knife to trim or slice off matchstick-thick shreds from the edge. Loosen the shreds and spread them out on a tray.

Chop and finely mince the pork, dried shrimps and ginger. Coarsely chop the water chestnuts. Mix them thoroughly in a basin with the salt, cornflour, pepper, sherry and beaten egg. Form the well-blended mixture into 20 balls of equal size. Roll the balls over the shredded swallow skin on the tray until each is thickly covered with shreds.

Spread oil on a large heatproof dish, and place the swallow skin meat balls on the dish in a single layer, not touching each other. Put the dish into a steamer, and steam steadily for 10–12 minutes. Meanwhile heat the Fukien Broth in a saucepan. Test and adjust the

seasoning, and when the broth boils, add the meat balls a few at a time. Allow the meat balls to simmer in the broth for 10 minutes. Sprinkle with chopped chives or spring onions, and serve either in individual bowls, or in a large tureen. This is one of the famous and characteristic soups of south-east coastal China.
Serves 6–10.

Braised Chicken in Wine Sediment Paste

1 young chicken (about 1.75 kg/3½ lb)
3 slices root ginger
7 ml (½ tablespoon) salt

2 stalks young leeks
oil for deep- or semi-deep-frying
30 ml (2 tablespoons) lard

Cooking Sauce

60 ml (4 tablespoons) red wine sediment paste
7 ml (½ tablespoon) sugar
30 ml (2 tablespoons) dry sherry

22 ml (1½ tablespoons) soya sauce
75–90 ml (5–6 tablespoons) stock (b)
15 ml (1 tablespoon) cornflour

Chop the chicken through the bone into about two dozen bite-sized pieces. Finely chop the ginger. Sprinkle and rub the ginger and salt on the chicken pieces. Leave to season for 1 hour. Mix the ingredients for the cooking sauce, except for the cornflour, in a bowl or basin. Blend the cornflour separately with 75 ml (5 tablespoons) water. Cut the leeks slantwise in 2.5 cm (1 in) slices.

Heat the oil in the deep-fryer (or 250 ml/½ pint oil in a large frying pan). When hot enough for a crumb dropped in it to sizzle, add the chicken, a few pieces at a time and allow them to fry for 3 minutes. Remove and drain.

Heat the lard in a saucepan, add the leeks and stir-fry them over a high heat for 1 minute. Add the chicken pieces, and pour the sauce mixture over them. Turn them around until well mixed. Reduce the heat to low, cover the pan and leave the contents to simmer for 10 minutes. Pour in the cornflour mixture. Turn the contents around a few times. When the sauce thickens, turn the contents out into a bowl for the diners to help themselves. An excellent dish with rice.
Serves 6–10.

Quick-Fried Sliced Chicken Breast with Sea Clams in Wine Sediment Paste

225–350 g ($\frac{1}{2}$–$\frac{3}{4}$ lb) chicken breast
2 dozen sea clams
3 slices root ginger
7 ml ($\frac{1}{2}$ tablespoon) salt
vegetable oil for deep-frying
2 stalks spring onion
22 ml (1$\frac{1}{2}$ tablespoons) lard
45 ml (3 tablespoons) red wine sediment paste
10 ml (2 teaspoons) sugar
30 ml (2 tablespoons) dry sherry
15 ml (1 tablespoon) soya sauce
15 ml (1 tablespoon) cornflour blended in 75 ml (5 tablespoons) stock (b)

Cut the chicken breast into small, thin slices. Clean the clams, and pour a kettleful of boiling water over them. When the shells open, remove the clam meat. Chop the ginger finely. Apply the salt, ginger and 15 ml (1 tablespoon) oil to the chicken and clam meat, and rub the mixture in evenly. Leave to season for 15 minutes. Cut the spring onions into small sections.

Heat the oil in the deep-fryer, or in a large frying pan if shallow-frying. Add the chicken and clams, fry gently for 1$\frac{1}{2}$ minutes, and drain.

Heat the lard in a frying pan. Add the chopped spring onions. Stir a few times, add the wine sediment paste, sugar, sherry, soya sauce and cornflour-stock mixture. Stir quickly until well mixed. As soon as the sauce thickens, add the clams and chicken pieces. Stir them together over a high heat for 45 seconds, and serve immediately in a well-heated dish.
Serves 6–8.

Crisp-Fried Pork Chops in Wine Sediment Paste with Peppers

1.2 kg (2$\frac{1}{2}$ lb) pork chops
7 ml ($\frac{1}{2}$ tablespoon) salt
pepper to taste
45 ml (3 tablespoons) wine sediment paste
7 ml ($\frac{1}{2}$ tablespoon) sugar
22 ml (1$\frac{1}{2}$ tablespoons) cornflour
30 ml (2 tablespoons) sherry
1 egg-white
2 red peppers
3 cloves garlic
oil for deep-frying
30 ml (2 tablespoons) lard
15 ml (1 tablespoon) sesame oil

Remove the pork meat from the bones, and cut it into small cubes. Sprinkle and rub the salt and pepper over the meat. Mix the wine sediment paste, sugar, cornflour, sherry and beaten egg-white into a paste. Apply this to the pork until every piece is well covered.

Cut the pepper into 2.5 cm (1 in) slices and chop the garlic coarsely.

Heat the oil in a deep-fryer (or heat 250 ml/½ pint oil in a large frying pan). When the oil is hot enough for a crumb dropped into it to sizzle, add the pork pieces, and deep-fry them over a high heat for 3½ minutes. (If shallow-frying, turn the pork pieces with a perforated spoon.) Drain them thoroughly.

Heat the lard in a frying pan. Add the pepper, and fry it over a high heat for 1 minute. Add the garlic, and return the pork pieces to the pan. Sprinkle them with the sesame oil, and turn them over a high heat for 1 minute. Transfer the contents to a well-heated dish to be eaten immediately.

Serves 6–8.

Shanghai and East-China Cooking

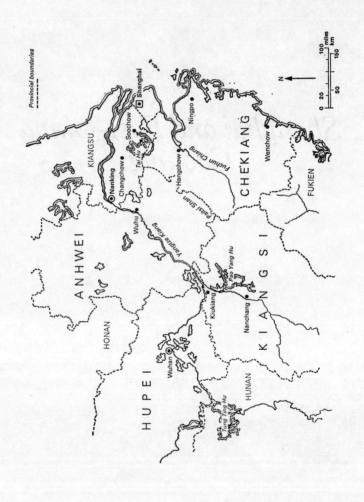

Shanghai and East-China Cooking

All Westerners who have lived in Shanghai seem to retain a nostalgia for the city. Its atmosphere was akin to that of Berlin of the 1930s, a combination of the old and decaying world with the young, new, and sometimes dangerous; it also represented a unique confluence of East and West. The city marked a particular junction of history and geography. Just north of Shanghai, where the Wampoo flows into the Yangtze, the great river broadens out to nearly a hundred miles wide as it empties itself into the China Sea. In relation to China as a whole, the Yangtze represents not only the boundary between north and south; it is also the great passageway between east and west. Ocean liners used to ply four or five hundred miles up to Wuhan and Wanhsien. From there, smaller and faster boats are able to negotiate the famous Gorges into Szechuan and the far west. The Yangtze is over 3,000 miles long. No wonder Shanghai, which is both river and sea port, situated strategically just off the estuary, has for nearly a century been one of the largest cities in China, and is nowadays considered one of the largest cities in the world. A poet of the Sung Dynasty once described the Great River from a pavilion window as 'flowing away emptily through the limitless skies and myriad centuries'; another writer, seeing it from the deck of a tossing boat, described it as 'stretching from horizon to limitless horizon, dotted here and there with a few lonely sails'.

The Yangtze was not the cradle of Chinese civilization; its first significance in Chinese history was relatively recently, around the time of Christ. By the time of the later Han Dynasty and the period of the Three Kingdoms, only a few decades later, the region must have already become quite heavily populated, for Tsao Tsao, one of the heroes of the Three Kingdoms, was said to have commanded a water-borne army of over three-quarters of a million men, and he composed poetry as they floated into battle. So many were the flags, masts and banners that they appeared like a forest which 'shaded the light of the sky'. Already the region was beginning to vibrate with life and excitement, and was teeming with people. The Yangtze and the area round it were to become the main artery of the flood of human life which is China.

For Westerners, Shanghai of the 1920s and 1930s was particularly fascinating because by then it had acquired all the trappings of Western material civilization, but was set in the very essence of China at its most diverse. Every type, trend, style and class in China could be found in Shanghai—the tycoons, the revolutionaries, the patriots, the traitors, and the pimps and prostitutes—incorporating all the vices and virtues of the nation. Western visitors were privileged observers, who could absorb the atmosphere and feel the heat without themselves being consumed.

As for Chinese food, few foreigners really knew much about it; besides, you could still eat good English food in more places in Shanghai than in London, till all hours of the morning, and take a silver or yellow taxi home. Chinese food was something exotic and 'native' which the Western palate did not yet appreciate.

But among the many Chinese who could afford to eat well, the discourse on food had already gone on for centuries. Great care was taken in the preparation of meals, not only for lavish entertainments and official banquets (during the early Republican days a first-class 'top banquet' for the entertainment of governors and war-lords was priced at $10,000; 'second-class', $5,000; and 'lowest class' $500; and the Chinese dollar then was equivalent in value to a US dollar in 1979), but also at home in individual households. But no matter how opulent the occasion, frugality was a constant theme in the Chinese kitchen. Nothing was wasted as would be apparent to anyone who joined an impromptu family luncheon after a night of mahjong playing. The left-over dishes of the previous night would be brought out again from the pantry and served cold, and your personal bowl of rice would be reheated by simply pouring a cup of boiling water over it. Oddly enough the procedure is strangely satisfying! For however affluent the Chinese may appear on the surface, there is always an underlying awareness of the possibility of shortage just around the corner, and famine or talk of famine has always been part of the Chinese racial memory. Nonetheless, the numerous bourgeoisie of the Yangtze ate well, and prepared their food with care. Their eating life was an intriguing combination of extravagance and frugality.

A distinctive style and character of the food of the Lower Yangtze area does not stand out as readily as that of Canton, with its profusion of seafood flavours and 'high savouriness'; or that of north

China and Peking, with its roast and barbecued dishes, its pronounced taste of garlic and thick soya-paste sauces. In fact, the cuisine of the region is in direct contrast to that of the Upper Yangtze, Szechuan. Where Szechuan food is hot, highly spiced and strong-tasting, the eastern emphasis is on dishes which taste fresh, pure and full of natural flavour.

The Lower Yangtze is full of flowing water, and the land is crisscrossed with innumerable streams and studded with ponds and lakes. Since the cooking of any region must reflect the geography of the region, it is natural that the character of this cuisine should reflect the purity of the water, and incorporate a host of freshwater products: shrimps, crab, duck, and a wide range of vegetation which flourishes in this area, especially plants growing in and beside the water. These local products are combined with the staple Chinese foods such as pork, pickles and chicken, to produce the dishes peculiar to the region.

There is also a tendency in Lower Yangtze food towards vegetable and vegetarian cooking. Although in China we usually eat rice plain—boiled or steamed—in Shanghai green vegetables are sometimes cooked together with the rice in the dish called simply Tsai Fan or Vegetable Rice.

Because the Yangtze is the greatest rice-producing region in China, all the rice-based products exist in abundance, among them the widely used Yellow Wine (most Chinese wines are grain-based). China's best-known rice wine is Shao Shing wine, which comes from the town of that name, just south of the Yangtze in the province of Chekiang. Because of the quality and profusion of the product, many dishes contain wine as one of the ingredients—giving rise to dishes with names like Drunken Chicken, Drunken Crabs, Drunken Spare-ribs, etc.

Rice is also often used as a stuffing when poultry is cooked whole, and stuffing of poultry seems a more common culinary practice than elsewhere. A variety of items apart from rice are used in the stuffing, including barley, glutinous rice, lotus nuts, gingko nuts, melon seeds, chestnuts, mushrooms and bamboo shoots. Eight Precious Duck is a dish of duck stuffed with eight different ingredients. A chicken stuffed in the same way is called Eight Precious Chicken. Eight Precious Rice, however, is a sweet steamed pudding, made of glutinous rice mixed and steamed with nuts, fruit-glacé and fruits, and layers of sweet bean paste. It resembles Christmas pudding, except that it is more colourful.

An instance of the restrained use of seasoning is that quite often a dish is salted partly by the addition of a small amount of chopped salted pickle (snow pickle) into the stir-frying of fresh ingredients, such as sliced or shredded pork, bamboo shoots, bean curd or vegetables, instead of salt or soya sauce being added in larger quantities. The same applies to the use of salt pork in conjunction with fresh meat, bean curd, fish or vegetables. Indeed, salt pork is more widely used here than in any other region. It is uncertain whether this is due to the accident of tradition, or for the practical consideration that salt pork keeps longer than fresh pork. Slices can be cut off and used in quick-cooked dishes to add flavour or meat content. Larger chunks are often used for cooking excellent soups. Salt pork is to the people of Shanghai much as salt beef is to the Jewish people.

Bean curd and its various side-products such as dried bean curds or bean-curd skin are used extensively in the vegetable or semi-vegetable dishes of the region. The same ingredients are sometimes actually shaped into replicas of ducks, chicken or fish, being of a texture and colour which can easily be transformed into a semblance of meat, fowl or fish, especially when red-cooked with soya sauce.

South of the Yangtze, bamboo grows in profusion everywhere. Young bamboo shoots, which resemble asparagus, are used in numerous dishes; they are subtly flavoured, with a crunchy texture, and much appreciated by connoisseurs. Along the Yangtze they are often quick-fried with shrimp eggs or crab eggs. In Chingkiang, a Yangtze port, the meat of fresh-water crab is incorporated into their version of Lion's Head Meat Balls. In the serving of Plain Sliced Boiled Pork in Shanghai, Shrimp-Egg Soya Sauce is often placed on the table as a dip.

In contrast to the use of fresh-water products as flavourers, for the richer and saltier meat dishes honey and unrefined crystal sugar are often used in a sweet sauce which is poured over substantial meat dishes, such as Braised Knuckle of Pork with Crystal Sugar Sauce, Steamed Ching Hua Ham with Honey Sauce, or Sliced Ham with Sliced Breast of Chicken with Sweet Sauce. Perhaps it is for this reason that the Shanghai and the east China people have a reputation for being sweet-toothed.

Because the region is so well irrigated, every village or hamlet having its own pond or stream, ducks are reared in great numbers. The farms around Nanking (a former capital of China) are said to provide 40 million ducks a year for the production of the famous Nanking Pressed Duck, dried duck which has to be steamed at length before cooking with other ingredients. The Soya Duck of

Hangchow is often regarded by connoisseurs as being more appealing than the more famous Peking Duck.

Steaming is probably employed more often here than in other regions as a method for long, slow cooking which distils the best out of meat or poultry. The original flavour of food cooked in this way is often better retained than in slow simmering where much of the flavour is dispersed into the liquid—though this latter can be an advantage if the soup is intended to be part of the dish. A third method used in east China cooking is to stew meat or poultry in a strong-tasting sauce for a good length of time, the final and felicitous result depending upon the exchange of flavours between meat and sauce in the course of the cooking. All three methods are popular in east China cooking, especially for the large meat and poultry dishes which are so much enjoyed during the autumn and winter.

But steaming is used not only in lengthy cooking. Short, sharp steaming (for perhaps 8–12 minutes) is also employed to cook diverse ingredients together in a single dish. The advantage of quick-steaming over quick-frying lies in the fact that in steaming, which is a static process, there is less mixing of ingredients, thus allowing each to maintain its own distinctive flavour.

In this region large marrows, squashes or melons are used as containers and steamed with whole chickens or ducks inside them, together with a variety of other ingredients. The fowl is brought to the table still inside the vegetable, a delectable sight. These dishes are called 'bells' or 'steamed bells', no doubt because of their shape. On a smaller scale mushrooms, aubergines, peppers, cucumbers and lotus roots are also often stuffed with various ingredients and steamed, making a colourful and appealing meal.

Leaves of the lotus, another natural product of the ponds, streams and lakes, are frequently and extensively used in wrapping food materials for cooking (again usually by steaming). Savoury rice wrapped in lotus leaves is called Choong. These triangular, cone-shaped parcels are often strung up together like sausages, and lengths of them are taken by travellers setting out on a journey, or can be seen hanging from a window or a hook in the kitchen. Whole chickens are sometimes similarly wrapped up into much larger parcels, which require several hours of steaming to cook through—for when served and unwrapped on the table, the flesh should be tender enough to take to pieces with a pair of chopsticks without the aid of a knife. During cooking, the contents of the package become imbued with the aromatic flavour of the dried lotus leaves.

East China is well known for 'paper-wrapped' dishes. These consist of morsels of chicken, beef, prawn, oyster, etc, wrapped up in non-inflammable cellophane paper in small packets like miniature envelopes, with a little seasoning in the form of shredded mushrooms, ginger, onion, or sauces. The packets are then deep-fried in hot oil, which cooks the contents almost instantly. In Szechuan some chilli pepper or chilli oil is added to the contents; in Canton, oyster sauce; while in Shanghai and east China the ingredients are often first marinated in wine, soya sauce and sugar. Heat is often better preserved when the food is wrapped and cooked in a layer of paper. When served, each envelope of paper-wrapped food is opened with chopsticks by the diner. All paper-wrapped dishes are considered excellent as an accompaniment to wine, for starting off a dinner party. Two or three dozen envelopes would be served, all bearing delectable 'messages', pregnant with eastern promise!

Steaming is also often used in this region for cooking small Paotzu, or Steamed Buns. In north China, whose food south-easterners often consider relatively rough or coarse, the steamed buns or Man Tou are often made and served plain, to take the place of rice. The Shanghai and eastern steamed buns are always prepared more elaborately, with a variety of stuffings. Apart from minced pork, other stuffings include crab eggs, young bamboo shoots, salted pickles with meat, or several ingredients, such as the Triple-ingredient Stuffed Paotzu of Yangchow. Sometimes the buns are even simply stuffed or filled with soup, by stuffing meat aspic inside the dough-casing before steaming. Often these savoury-stuffed buns are made much smaller than is customary in the 'coarser' north. These small buns are called Hsiao Lung Pao, or Little Bell Steamed Buns, and can be eaten in one or two mouthfuls, while the solid steamed buns of the north are often equal in weight to three-quarters of a bowl of rice: two buns are quite enough to fill most stomachs!

Pasta specialities include a range of 'fish noodles', semi-soup dishes incorporating noodles and fish which the people of the Lower Yangtze consume as a whole meal. Shanghai is famous for its Cold Tossed Noodles, which are a summer speciality of the region.

Parallel to the use of wine in cooking, the region is well known for its production of quality vinegar, the best-known being the Chingkiang aromatic vinegar. This is used in the famous Westlake Whole Fish in Vinegar Sauce, and in marinading the freshly caught live shrimps from the same lake (the celebrated West Lake of Hangchow). In the long-cooked fish dishes of the Lower Yangtze, where the aim is to make the bones soft enough to be edible, the addition of a small amount of vinegar into the cooking is essential. In one dish, small fish of the sardine or herring variety are first marinated in vinegar, wine and soya sauce, then placed in a casserole or heatproof dish in thick layers alternated with sliced onion and cooked over a low heat for 5–6 hours. The result is a complete and very satisfying meal.

Viewed by the outsider, this lush, well-watered region of the Lower Yangtze seems a place for easeful living, as it was indeed regarded as such by the poets and writers of old; but in fact the people of Shanghai are some of the most ambitious and enterprising in the whole of China. They are always prepared to work, fight and spend to achieve their ambitions. They are naturally lavish spenders, and fiercely competitive. It is in their tradition to think big and act big. Southerners who come into contact with them are usually impressed with their style; northerners think of them as irrepressible showmen with few scruples. Yet when it comes to food their habits seem to reflect the true nature of the region, which is full of fresh-water produce and abundant rice harvests. There is nothing rough or fierce about the food; the seasonings are mild, the flavours delicate and refined. There is a constant suggestion that foods should be given the opportunity to develop their natural taste and flavour, which can only be too easily overshadowed or suppressed by pungent ingredients. Stir-fried foods are quite often cooked plain, seasoned only by salt and pepper added during the later phase of the cooking or after the food has been served. Wine is used liberally and vinegar frequently, both being local products made from rice, which is harvested in vast quantities along the Yangtze. The river-ports along the Yangtze are all prosperous little townships whose comfortable bourgeois inhabitants owe their wealth to rice. Their cooking may not have the immediate impact of the cuisine of the west or south, but the food is delicately prepared and always given the maximum opportunity to develop its natural flavour. Many of these Chiang-Nan (South of the River) dishes were incorporated into the repertoire of Imperial Court Dishes after Emperor Chien-Lung made his famous incognito tours of the south during the height of the Manchu power. He had never eaten anything quite like it in the north!

There is frequent emphasis in Chinese cuisine on 'legitimacy' (Cheng Chung), which in this case means authenticity. 'Authentic' dishes are evolved rather than invented; and the best food and cooking in China is invariably the authentic 'food of the people', developed over the centuries from the natural produce of the region concerned, and which has triumphantly stood the test of time.

Soups

There seem to be more soups in the cooking of east China and the Lower Yangtze than anywhere else in China, although none carries a particularly pronounced flavour or creates an immediate impact on the palate. But is this not the very character of the cuisine itself —wanting not to make an overwhelming impression, but to bring out the natural subtle flavour of the ingredients for the appreciation of the discerning palate?

Ham and Chicken Clear Soup of Yangchow
(Adapted from the famous Fu-Choon Tea House, Yangchow.)

1 small chicken (about 1.25 kg/ 2½ lb)

1 medium chicken (about 1.5 kg/3½ lb)

675 g (1½ lb) ham

1 pair pig's trotters (about 675 g/1½ lb)

6 medium Chinese dried mushrooms

100 g (¼ lb) bamboo shoots

2 stalks spring onion

15 ml (1 tablespoon) dried shrimps

1.75 litres (3½ pints) water

3 slices root ginger

10 ml (2 teaspoons) salt (or to taste)

45 ml (3 tablespoons) Chinese yellow wine or sherry

Clean both chickens thoroughly and remove the heads and feet if still attached. Eliminate any bristles on the ham and trotters, and trim back the hooves of the trotters. Soak the mushrooms in water for 20 minutes; remove and discard the stalks. Cut the bamboo shoots into small wedge-shaped triangular pieces. Cut the spring onions into short sections. Remove the breast from the smaller chicken, and chop it finely into a 'white mince'. Remove the legs and finely chop the rest of the chicken through the bone into a 'red mince'. Soak the shrimps in water for 30 minutes and drain them.

Parboil the second chicken with the ham and trotters for 10 minutes in boiling water and drain. Place them with the shrimps and ginger in a casserole or extra-large double-boiler and simmer for 15 minutes. Skim off any excess grease and impurities. Remove the trotters, and strain the soup through a doubled cheesecloth. Clean the casserole and return the soup to it. Add one of the spring onions and the 'white mince'. Bring to the boil and simmer for 15 minutes. Strain the soup through a doubled cheesecloth, and add it to the chicken, bamboo shoots and ham in the heatproof dish along with the balance of spring onion, and yellow wine or sherry. Continue to steam for a further 15 minutes.

Serve in the heatproof dish, which is brought steaming to the table. The dish is appreciated for the purity and freshness of the soup, and the uncomplicated taste of chicken enhanced only by the flavour of the ham. What is aimed at here is a lightness and delicacy of composition.

Serves 10–12.

'Semi-Soup' Composition of Shredded Ingredients
(Adapted from East China Garden Restaurant, Nanking.)

2 pairs chicken kidneys and liver
75 g (3 oz) pig's kidney
50 g (2 oz) bamboo shoots
75 g (3 oz) cooked breast of chicken
50 g (2 oz) cooked duck
25 g (1 oz) cooked chicken skin
225 g (½ lb) dried bean curd
75 g (3 oz) ham

30 ml (2 tablespoons) lard
45 ml (3 tablespoons) fresh peeled shrimps
50 g (2 oz) bean sprouts
375 ml (¾ pint) chicken stock (a)
30 ml (2 tablespoons) soya sauce
salt and pepper to taste

Cut the chicken kidney and liver and bamboo shoots into thin slices. Chop the cooked chicken, duck and chicken skin into matchstick-thick shreds. Cut the dried bean curd and ham into similar shreds. Parboil the chicken kidney and liver and bamboo shoots for 2 minutes and drain them.

Heat the lard in a frying pan. Add the shrimps and bean sprouts, and quickly stir-fry for 45 seconds and then remove from the heat.

Place the shredded chicken, duck, chicken skin, chicken kidney and liver, bamboo shoots and bean curd in a pan with the chicken stock. Bring to the boil and simmer for 15 minutes. Add the shrimps, bean sprouts, shredded kidney and lard from the frying pan, and the soya sauce and seasoning. Cook for 2 minutes. Finally sprinkle with shredded ham.

Serve in a deep-sided dish or heatproof glass dish. This dish of

multicoloured shreds immersed in a savoury but not strongly flavoured soup, has a light, pleasant, uncloying appeal. The dried bean curd adds the necessary bulk to consume with rice, for which this dish acts as a traditional supplement.
Serves 8–10.

West Lake Watercress (or Spinach) Soup
(Adapted from the Pavilion of Pavilions Restaurant, Hangchow.)

225 g (½ lb) spinach or water-cress
500 ml (1 pint) chicken-and-ham stock (b)
45 ml (3 tablespoons) shredded

cooked chicken flesh
45 ml (3 tablespoons) chicken fat
45 ml (3 tablespoons) shredded ham

Remove and discard the tougher stems and discoloured leaves of the spinach or watercress. Heat a panful of water. When it boils drop the spinach (or watercress) in for not more than 10 seconds, and drain it immediately. The chicken and ham stock can be prepared by simmering a 675 g (1½ lb) ham bone, or 100 g (¼ lb) ham in chicken stock for 30 minutes. Skim away any excess fat. Bring the stock to the boil in a saucepan and season to taste.

Place the parboiled spinach (or watercress) at the bottom of a large tureen. Pour the boiling soup into the tureen. Add the chicken fat, and garnish with the shredded ham.
Serves 6.

Fish Head Soup
(Adapted from the Pavilion of Pavilions Restaurant, Hangchow. This dish has only been created since the Liberation, and has been much 'acclaimed by the customers from home and abroad, and appreciated by the masses'.)

1 large fresh-water fish head (about 900 g/2 lb)
2 stalks spring onion
225 g (½ lb) ham
37 ml (2½ tablespoons) lard

3 slices root ginger
30–45 ml (2–3 tablespoons) white wine or dry sherry
10 ml (2 teaspoons) salt
125 ml (¼ pint) milk

Clean and cut the fish head vertically into two halves, dip these into a pan of boiling water for 15 seconds and remove. Cut the spring onions into medium-sized sections, and the ham into small slices.

Heat the lard in a large saucepan, tilting the pan so that the surface is evenly covered. Place the two halves of the fish head face-side down in the pan to fry for 1 minute. Turn them over, add the ginger and half the onion and fry for 2 minutes; add the wine, and pour in 1 litre (2 pints) water. Bring to the boil over a high heat and boil vigorously for 10 minutes. Add the salt, then remove the fish head halves and place them in a deep-sided dish or tureen.

Remove the ginger and spring onion from the soup in the pan, as well as all impurities. Add the milk. Bring this slowly to the boil. As soon as it boils, pour the soup over the fish heads in the deep-sided dish.

Garnish the fish head with ham and the remainder of the spring onion. The main appeal of the dish lies in its freshness and light savouriness. A dish most appreciated by the people of the lower Yangtze.

Serves 6–10.

Yellow Beans (or Green Peas) and Shredded Pork Soup
(Adapted from Teh Hsing Restaurant, Shanghai.)

225 g (½ lb) yellow beans (soya beans) or fresh peas
50–75 g (2–3 oz) leg of pork
22 ml (1½ tablespoons) lard
5 ml (1 teaspoon) salt
37 ml (2½ tablespoons) soya sauce
250 ml (½ pint) stock (b)
15 ml (1 tablespoon) coarsely chopped spring onion

Soak the yellow beans in water for 24 hours; if green peas are used no soaking is necessary. Place them in a blender and grind at a medium speed for a minute. Cut the pork into matchstick-thick shreds.

Heat 15 ml (1 tablespoon) lard in a saucepan. Add the shredded pork and the salt, and stir-fry for 2 minutes. Add the ground beans, or peas, soya sauce, and stock. Bring to a gentle boil, and simmer for 30 minutes.

Pour the contents into a large soup bowl and sprinkle with the spring onion and lard. Very much a 'dish of the people'.

Serves 6–8.

Bamboo Shoot Soup

(Adapted from the Kung Deh-Ling, Buddhist Restaurant, Shanghai.)

225 g (½ lb) fresh bamboo
  shoots
75 g (3 oz) bean curd skin
30 ml (2 tablespoons) oil
2 slices root ginger

1 litre (2 pints) water
12 ml (2½ teaspoons) salt
45 ml (3 tablespoons) Kaoliang
  spirit

Remove the outer leaves of the shoots, and cut them into sections of equal length. Soak the bean curd skin for 2 hours in water. Drain and cut it into 6.25–7.5 cm (2½–3 in) long sections.

Heat the oil in a casserole. Add the ginger, bamboo shoots, bean curd skin and salt. Stir them over a medium heat for 5 minutes. Pour in 1 litre (2 pints) water; bring the contents to a gentle boil, add the Kaoliang spirit and simmer gently (place an asbestos sheet under the casserole) for 1 hour.

Serve in the casserole at the dining table. The dish is generally in season during the late summer and early autumn, and is a favourite seasonal dish, also called Phoenix Tail Soup.
Serves 6–8.

Mushroom Soup with Crispy Rice Croûtons

(Adapted from the Pine Moon in the Spring Breeze Restaurant, Shanghai.)

10 large Chinese dried mushrooms
225 g (½ lb) fresh firm button
  mushrooms
750 ml (1½ pints) stock (b)
45 ml (3 tablespoons) dried
  shrimps

30 ml (2 tablespoons) left-over
  rice
22 ml (1½ tablespoons) sesame
  oil
oil for deep-frying
5 ml (1 teaspoon) salt
22 ml (1½ tablespoons) soya
  sauce

Soak the dried mushrooms in 250 ml (½ pint) water for 30 minutes; retain the water; remove and discard the stalks. Clean the fresh mushrooms and remove the stalks (use the latter to boil with the stock).

Heat the stock in a saucepan. Add the fresh mushrooms, half the dried mushrooms, fresh mushroom stalks, water from the dried mushrooms, and dried shrimps. Simmer gently for 45 minutes. Strain away all the solids. Mould the rice into more or less equal-sized pieces binding them with a little water.

Strain the stock through a cheesecloth into a large saucepan. Bring to the boil gently, add the balance of the dried mushrooms and simmer gently for 5 minutes then add the fresh mushrooms, and simmer gently together for a further 5 minutes. Adjust the seasoning.

Place the oil at the bottom of a very large tureen. Pour the boiling soup into the bowl. Quickly deep-fry the rice in hot oil for no more than 1 minute. Drain and sprinkle it over the soup in the soup bowl, and serve. The soup should have a marked mushroomy taste, combining the flavour of both types of mushrooms.
Serves 6–8

The Famous Triple-Shred Soup of Shanghai
(Adapted from the Teh Hsing Restaurant, Shanghai.)

75 g (3 oz) cooked ham	*1 large Chinese dried mush-*
75 g (3 oz) cooked breast of	*room*
chicken	*5 ml (1 teaspoon) salt*
75 g (3 oz) cooked leg of pork	*750 ml (1½ pints) stock (c)*
75 g (3 oz) bamboo shoots	*7 ml (½ tablespoon) lard*

Cut the ham, chicken breast, pork and bamboo shoots into matchstick-sized shreds. Arrange them neatly in separate piles in a large heatproof dish. Soak the mushroom for 15 minutes, remove the stalk, and place it cap-side-down in the centre amongst the shredded ingredients. Sprinkle the pork and chicken with salt.

Put the heatproof dish containing the various shredded ingredients into a steamer, and steam steadily for 30 minutes. Meanwhile, heat the stock in a saucepan. When it boils, add the salt and lard.

Turn the contents of the heatproof dish in one motion into a large deep-sided dish. Carefully pour the stock from the saucepan into the dish so that the heaps of ingredients are undisturbed and serve. The dish is appreciated for its purity and clarity.
Serves 6–8.

Mussel Soup with Bean Curd
(Adapted from the Tsai Kan Hsiang Restaurant, Yangchow.)

3 large Chinese dried mushrooms	*2 young leeks*
3 stalks golden needles (tiger	*375–500 ml (¾–1 pint) mussels*
lily buds)	*3 slices root ginger*
2 cakes bean curd	*500 ml (1 pint) stock (b)*

10 ml (2 teaspoons) salt
15 ml (1 tablespoon) soya sauce
pepper to taste
10 ml (2 teaspoons) lard

30 ml (2 tablespoons) dry
sherry or Chinese yellow wine
30 ml (2 tablespoons) coriander
leaves

Soak the dried mushrooms for 20 minutes, discard the stalks and
cut the caps into quarters. Soak the golden needles for 10 minutes
and cut them into reasonably long sections. Cut each cake of bean
curd into a dozen pieces, and the leeks into small slices. Clean the
mussels thoroughly with a brush, and rinse them two or three
times under running water.

Heat 750 ml (1½ pints) water in a large saucepan. When it boils,
add the mussels and ginger. Allow the contents to reboil; after 15
seconds remove the pan from the heat, skim off any impurities
and pour away half the water.

Meanwhile, heat the stock in another saucepan. Add the dried
mushrooms, golden needles, leeks, bean curd and salt. Bring to the
boil, and simmer for 10 minutes. Pour the contents into the saucepan containing the mussels. Add the soya sauce and season with
pepper and salt. Bring the soup to the boil again, and simmer
gently for 5–6 minutes. Add the lard and sherry or yellow wine and
sprinkle with the coriander leaves.

Serve in a large tureen or casserole. This is a favourite dish of
the coastal people and the fishing community of the Yangtze delta.
Serves 6–8.

Fish-Soup Noodles

675 g (1½ lb) small fish
(whiting, herring, sardines,
etc)
3 slices root ginger
3 stalks spring onion
675 g (1½ lb) egg noodles
45 ml (3 tablespoons) vegetable
oil

1 litre (2 pints) stock (b)
salt and pepper to taste
15 ml (1 tablespoon) cornflour
blended in 90 ml (6 tablespoons) water or milk
60 ml (4 tablespoons) fresh
shelled shrimps

Clean the fish thoroughly and gut them if this has not been done
already. Cut the ginger into shreds, and the spring onion into
small sections. Boil the noodles for 6–7 minutes, drain, and divide
them among six bowls.

Place the fish and ginger in a dry pan. Heat over a low heat until all the moisture has evaporated (about 7–8 minutes). Add the oil and stir-fry slowly, still over a low heat, for 9–10 minutes, until the fish has disintegrated. Pour in the stock. Bring the contents to the boil, and simmer gently for 45 minutes. Double-strain the soup, first through a filter, and then through cheesecloth into another saucepan. Place the pan over a medium heat, and adjust the seasoning. When the contents reboil, add the blended cornflour and shrimps; stir and simmer for 2–3 minutes. The soup should now be quite white.

Sprinkle the top of the noodles with 2.5 ml ($\frac{1}{2}$ teaspoon) lard and some of the spring onions. Pour a helping of the white fish soup and shrimps over each bowl of noodles.
Serves 6.

Chicken and Duck

Chi Ko Chiang or Braised Chicken on the Bone
(Adapted from Teh Hsing Restaurant, Shanghai.)

1 medium chicken (about 1.35 kg; 3 lb)
4 stalks spring onion
52 ml (3½ tablespoons) vegetable oil
45 ml (3 tablespoons) dry sherry
45 ml (3 tablespoons) soya sauce
15 ml (1 tablespoon) soya or yellow bean paste
6 ml (1¼ teaspoons) sugar
250 ml (¼ pint) stock (b)
22 ml (1½ tablespoons) lard
15 ml (1 tablespoon) cornflour blended in 45 ml (3 tablespoons) water

Remove the head, neck, and feet of the chicken if still attached. Chop the body and legs of the chicken, through the bone, into medium-sized pieces. Cut the spring onions into medium-sized sections.

Heat the oil in a large saucepan or casserole. Add the chicken pieces, and turn them over a high heat for 5–6 minutes. Add the sherry, soya sauce, soya paste and sugar. Turn the chicken pieces with the other ingredients for 3 minutes. Pour in the stock. When it starts to boil, mix the chicken pieces around a few times, and reduce the heat to low. Leave to simmer for 12–15 minutes, when the sauce in the pan should be reduced to less than half. Add the spring onion and lard. Turn the contents around a few times and

add the cornflour mixture. When the sauce thickens, turn once more and serve. Serve in a deep-sided, well-heated dish.
Serves 6–8.

Quick-Fried Chicken Kidney
(Adapted from the Lao Yung Shuan Restaurant, Shanghai.)

8 medium Chinese dried mush-rooms

75–100 g (3–4 oz) bamboo shoots

8 medium chicken kidneys

7 ml (½ tablespoon) salt

1 large onion

30 ml (2 tablespoons) vegetable oil

30 ml (2 tablespoons) dry sherry

15 ml (1 tablespoon) light-coloured soya sauce

90 ml (6 tablespoons) stock (b)

12 ml (¾ tablespoon) cornflour blended in 45 ml (3 table-spoons) water

15 ml (1 tablespoon) lard

Soak the mushrooms in water for 20 minutes. Remove the stalks. Cut the bamboo shoots into medium-sized thin slices. Remove the membrane from the kidneys but otherwise retain the original shape. Rub them with the salt. Cut the onion into quarters.

Heat the oil in a frying pan. Add the onion to fry at medium heat for 2 minutes, turn it in the oil a few times and remove. Add the bamboo shoots and mushrooms and stir-fry for 1 minute, fol-lowed by the sherry, soya sauce, stock and kidney. Turn the heat to high, allowing the pan's contents to cook vigorously for 3 minutes. Add the blended cornflour mixture and the lard. Stir a couple more times, and serve quickly. This is one of the better known Shanghai dishes.
Serves 5–6.

Braised Chicken Drumsticks
(Adapted from the Yung Hua Restaurant, Shanghai.)

1 small onion

3 stalks spring onion

10 chicken drumsticks

3 slices root ginger

52 ml (3½ tablespoons) lard or vegetable oil

5 ml (1 teaspoon) curry powder

7 ml (½ tablespoon) salt

45 ml (3 tablespoons) tomato

purée

30 ml (2 tablespoons) dry sherry

10 ml (2 teaspoons) sugar

90 ml (6 tablespoons) chicken stock (a)

15 ml (1 tablespoon) cornflour blended in 45 ml (3 table-spoons) water

Chop the onion into small pieces. Tie knots in the spring onions (for easy removal).

Place the drumsticks in a pan of boiling water to blanch for 3 minutes, then drain. Transfer to a heatproof dish, add the ginger, spring onions and 250 ml (½ pint) water. Put the dish into a steamer and steam for 1 hour. Take the drumsticks out individually and remove the bones, leaving the drumsticks as intact as possible. Put them back into the steamer for a further hour.

Meanwhile heat 37 ml (2½ tablespoons) lard in a frying pan. Add the onion to stir-fry for 1 minute, then add the curry and stir-fry it with the onion for 1 minute more. Add the salt, tomato purée, sherry, sugar and stock (from the basin in which the drumsticks were steamed). Stir them over a high heat into a consistent mixture. Finally, add the remaining 15 ml (1 tablespoon) lard and the corn-flour and mix until the sauce thickens.

Serve on a round dish with the drumsticks radiating from the centre and the thick red sauce poured evenly over them.
Serves 10.

Melon Chicken

0.9–1 kg (2–2½ lb) young chicken
6 large Chinese dried mush-rooms
50 g (2 oz) bamboo shoots
1 large water melon (about 2.2–2.65 kg/5–6 lb)

3 slices root ginger
12 ml (2½ teaspoons) salt
50–75 g (2–3 oz) ham
45 ml (3 tablespoons) dry sherry
10 ml (2 teaspoons) shrimp sauce

Remove the head, feet and innards of the chicken. Parboil the cleaned chicken in boiling water for 5–6 minutes and drain it. Soak the mushrooms in water for 20 minutes; drain and discard the stalks. Cut the bamboo shoots into medium-sized thin slices. Remove the top fifth of the melon by slicing it off horizontally. Keep the 'lid'. Scoop out all the pulp, seeds and flesh of the melon, leaving a large cavity.

Place the chicken, ginger and salt in a casserole, and pour in 1 litre (2 pints) water. Add the mushrooms, bamboo shoots and ham, spreading them evenly over the chicken in the liquid in the casserole. Bring to the boil, place an asbestos sheet under the casserole, and simmer very gently for 2 hours.

F

Put the melon in a large heatproof bowl so that it stands upright securely and transfer the chicken into the cavity. Pour in the soup from the casserole. Discard the ginger, and use tongs or chopsticks to transfer the bamboo shoots, ham and mushrooms from the casserole into the melon. Add the pieces of melon flesh from the inside of the melon, cut into regular-sized, 12 g (½ oz) chunks. Sprinkle the contents with the sherry and shrimp sauce. Insert the bowl with the melon in it into a steamer, and steam for 15 minutes.

Close the top of the melon with the sliced-off 'lid', and bring the whole melon to the table still standing in the heatproof bowl. Open the lid and allow the diners to help themselves with their chopsticks and spoons.

Serves 6–10.

Quick-Fried Chicken with Chestnut
(Adapted from the Metropolitan Catering Co, Shanghai.)

100 g (¼ lb) breast of chicken
5 ml (1 teaspoon) salt
22 ml (1½ tablespoons) corn-flour
45 ml (3 tablespoons) stock (b)
22 ml (1½ tablespoons) dry sherry
15 ml (1 tablespoon) soya sauce
5 ml (1 teaspoon) sugar
3 stalks spring onion
125 ml (¼ pint) vegetable oil for shallow-frying
100 g (¼ lb) peeled chestnuts
10 ml (2 teaspoons) lard
10 ml (2 teaspoons) sesame oil

Dice the chicken into small cubes. Sprinkle and rub these with salt and 7 ml (½ tablespoon) cornflour. Add the remaining cornflour to the stock, sherry, soya sauce, and sugar in a bowl. Blend until smooth. Cut the spring onions into small sections.

Heat the oil in a large frying pan. When a crumb dropped in the oil will sizzle, add the chicken and chestnuts. Stir them in hot oil for 45 seconds, and drain. Pour away most of the oil. Add the onions. Stir them in the remaining oil in the pan for 15 seconds. Pour in the blended mixture from the bowl and stir until the sauce thickens. Return the chicken and chestnuts to the pan; stir and mix with the sauce for 30 seconds. Add the lard, followed by the sesame oil. Stir once more and serve immediately.

Serves 4–5.

Drunken Chicken

(Adapted from the Restaurant of the First-rank Scholars, Shanghai.)

1 medium-sized young chicken (about 1.5 kg/3½ lb)
6 slices root ginger
15–20 ml (1–1⅓ tablespoons) ground cinnamon, cloves or nutmeg or, if available, 12 ml (¾ tablespoon) five-spice mixture in pieces, not powder
3 stalks spring onion
30 ml (2 tablespoons) wine sediment paste (otherwise use 30 ml/2 tablespoons brandy)
90 ml (6 tablespoons) dry sherry

Plunge the chicken into a large pan of boiling water, parboil it for 5 minutes, and drain. Cool by plunging into a basin of cold water. Drain again and dry.

Heat a large pan of water, adding the ginger. When the water starts to boil, add the chicken. Reduce the heat as soon as the contents reboil, and simmer gently for 30 minutes. Remove and drain the chicken, and chop it into quarters.

When the chicken pieces are cool, rub them with the salt, ground cinnamon, cloves and nutmeg (or add the five-spice mixture) and freshly-cut spring onion sections. Mix thoroughly. Place the chicken in a large basin in the refrigerator for 5–6 hours.

Shake the chicken pieces free of seasoning ingredients, and transfer them to a bowl or ceramic casserole with a lid. Sprinkle and rub the chicken with wine sediment paste or brandy, then add the dry sherry. Cover the bowl or casserole firmly, shake to mix the contents, and chill in the refrigerator overnight.

Take out the chicken quarters. Chop each quarter again through the bone into 5–6 pieces. Arrange neatly on a serving dish, placing the irregular pieces at the bottom and the meatier pieces on top. A good starter for a multi-course dinner.
Serves 6–10.

Nanking Braised Duck

(Adapted from the East China Garden Restaurant, Nanking.)

225 g (½ lb) duck meat (uncooked, carved from breast, sides and legs)
100 g (¼ lb) winter bamboo shoots
8 medium Chinese dried mushrooms
5 ml (1 teaspoon) sugar
22 ml (1½ tablespoons) soya sauce
15 ml (1 tablespoon) vinegar
75 ml (5 tablespoons) chicken stock or duck stock

45 ml (3 tablespoons) vegetable   2 ml (½ teaspoon) salt
   oil   15 ml (1 tablespoon) duck fat
22 ml (1½ tablespoons) dry
   sherry

Cut the duck meat into small, thin slices, and the bamboo shoots
into similar-sized slices. Soak the dried mushrooms in water for
20 minutes, drain, and remove the stalks. Mix the sugar, soya
sauce, vinegar, monosodium glutamate and 15 ml (1 tablespoon)
stock into a 'cooking sauce'.

Heat the oil in a frying pan. Add the bamboo shoots and mushrooms. Stir-fry over a high heat for 1½ minutes. Add the sauce
and continue to stir-fry for 1 minute. Add the sherry and remaining
stock and stir well. When the sauce starts to boil, add the duck
slices, and pour in the duck fat. Continue to stir-fry over a high
heat for 2 minutes. Heat and freshness are essential to the quality
and success of the dish, which must be served and eaten quickly.
Serves 6–8.

Duck and Chicken Rice with Vegetables
(Adapted from the Fu-Choon Tea House, Yangchow.)

1 medium-sized duck (about 1.5   300 g (11 oz) spring greens
   kg/3½ lb)   (green cabbage)
1 medium-sized boiling fowl   300 g (11 oz) broccoli
   (same weight as duck)   900 g (2 lb) rice
225 g (½ lb) belly of pork   2 litres (4 pints) water
225 g (½ lb) ham   100 g (¼ lb) snow pickle
450 g (1 lb) bamboo shoots   20 ml (4 teaspoons) salt
                                    45 ml (3 tablespoons) lard

Parboil the duck, chicken and pork for 10 minutes and drain. Dice
the ham and bamboo shoots into small cubes. Cut the cabbage and
broccoli into medium-sized slices. Wash the rice in 2 changes of
water.

Boil the water in a large pot or casserole. Add the chicken, duck
and pork. When contents reboil, reduce the heat to low and simmer
gently for 1½ hours. Take out the meat and retain the stock. Cut
the duck and chicken meat from the carcase into medium-sized
pieces. Cut the pork into similar-sized pieces. Chop the pickles into
small pieces. Return the duck, chicken and pork to the stock in the
pot. Add the rice and 5 ml (1 teaspoon) salt, and, using a wooden
spoon, stir the contents slowly but continually over a low heat.

In about 18–20 minutes the rice will have absorbed most of the stock in the container.

Meanwhile, heat the lard in a large frying pan. Add the cabbage, broccoli and salt. Stir them together over a medium heat for 2 minutes. Add the pickles, and continue to stir-fry for 1 minute.

Now spread the diced ham and the vegetables in the frying pan, over the top of the contents of the pot. Cover and leave to cook very gently for 5 minutes. Turn the heat off, and allow the ingredients to cook in their own heat for a further 15 minutes.

Place the pot at the centre of the table. Arrange four small saucer-sized dishes of good quality soya sauce around the pot. Remove the lid and let the diners help themselves to a bowlful of rice and vegetables, dipping the larger pieces of food in the soya sauce as they pick or spoon them out from the pot.
Serves 12–15.

Cold Soya Duck

1 medium duck (about 1.5 kg/ 3½ lb)
22 ml (1½ tablespoons) sugar
45 ml (3 tablespoons) soya sauce
5 ml (1 teaspoon) salt
10 ml (2 teaspoons) cinnamon bark
4 pieces star anise
4 slices root ginger
2 medium onions
1 ml (¼ teaspoon) cochineal or red colouring
12 ml (¾ tablespoon) cornflour

Remove the innards, neck and head, parboil the duck for 10 minutes, and drain. Place it in a pot or casserole. Add 10 ml (2 teaspoons) sugar, the soya sauce, salt, sherry, cinnamon, anise, ginger, sliced onions, red colouring and enough water to cover the duck. Bring the contents to the boil, cover, reduce the heat to low, and simmer for 1½ hours, turning the bird over twice. Remove it from the pot to drain and cool.

When the duck is cold, chop it through the bone into bite-sized pieces, and arrange them neatly on a serving dish. Skim off any excess fat from the liquid in the pot. Remove all solids and reduce the liquid by a third through boiling. Use half the liquid to make a sauce, by adding the balance of sugar, the cornflour (blended first in 45 ml/3 tablespoons stock or water) and mix them together thoroughly. Put the pan over a medium heat until the sauce thickens. Allow the sauce to cool. When cold, pour it over the duck and

serve. It is a favourite Soochow dish in the summer. The interesting
flavour lies in the trace of saltiness within its general fresh sweet-
ness.
Serves 8–10.

Hangchow Steamed Spiced Duck
(Adapted from the Tien Hsiang Lou, or Restaurant of Heavenly
Aroma, Hangchow.)

2.2 kg (5 lb) duck
20 ml (1⅓ tablespoons) salt

7 ml (½ tablespoon) bicarbonate
of soda
soya sauce for marinating

After cleaning the duck and removing the giblets, hang it up to dry
for 3–4 hours. Then rub it thoroughly inside and out with a mixture
of salt and bicarbonate of soda. Place a bamboo or wooden frame
at the bottom of a large jar, and place the duck on top. Weigh
down the bird with a 6.6 kg (15 lb) weight placed on top, again
over a wooden or bamboo frame. After 36 hours of pressing turn
the bird around, and subject it to another 36 hours of pressing (at a
temperature of about zero°C; at 10°C the time should be reduced
by a third).

Drain the duck, and hang it up to dry for 2–3 hours. Place the
duck in another jar and pour in enough soya sauce to cover it.
Allow the duck to stand in the soya sauce for 36 hours then
turn it around and immerse it for a further 36 hours. Remove
and drain.

Dip the duck in a pan of boiling soya sauce for 10 seconds.
Drain, and insert a wooden or bamboo frame inside the duck to
extend the cavity and facilitate the movement of air. Hang the duck
by the nose in an airy and sunny spot to sun and dry for 3 days (2
days in summer).

Put the duck on a raised frame in a deep-sided heatproof dish,
insert it into a steamer, and steam vigorously for 2 hours.

Chop the duck through the bone into large bite-sized pieces and
arrange these neatly on a serving dish. To be consumed in conjunction with green vegetables (lettuce, quick-fried spinach, young
cabbage, celery etc) and Steamed Buns (see page 63). This dish
enjoys as much fame in China as the Peking Duck which is so well
known abroad.
Serves 6–8.

Pork

Steamed Pork in Soya Cheese Sauce
(Adapted from City Catering Co, Soochow.)

900 g (2 lb) belly of pork
15 ml (1 tablespoon) red soya
 cheese
5 ml (1 teaspoon) salt
7 ml (½ tablespoon) sugar
5 ml (1 teaspoon) red rice (or
 ½ drop cochineal blended in
 30 ml/2 tablespoons water)

2 medium onions
4 slices root ginger
30 ml (2 tablespoons) dry sherry
45 ml (3 tablespoons) vegetable
 oil
6 large lettuce leaves
5 ml (1 teaspoon) salt

Parboil the pork for 4–5 minutes. Drain and cut through lean and fat into 20 pieces, each with the skin attached. Score the skin of each piece with half-a-dozen criss-cross cuts. Mix the red soya cheese with the salt, sugar, cochineal (if red rice is available, it will need to be soaked in 30 ml/2 tablespoons water blended with cheese, sugar and salt). Apply the mixture to the pork, placed skin-side down in a basin or deep-sided heatproof dish. Cut the onion into thin slices, and place them on top of the pork together with the ginger. Sprinkle with sherry. Place the basin or dish in a steamer, and steam steadily for 3 hours. Remove and discard the ginger and onion.

Turn the pork out of the basin or dish in one motion on to a large serving dish. Heat the oil in a large frying pan. Add the lettuce leaves, sprinkle them with 3 ml (⅔ teaspoon) salt, and stir-fry for 1 minute over a high heat. Surround the pork pudding with lettuce. *Serves 6–8.*

Shredded Pork with Snow Pickle

225 g (½ lb) lean pork
225 g (½ lb) belly of pork
225 g (½ lb) bamboo shoots
15 ml (1 tablespoon) cornflour
52 ml (3½ tablespoons) vegetable oil

37 ml (2½ tablespoons) snow
 pickle
22 ml (1½ tablespoons) soya
 sauce
22 ml (1½ tablespoons) dry
 sherry

Cut the pork into double-matchstick-thick shreds. Cut the bamboo shoots into similar-sized strips. Sprinkle and rub the pork with the cornflour and 7 ml (½ tablespoon) oil. Chop the pickles into small pieces.

Heat the oil fiercely in a large frying pan. Add the shredded pork, and stir-fry over a high heat for 1½ minutes. Add the pickle, soya sauce, bamboo shoots and sherry. Continue to stir-fry over a high heat for 2 minutes. Serve immediately.
Serves 4–6.

Sliced Pork with Heart of Spring Cabbage
(Adapted from the City Catering Co, Shanghai.)

275 g (⅔ lb) belly of pork
450 g (1 lb) green cabbage
37 ml (2½ tablespoons) vegetable oil
2 ml (½ teaspoon) salt
30 ml (2 tablespoons) soya

sauce
5 ml (1 teaspoon) sugar
60 ml (4 tablespoons) stock (b)
10 ml (2 teaspoons) cornflour
  blended in 30 ml (2 tablespoons) water

Cut the pork across lean and fat into thin slices (after removing the skin). Cut the cabbage into pieces of approximately the same size.

Heat oil in a large frying pan. Add cabbage and salt. Stir-fry for 1 minute. Sprinkle with half the soya sauce, half the sugar and all the stock. Continue to stir-fry for 1½ minutes over a high heat. Reduce the heat to low, cover the pan and simmer for 3 minutes. Remove the cabbage and arrange it around the sides of a large serving dish. Add the lard to the pan. Increase the heat to high. Add the pork pieces. Stir-fry over a high heat for 1½ minutes. Add the balance of soya sauce and sugar. Continue to stir-fry for 1½ minutes. Pour in the blended cornflour. Stir and cook for a further 45 seconds.

Pour the pork from the frying pan into the centre of the spring cabbage, and serve. The attraction of the dish lies in its freshness and uncomplicated flavouring.
Serves 6–8.

Casserole of Salt Pork with Heart of Cabbage and Bean Curd

225 g (½ lb) salt pork
350 g (¾ lb) heart of cabbage
  (or spring greens)
2 cakes bean curd
37 ml (2½ tablespoons) vegetable oil

250 ml (½ pint) stock (b)
22 ml (1½ tablespoons) soya
  sauce
chicken stock cube
7 ml (½ tablespoon) lard
30 ml (2 tablespoons) dry sherry

Cut the pork into small pieces. Cut the cabbage into slightly larger pieces, and each piece of bean curd into 10–12 pieces.

Heat the oil in a large frying pan. Add the pork and cabbage, and stir-fry over a high heat for 3 minutes. Add the stock, soya sauce, stock cube, lard and sherry. Cook over a high heat for 1 minute, turning the contents gently.

Place the bean curd pieces at the bottom of a metal casserole. Pour the contents of the frying pan over the bean curd. Place the casserole over a low heat, and simmer gently for 20 minutes.

Serve in the casserole, for the diners to help themselves.
Serves 6–8.

Yangchow Double-Grilled Roast Pork
(Adapted from the Yangchow Restaurant, Yangchow.)

2.65 kg (6 lb) belly of pork with skin and rib-bone attached

Dips and Accompaniments

*1 dozen Lotus Leaf or Thousand-
    Thread Steamed Buns
2 saucers sweet soya paste
2 saucers spring onions cut into
5 cm (2 in) sections
2 saucers each containing 45 ml
    (3 tablespoons) Aromatic Salt
    and Pepper Mix (see page 68)*

Cut the pork into 2 pieces for easier handling. Pour a kettleful of water over the skin, dry and clean thoroughly.

Place the pork under a moderate grill, skin-side up, for 6 minutes; turn it over and grill the bone-and-meat side for 6 minutes. Turn the pork over again and grill the skin side for a further 6 minutes, when some black spots will have appeared on the skin. Scrape the black spots away with a knife, and repeat the grilling, but reduce the time to 5 x 5 x 5 minutes. As more burnt black spots appear on the skin, scrape them away.

Now place the pieces of pork on a wire rack and put them in a cool-moderate oven at 150°C (300°F)/Gas 2. Roast the pork for 30 minutes, beginning skin-side down, for 10 minutes and ending with skin-side up for 10 minutes. By this time both sides will be thoroughly cooked.

Bring the pieces of pork to the table or to a side table, and place them on a heavy chopping board. Cut the crackling from the meat, having first removed the bones. Cut the meat into thin slices

F*

and the crackling into squares, and eat them sandwiched in Lotus Leaf or Thousand-Thread Steamed Buns, brushed with sweet soya-paste sauce, with helpings of spring onion. Some pieces of crackling are eaten independently after being sprinkled with Aromatic Salt and Pepper Mix. When properly cooked—the recipe may require one or two experimental runs—the dish should measure up to its high reputation.
Serves 6.

Tung-Po Casserole of Pork

(Soo Tung Po was the famous Chinese poet of the Sung Dynasty who reputedly invented the dish. This recipe is adapted from the Tien Choon Restaurant, Hangchow.)

900 g (2 lb) belly of pork (with at least 3 layers of lean and fat)
2 medium onions
10 ml (2 teaspoons) sugar

75 ml (5 tablespoons) soya sauce
75 ml (5 tablespoons) dry sherry
4 slices root ginger

Cut the pork through the skin into quarters. Plunge them into boiling water, parboil for 5 minutes and drain. Cool by soaking in cold water and drain when cold. Cut the onion into thin slices.

Line the bottom of a casserole with half the sliced onion. Place the pieces of pork in a basin. Blend the sugar, soya sauce and sherry together and pour the mixture over the pork. Turn the pork pieces over a number of times, so that skin and meat are evenly coated. Marinate for one hour or more.

Place the pork skin-side-down on top of the layer of sliced onions. Cover with chopped ginger and the remainder of the onion. Pour the rest of the marinade over the contents. Cover the casserole and place it in a preheated oven at 200°C (400°F)/Gas 6 for 15 minutes; reduce the heat to 150°C (300°F)/Gas 2 to cook for 1 hour, and then cook at 140°C (275°F)/Gas 1 for a further 1½ hours.

Discard the ginger and onion. Arrange the pieces of pork skin-side up, with one piece on top of the other three. Skim away any excess fat, and pour the gravy from the casserole over the pork. Because of the long cooking the pork should have the tenderness of bean curd, and can be broken up with chopsticks.
Serves 6–8.

Lion's Head Clear-Simmered Meat Balls
(Adapted from the City Catering Co, Hangchow.)

900 g (2 lb) belly of pork
12 ml (2½ teaspoons) salt
1 egg
22 ml (1½ tablespoons) corn-

flour
30 ml (2 tablespoons) dry
sherry
4–5 lettuce leaves

Remove the skin from the pork, and chop the meat finely. Add the salt, beaten egg, cornflour and sherry and mix them thoroughly with the minced pork using a wooden spoon, for at least 5–6 minutes. Form the mixture into 4 large meat balls. Tear the lettuce into shreds.

Heat 750 ml (1½ pints) water in a casserole. When it starts to boil, lower the meat balls into the boiling water. When the contents start to re-boil, reduce the heat to low and insert an asbestos sheet under the pot. Simmer very gently for 1½ hours. Skim off excess fat from the soup and strew the shredded lettuce over the surface. Close the lid and simmer for a further 15 minutes.

Serve in the casserole, or transfer contents to a large bowl. The quickly-cooked vegetables make a fresh contrast with the long-cooked meat. This is a much lighter dish than the other Lion's Head versions traditional to other parts of China.

Serves 6–7.

Shanghai Spare-Ribs with Two Types of Dips
(Adapted from the Old Yung Swen Restaurant, Shanghai.)

900 g (2 lb) spare-ribs
2 ml (½ teaspoon) salt
22 ml (1½ tablespoons) soya
sauce

22 ml (1½ tablespoons) dry
sherry
oil for deep-frying

Dip 1

15 ml (1 tablespoon) sugar
22 ml (1½ tablespoons) wine
vinegar

22 ml (1½ tablespoons) soya
sauce
15 ml (1 tablespoon) water

Dip 2

Aromatic Salt and Pepper Mix (page 68)

Cut the spare-ribs into individual ribs, and chop them into long segments. Give each piece of rib a hammer blow or two with the back of the chopper to loosen the meat. Mix the salt, soya sauce and sherry and rub this over the ribs. Leave to season for 1 hour.

Heat the oil in the deep-fryer. When a crumb dropped into it sizzles, place half the spare-ribs in a wire basket in the oil, fry for 30 seconds and remove. Allow the oil time to regain its heat, and fry the balance of the spare-ribs for 30 seconds also. Now put both lots of spare-ribs in the wire basket, and when the oil is hot again, lower them into it to fry for 1½ minutes. Drain thoroughly on absorbent paper and transfer to a well-heated serving dish.

Heat 22 ml (1½ tablespoons) oil in a small pan. Mix the ingredients for the dip in a bowl and pour this into the pan. Stir for 45 seconds over a medium heat. Pour the hot sweet and sour mixture into a saucer. The diner dips the spare-ribs either in this or in the Salt and Pepper Mix before eating.

Serves 5–6.

Shanghai Pork Chop

Repeat the recipe on page 165, but using a 6.75 g (1½ lb) leg of pork instead of spare ribs. Cut the meat into small cubes. Instead of seasoning with soya sauce, sherry, etc, make a batter with 30 ml (2 tablespoons) cornflour, 5 ml (1 teaspoon) salt and 1 egg. Coat the pork in the batter mixture.

Deep-fry the pork pieces in the same manner as the spare-ribs: 30 seconds at first, then 1½ minutes more in very hot oil. Drain and serve with the same dips as in the previous recipe. An excellent dish to start a meal.

Serves 5–6.

Pork Stuffed Cucumber
(Adapted from the City Catering Co, Soochow.)

1 large cucumber	15 ml (1 tablespoon) dry sherry
225 g (½ lb) lean and fat pork	2 slices root ginger
15 ml (1 tablespoon) soya sauce	22 ml (1½ tablespoons) cornflour
1 ml (¼ teaspoon) sugar	oil for deep-frying

Sauce

250 ml (½ pint) stock (b)	sauce
30 ml (2 tablespoons) sherry	½ chicken stock cube
15 ml (1 tablespoon) soya	5 ml (1 teaspoon) sesame oil

Cut the cucumber into 5 cm (2 in) sections. Scoop out three-quarters of the pulp and seeds to make each section into the shape of a cup. Mince the pork, add the soya sauce, sugar, sherry and finely chopped ginger and mix thoroughly. Fill the cucumber cups with the mixture and sprinkle and rub the cornflour over the top of the filling. Heat the sauce ingredients in a small pan. Remove and stir as soon as this boils.

Place half the cucumber and pork cups in a wire basket, pork-side down, deep-fry for 1½ minutes and remove. Repeat with the second half of the cucumber cups. Arrange the cucumber cups on a glass or heatproof dish. Pour the sauce over them. Cover the dish, and put it in a preheated oven at 180°C (350°F)/Gas 4. Leave to cook for 25–30 minutes. Serve in the cooking dish.
Serves 6–8.

Fish and Shellfish

Shanghai Braised Carp

(Adapted from the Lao Cheng Hsing Restaurant, Shanghai.)

2 carp (about 1.2–1.35 kg/2½– 3 lb)
7 ml (½ tablespoon) salt
2 slices root ginger
100 g (¼ lb) belly of pork
4 stalks spring onion
75 g (3 oz) bamboo shoots
30 ml (2 tablespoons) snow pickles
oil for deep-frying

45 ml (3 tablespoons) soya sauce
7 ml (½ tablespoon) sugar
90 ml (6 tablespoons) stock (b)
½ chicken stock cube
30 ml (2 tablespoons) dry sherry
15 ml (1 tablespoon) cornflour blended in 45 ml (3 tablespoons) water
10 ml (2 teaspoons) sesame oil

Clean the carp thoroughly under running water, and scrape away the scales. Rub with salt and finely-chopped ginger. Leave to season for 30 minutes. Dice the pork into small cubes. Cut the spring onions into short sections and the bamboo shoots into small, thin slices, and chop the pickles into small pieces.

Heat the oil in the deep-fryer. When a crumb dropped into it sizzles, lower the carp in a wire basket into the hot oil to fry for 1 minute. Remove and drain.

Heat 30 ml (2 tablespoons) oil in a large frying pan or wok. Add the pork cubes and stir them around over a high heat for 30 seconds. Add the spring onion, soya sauce, sugar, stock and crushed stock cube. Stir the mixture until it starts to boil and froth over a high heat. Lower the fish into the pan, and baste for 30 seconds. Turn it over and baste for a further 30 seconds. Sprinkle the fish with the sherry. Reduce the heat to low, and place a lid over the pan to cook slowly for 20 minutes.

Transfer the fish carefully to a well-heated oval dish. Return the pan to the heat. Add the cornflour mixture, lard and sesame oil. Stir quickly over a high heat. When the sauce thickens and boils, pour it over the length of the fish.

Although not a banquet dish, carp cooked in this way is always most acceptable for a domestic dinner.
Serves 6–8.

Filleted Yellow Fish with Bêche de Mer (Sea Cucumber)
(Adapted from the Pavilion of First Rank Scholar,
Chuan Yuan Lou, Shanghai.)

225 g (½ lb) bêche de mer (sea cucumber)
450 g (1 lb) yellow fish (any suitable fish may be used)
12 ml (2½ teaspoons) salt
3 stalks spring onion
1 egg
30 ml (2 tablespoons) lard
625 ml (1¼ pints) stock (b)

1 chicken stock cube
45 ml (3 tablespoons) dry sherry
30 ml (2 tablespoons) wine vinegar
1 ml (¼ teaspoon) white pepper
15 ml (1 tablespoon) cornflour (blended in 60 ml/4 tablespoons water)
50 g (2 oz) ham

Soak the *bêche de mer* in water overnight. Parboil it in fresh water for 15 minutes, drain and cut it into medium-sized pieces. Fillet the fish, remove all bones carefully, and cut it into similar-sized pieces. Rub them with 5 ml (1 teaspoon) salt. Cut each spring onion stalk in two. Tie each section in a knot (for easy removal). Chop the ham coarsely. Beat the egg lightly for 15 seconds with a fork.

Heat 22 ml (1½ tablespoons) lard in a deep frying pan. Add the spring onions and stir in the hot fat for 30 seconds. Add the stock, balance of salt and stock cube. When the soup has boiled for 1 minute, remove the spring onion. Add the sherry, vinegar, pepper, fish and *bêche de mer*. Allow the contents to simmer for 5 minutes. Add the cornflour mixture. Stir until the soup has thickened somewhat. Add the remainder of the lard, and stir gently.

Pour the soup and fish into a large glass bowl or tureen and

sprinkle the top with the chopped ham. A dish much loved by the elderly.
Serves 6–8.

Double Deep-Fried Quick-Braised Eels
(Adapted from the Lao Cheng Hsing Restaurant, Shanghai.)

1.2–1.35 kg (2½–3 lb) eel (or eels)
45 ml (3 tablespoons) dry sherry
3 stalks spring onion
8–10 slices root ginger
oil for deep-frying
22 ml (1½ tablespoons) soya sauce
15 ml (1 tablespoon) soya paste or hoisin sauce
7 ml (½ tablespoon) sugar
pinch five-spice powder
60 ml (4 tablespoons) stock (b)
½ chicken stock cube
60 ml (4 tablespoons) aromatic vinegar

Ask the fishmonger to gut and clean the eels thoroughly. Parboil them for 5 minutes, and drain. Rub them with the sherry. Leave to dry in an airy spot for 1 hour. Chop the spring onion into small pieces. Cut the ginger into shreds.

Heat the oil in a deep-fryer. Lower the eel in a wire basket to deep-fry for 4 minutes. Remove and drain. Ease the flesh of the eel off the bones. Cut it into regular bite-sized strips. Place them in the wire basket once more, lower them into the hot fat to deep-fry for 1 minute, and drain.

Heat 22 ml (1½ tablespoons) oil in a frying pan. Add the soya sauce, soya paste, sugar, five-spice powder, stock and stock cube. Stir-fry quickly for 45 seconds. Add the strips of eel, sprinkle them with spring onions and turn them in the sauce for 1 minute until every piece of eel is well covered with sauce. Sprinkle the contents with pepper. Turn once more.

Serve in a well-heated dish to be eaten immediately. The shredded ginger should be soaked in vinegar and served in two saucer-sized dishes for the diners to use as dips when required.
Serves 6–8.

Steamed Fish
(Adapted from the Yung Hua Restaurant, Shanghai.)

900 g (2 lb) fish (shad, bream, mullet, salmon, trout, etc)
15 ml (1 tablespoon) salt
6 medium Chinese dried mushrooms
8 slices ham

8 slices bamboo shoots (same   3 slices root ginger
   size as ham)   22 ml (1½ tablespoons) lard
7 ml (½ tablespoon) sugar   45 ml (3 tablespoons) dry
45–60 ml (3–4 tablespoons)   sherry
   pork fat (diced into tiny   3 stalks spring onion
   cubes)

After cleaning the fish thoroughly by brushing it with a stiff brush
under running water, score it half-way through the flesh in 3 hori-
zontal slices along each side. Rub the fish with the salt, and place
it on a large heatproof dish. Soak the mushrooms in water for 20
minutes, remove and discard the stalks. Dress the full length of the
dish neatly with the ham, mushrooms, bamboo shoots and sprinkle
this evenly with the sugar, ginger and diced pork fat. Heat the lard
and sherry together, and as soon as the lard melts, pour the mixture
evenly over the length of the fish. Cut the spring onions into 7.5
cm (3 in) sections, and arrange them on top.

Put the fish in the heatproof dish into a steamer, and steam
vigorously for 15–16 minutes (no longer). The secret of this dish
is in the timing. So long as the fish is not over cooked, which
hardens the flesh and causes it to lose its flavour, or undercooked
and served partly raw, the dish is very fresh and tasty. The diced
pork fat, bamboo shoots, ginger and onion are used only as flavouring during the cooking and are not meant to be eaten. Only the ham
and mushrooms are nibbled at with the fish.
Serves 6–8.

Triple-Fried Crispy Yellow Fish
(Adapted from the Pavilion of the First Rank Scholar, Shanghai.)

0.9–1.2 kg (2–2½ lb) fish   ½ beaten egg
   (ideally yellow fish, a pro- 3 stalks spring onion
   duct of the Yangtze and China 3 sprigs of parsley
   Sea, but almost any medium-   oil for deep frying
   sized fish can be used)   15 ml (1 tablespoon) lard
60 ml (4 tablespoons) plain   pinch five-spice powder
   flour   5 ml (1 teaspoon) salt
60 ml (4 tablespoons) self-rais- pinch black pepper
   ing flour   30 ml (2 tablespoons) dry sherry
60 ml (4 tablespoons) water

Fillet the fish (be sure to remove all the bones) and cut it into small slices. Mix the plain and self-raising flour, water and beaten egg into a batter and coat the fish pieces with it. Chop the spring onions and parsley.

Place half the pieces of fish in a wire basket, deep-fry in hot oil for 2 minutes, and drain. Fry the rest for the same length of time. Finally, deep-fry all the pieces together for 2 minutes, and drain them.

Heat the lard in a frying pan. Add the parsley, spring onion, five-spice powder, salt, pepper, sherry and lard. Stir the ingredients around a few times. Pour the fried fish pieces into the pan, and turn quickly over a high heat with the other ingredients for 1 minute. Serve on a well-heated dish. This is a good starter for a meal, or to eat with rice.
Serves 5–6.

Braised Fish with Bean Curd
(Adapted from the Metropolitan Catering Co, Shanghai.)

675 g (1½ lb) fish (carp, pike, bream, mullet, etc)
7 ml (½ tablespoon) salt
45 ml (3 tablespoons) vegetable oil
2 cakes bean curd
2 slices root ginger
30 ml (2 tablespoons) snow pickle
2 stalks spring onion
30 ml (2 tablespoons) soya sauce
30 ml (2 tablespoons) dry sherry
7 ml (½ tablespoon) sugar
375 ml (¾ pint) stock (b)
½ chicken stock cube
15 ml (1 tablespoon) lard

Clean the fish and cut it into 6 pieces. Rub these with the salt and 7 ml (½ tablespoon) oil. Cut each piece of bean curd into 10 pieces. Chop the ginger and pickle coarsely, and the spring onions into small sections.

Heat the oil in a saucepan or deep frying pan. Add the pieces of fish and the chopped pickle and ginger. Turn them together in the hot oil over a high heat for 1 minute. Add the soya sauce, sherry, sugar, stock and stock cube. When the contents boil, add the bean curd. When they reboil, place a lid over the pan, reduce the heat to low and leave to simmer for 5 minutes. Remove the lid, add the lard, and sprinkle the surface with spring onion. Turn the heat to high for a few seconds, then transfer the contents to a bowl or deep-sided dish and serve. A typical Shanghai home-cooked dinner dish.
Serves 6–8.

Quick-Fried Sliced Fish
(Adapted from the City Catering Co, Hangchow.)

350 g (8 lb) filleted fish
5 ml (1 teaspoon) salt
30 ml (2 tablespoons) cornflour
1 egg-white
2 stalks spring onion
oil for deep-frying
15 ml (1 tablespoon) lard

3 cloves garlic
60 ml (4 tablespoons) stock
  (b)
30 ml (2 tablespoons) dry
  sherry
4 ml (¾ teaspoon) salt

Cut the fish into a dozen slices. Sprinkle and rub these with the salt and 15 ml (1 tablespoon) cornflour, and wet with the beaten egg-white. Mix the remaining cornflour with 30 ml (2 tablespoons) water until well blended. Chop the spring onions into small sections.

Heat the oil in a deep-fryer. Place the batter-coated fish in a wire basket, lower it into the hot oil to fry for 20 seconds, and remove.

Heat the lard in a frying pan. Add the chopped onion, crushed garlic, stock, sherry and salt. When the contents start to boil, add the cornflour mixture. Stir until the sauce has thickened. Return the pieces of sliced fish into the pan. Let them cook in the sauce for 1½ minutes. Serve on a well-heated dish, to be eaten immediately. *Serves 6–8.*

Sliced Fish in Vinegar Sauce
(Adapted from the City Catering Co, Hangchow.)

Repeat the recipe above, but, when preparing the sauce, instead of adding salt, use 45 ml (3 tablespoons) wine vinegar or Chinese aromatic vinegar, plus 5 ml (1 teaspoon) sugar and 5 ml (1 teaspoon) sesame oil, and cook these together with the slices of fish for 1½ minutes after the sauce has been thickened with the cornflour mixture.

Plain Quick-Fried Large Shrimps
(Adapted from the City Catering Co, Soochow.)

350 g (¾ lb) shrimp meat
7 ml (½ tablespoon) salt
22 ml (1½ tablespoons) cornflour
1 egg white
2 slices root ginger
vegetable oil for deep-frying, or

250 ml (½ pint) for shallow-
  frying
15 ml (1 tablespoon) lard
22 ml (1½ tablespoons) dry
  sherry
30 ml (2 tablespoons) stock (b)
10 ml (2 teaspoons) sesame oil

Rub the shrimps with the salt, 15 ml (1 tablespoon) cornflour and beaten egg-white. Mix the remainder of the cornflour with 30 ml (2 tablespoons) water until well blended. Chop the ginger finely.

Heat the oil in a frying pan or deep-fryer. Add the shrimps and fry for no more than 1 minute. Remove and drain.

Heat the lard in a frying pan. Add the ginger and stir it in the fat a few times. Add the sherry, stock and cornflour mixture. Stir until the sauce thickens. Put the shrimps in the pan. Add the sesame oil and stir and turn them around quickly for 30 seconds. Serve immediately on a well-heated dish. The simple flavour and freshness of the shrimps are characteristic of the dish.
Serves 5–6.

Quick-Fried Crab Meat
(Adapted from the City Catering Co, Soochow.)

50–75 g (2–3 oz) lean and fat pork
2 slices root ginger
2 stalks spring onion
30 ml (2 tablespoons) lard
225 g (½ lb) crab meat
15 ml (1 tablespoon) soya sauce
5 ml (1 teaspoon) sugar
30 ml (2 tablespoons) dry sherry
15 ml (1 tablespoon) cornflour blended in 45 ml (3 tablespoons) water
pepper to taste
7 ml (½ tablespoon) salt
30 ml (2 tablespoons) stock (b)

Chop the pork and ginger coarsely. Slice the spring onion into small, thin shavings.

Heat the lard in a frying pan. When hot add the pork and ginger, and stir-fry over a high heat for 1½ minutes. Add the spring onion and crab meat. Mix with the other ingredients and stir-fry for 30 seconds. Add the soya sauce, sugar and sherry. Continue to stir-fry for 1 minute. Reduce the heat to low and add the cornflour mixture. Turn and blend it together with the other ingredients. Sprinkle with pepper to taste, and serve. This is a well-known dish of the Lower Yangtze, and is excellent with rice.
Serves 5–6.

Braised Crab Meat with Bean Curd
(Adapted from the City Catering Co, Soochow.)
Repeat the recipe above, but cut 2 cakes of bean curd into a dozen pieces each and heat them in 125 ml (¼ pint) stock and 15

ml (1 tablespoon) soya sauce for 5 minutes. Put the whole of the previous dish on top of the pieces of bean curd to simmer together for 3 minutes. Serve in a bowl. The incorporation of bean curd enlarges the dish more than two-fold, without detracting from the flavour: a useful variation if extra guests arrive unexpectedly for dinner.

Quick-Fried Shrimps with Tomato and Crispy Rice
(Adapted from the Pavilion of Pavilions Restaurant, Hangchow.)

350 g (¾ lb) large shrimps
5 ml (1 teaspoon) salt
6 medium tomatoes, skinned
90 ml (6 tablespoons) cooked rice
oil for deep-frying
125 ml (¼ pint) chicken stock (a)

22 ml (1½ tablespoons) soya sauce
30 ml (2 tablespoons) dry sherry
5 ml (1 teaspoon) cornflour blended in 45 ml (3 tablespoons) water

Rub the shrimps with the salt. Cut each tomato into quarters. Mould the rice into small cakes, binding these with a little water.

Heat the oil in a deep-fryer. Place the shrimps in a wire basket, fry for 15 seconds and drain. Heat 22 ml (1½ tablespoons) oil in a frying pan. Add the tomatoes and stir them over a high heat for 30 seconds. Pour in the stock, soya sauce and sherry. Add the cornflour mixture. Stir until the stock thickens. Reduce the heat and allow the contents to cook gently for 2 minutes. Add the shrimps, and mix them with the sauce and tomatoes. Meanwhile, deep-fry the rice cakes in hot oil for 2½ minutes and drain.

Place the hot crispy rice cakes at the bottom of a well-heated dish and pour the shrimp and tomato mixture from the frying pan on top of them. The rice should sizzle loudly when the shrimp sauce is poured over it, which adds to the drama of the dish. A colourful and interesting dish to serve at a dinner party.
Serves 6–8.

Vegetables and Bean Curd Dishes

Quick-Fried Winter Mushrooms and Winter Bamboo Shoots

(Quick-Fry of Two Winters—adapted from the Pine Moon in the Spring Breeze Restaurant, Shanghai.)

12 large Chinese dried winter mushrooms

350 g (¾ lb) winter bamboo shoots (or canned bamboo shoots)

10 ml (2 teaspoons) cornflour

45 ml (3 tablespoons) cold stock (b)

37 ml (2½ tablespoons) vegetable oil

22 ml (1½ tablespoons) soya sauce

5 ml (1 teaspoon) sugar

2 ml (½ teaspoon) salt

75 ml (5 tablespoons) mushroom water

15 ml (1 tablespoon) sesame oil

Soak mushrooms in 125 ml (¼ pint) hot water for 30 minutes. Retain the water and remove the mushroom stalks. Cut the bamboo shoots into small, thick, triangular pieces. Mix the cornflour in the cold stock until well blended.

Heat the oil in a medium-sized frying pan. Add the mushrooms and turn them a few times over a high heat. Push them to one side, and add the bamboo shoots. Stir and turn them in the hot oil for 1 minute. Bring over the mushrooms to mix with the bamboo shoots. Sprinkle with the soya sauce, sugar, salt and mushroom water. Turn and stir together for 1 minute. Reduce the heat and leave to cook for 3 minutes. Add the cornflour in stock, and mix it with the other ingredients. As soon as the sauce thickens, sprinkle with sesame oil, and the dish is ready. Serve in a well-heated dish. Because of its subtlety of flavours, the dish is considered a delicacy, suitable for a dinner party or banquet.

Serves 5–6.

Lo-han Tsai, or Buddhists' Hot Vegetable Ensemble

(Adapted from the Pine Moon in the Spring Breeze Restaurant, Shanghai.)

8 medium Chinese dried mushrooms

10 medium-large button mushrooms

100 g (¼ lb) Chinese grass mushrooms

6 strands golden needles (tiger lily buds)

50 g (2 oz) transparent pea-starch noodles

50–75 g (2–3 oz) French beans (or mange tout)

6 asparagus tips

4–5 chestnuts

50 g (2 oz) bean curd skin

60 ml (4 tablespoons) wood ears

75 ml (5 tablespoons) vegetable oil

90 ml (6 tablespoons) mushroom water

7 ml (½ tablespoon) sugar

52 ml (3½ tablespoons) soya sauce

75–100 g (3–4 oz) bamboo shoots

500 ml (1 pint) stock (b)

50–75 g (2–3 oz) broccoli

7 ml (½ tablespoon) salt

50–75 g (2–3 oz) cauliflower

22 ml (1½ tablespoons) hoisin sauce

15 ml (1 tablespoon) cornflour blended in 75 ml (5 table-spoons) water

15 ml (1 tablespoon) sesame oil

Soak the dried mushrooms in 125 ml (¼ pint) hot water for 30 minutes. Retain the water, remove the mushrooms and cut off the stalks. Clean the button mushrooms, cut the caps into quarters and the stalks into halves. Drain the grass mushrooms. Soak the golden needles for 10 minutes, drain them and cut the stems into quarters. Soak the pea-starch noodles for 5 minutes, and drain them. Top and tail the French beans, and remove any tough parts from the asparagus. Boil the chestnuts for 20 minutes, remove the shells and cut each chestnut into quarters. Soak the bean curd skin for 30 minutes and cut it into medium-sized sections; soak the wood ears for 10 minutes, and drain them.

Heat 45 ml (3 tablespoons) oil in a large saucepan or casserole. When hot add the dried mushrooms. After turning them around a few times, add all the other mushrooms, and stir-fry them together over a high heat for 2 minutes. Add the wood ears, bean curd skin and golden needles, followed by the mushroom water, sugar, soya sauce and bamboo shoots, and bring them to boil. Pour in half the stock, and add the transparent noodles. Stir and mix the ingredients together. When the contents start to boil, reduce the heat and simmer for 10 minutes.

Meanwhile heat the remaining oil in another saucepan. Add the chestnuts, asparagus, French beans and broccoli. Sprinkle them with salt, and stir-fry over a high heat for 3 minutes. Add the cauliflower, hoisin sauce and the balance of the stock. Bring the contents to the boil. Reduce the heat and allow to simmer for 5 minutes. Stir in the cornflour mixture. When the sauce in the pan has thickened, pour the contents into the saucepan containing the mushrooms. Mix the ingredients of the two saucepans together and allow them to simmer for 5–6 minutes. Sprinkle with sesame oil.

Serve in a large tureen or in the casserole in which it has cooked. This is an excellent dish to consume with rice. In China, the 'ensemble' of vegetables sometimes takes the place of meat, if the latter is not readily available. The dried vegetables—particularly the golden needles—give the dish its characteristic musty, woody flavour.

Serves 8–10.

Sweet and Sour Cucumber
(Adapted from the Metropolitan Catering Co, Shanghai.)

1 medium-large cucumber
3 slices root ginger
9 ml (1¾ teaspoons) salt
15 ml (1 tablespoon) sesame oil

22 ml (1¼ tablespoons) sugar
22 ml (1½ tablespoons) wine vinegar

Cut the cucumber into medium-sized sections. Cut each section vertically in half. Scrape away any seeds and pulp. Now cut each section of cucumber vertically into 3–4 strips. Finely chop or grate the ginger. Rub the cucumber pieces with the salt, ginger and sesame oil. Leave them to season for 30 minutes. Meanwhile mix the sugar and vinegar in a bowl until well blended. Pour this mixture over the cucumber, turn the pieces until well coated and rearrange them neatly before serving.

An excellent side-dish with any rice or succulent food.
Serves 4–6.

Quick-Fried Shrimps and Cucumber
(Adapted from the Metropolitan Catering Co, Shanghai.)

2 slices root ginger
1 medium cucumber
225 g (½ lb) fresh shrimps
5 ml (1 teaspoon) salt
2.5 ml (½ teaspoon) sesame oil

22 ml (1½ tablespoons) soya sauce
5 ml (1 teaspoon) sugar
30 ml (2 tablespoons) dry sherry
37 ml (2½ tablespoons) lard

Chop the ginger. Cut the cucumber into 5 cm (2 in) sections, cut these vertically in half and then cut each piece vertically again into 3–4 strips. Wash the shrimps thoroughly, remove the heads and legs, but leave the shells on. Rub the shrimps with salt, ginger and sesame oil. Mix the soya sauce with the sugar and sherry in a small bowl.

Heat the lard in a frying pan over a high heat. Add the shrimps, turn them over 2–3 times and add the cucumber. Turn this over and stir-fry with the shrimps for 30 seconds. Pour in the soya-sugar-sherry mixture. Stir the contents together for 1 minute and serve immediately. The diners should remove the shrimp shells with their teeth as they eat. A dish often used to start a family dinner.

Serves 6–8.

Stir-Fried Spinach in Shrimp Sauce with Bean Curd Cheese
(Adapted from the Metropolitan Catering Co, Shanghai.)

15 ml (1 tablespoon) dried shrimps
675 g (1½ lb) leaf spinach
2 cloves garlic
52 ml (3½ tablespoons) vegetable oil
5 ml (1 teaspoon) salt
10 ml (2 teaspoons) bean-curd cheese
15 ml (1 tablespoon) shrimp sauce
22 ml (1½ tablespoons) lard

Soak the dried shrimps in warm water for 30 minutes, and drain them. Clean the spinach leaves, eliminating the tougher stems and discoloured leaves. Crush and chop the garlic.

Heat the oil in a large frying pan or saucepan over a high heat. Add the shrimps. Stir them in the hot oil for 1 minute to flavour the oil. Add the spinach, and turn it quickly with the oil and shrimps until every leaf is well coated. Sprinkle the spinach with the salt, bean curd cheese and shrimp sauce, and continue to stir-fry over a high heat for 1 minute. Reduce the heat to medium, add the garlic and allow the contents to cook for 1 minute more. Add the lard. When it has all melted, turn the leaves over 2–3 times. (Chicken fat or butter can be used instead of lard for 'glossing' the spinach just before dishing out.) Serve immediately.

Serves 6–8.

Braised Hearts of Spring Cabbage or Spring Greens
(Adapted from the City Catering Co, Soochow.)

3 small spring cabbages (about 675 g/1½ lb in all)

52 ml (3½ tablespoons) vegetable oil

5 ml (1 teaspoon) salt

45 ml (3 tablespoons) soya sauce

90 ml (6 tablespoons) stock (b)

5 ml (1 teaspoon) sugar

15 ml (1 tablespoon) lard or chicken fat

Cut the cabbage into 3.75 cm (1½ in) thick slices, removing any rough stems and discoloured leaves.

Heat the oil in a saucepan. Add the cabbage, sprinkle with salt and stir over a high heat for 1 minute. Reduce the heat to medium and sprinkle the contents of the pan with the soya sauce, stock and sugar. Stir and turn for 1½ minutes. Reduce the heat to low, cover the saucepan and leave the contents to cook gently for 5–6 minutes. Add the lard or chicken fat and turn the leaves over a few more times.

Serve in a large bowl or deep-sided dish. The flavour can be varied by adding dried shrimps to the oil (as in the recipe on page 178) during the initial part of the cooking.

Serves 6–8.

Quick-Fried Bean Sprouts
(Adapted from the City Catering Co, Soochow.)

450 g (1 lb) bean sprouts

4–5 stalks spring onion

2 cloves garlic

45 ml (3 tablespoons) vegetable oil

5 ml (1 teaspoon) salt

15 ml (1 tablespoon) soya sauce

2.5 ml (½ teaspoon) sugar

15 ml (1 tablespoon) lard or chicken fat

Wash and dry the bean sprouts thoroughly. Cut the spring onions into small sections and divide them equally into green and white parts. Crush and chop the garlic.

Heat the oil in a large frying pan or saucepan. Add the white parts of the spring onions. Stir them in the hot oil for 30 seconds to flavour it. Add the bean sprouts and sprinkle them with the salt. Turn and stir-fry them over a high heat for 1½ minutes. Add the soya sauce, sugar and garlic. Continue to stir-fry over a high heat for 1½ minutes. Add the lard and the green parts of the spring

onion. Turn and stir for a further 30 seconds. Eat fresh from the
pan: heat is an integral part of the flavour of this dish.
Serves 6–8.

Quick Double-Fried Eggplant (Aubergine) in Soya Paste Sauce
(Adapted from the Metropolitan Catering Co, Shanghai.)

*675 g (1½ lb) eggplants (auber-
gines)*
2 slices root ginger
*vegetable oil for shallow-frying
(about 250 ml/½ pint) or
deep-frying*
22 ml (1½ tablespoons) lard
*22 ml (1½ tablespoons) soya
paste*

*15 ml (1 tablespoon) soya
sauce*
2.5 ml (½ teaspoon) chilli sauce
2.5 ml (½ teaspoon) sugar
30 ml (2 tablespoons) stock (b)
*30 ml (2 tablespoons) dry
sherry*

Cut the eggplants into medium-sized, thin strips. Score shallow
criss-cross cuts over the surfaces at intervals. Chop the ginger
coarsely.

Heat the oil in the deep-fryer (or in a frying pan if shallow-frying)
until a crumb sizzles when dropped into it. Add the eggplant strips
and stir them in the hot oil over a high heat for 30–40 seconds.
Remove and drain.

Heat the lard in a frying pan. Add the ginger. Stir it around a
few times over a medium heat. Add the soya paste, soya sauce,
chilli sauce, sugar and stock and mix with the fat into a thick
paste. Add the eggplant and turn and mix it with the sauce until
every strip is well covered. Reduce the heat to low, and leave to cook
for 2 minutes. Sprinkle the contents with sherry, and increase the
heat to high. Stir-fry quickly for 15 seconds and serve immediately.
This is another case where the heat is an essential part of the dish.
Serves 5–6.

Braised Winter Melon
(Adapted from the Metropolitan Catering Co, Shanghai.)

*675–900 g (1½–2 lb) winter
melon or marrow*
15 ml (1 tablespoon) cornflour
90 ml (6 tablespoons) milk
oil for deep-frying

22 ml (1½ tablespoons) lard
125 ml (¼ pint) stock (b)
10 ml (2 teaspoons) salt
15 ml (1 tablespoon) butter

After removing the skin, pips and pulp of the melon or marrow, cut it into medium-sized thin strips. Score shallow criss-cross cuts over the surface of each strip. Mix the cornflour with the milk until well blended.

Heat the oil in a deep-fryer. When a crumb dropped into it sizzles, add the winter melon strips. Deep-fry for 3 minutes. Remove and drain.

Melt the lard in a frying pan. Add the stock, followed by the winter melon. Sprinkle with salt. Leave to simmer for 3 minutes, covered. Remove the lid, and add the butter and cornflour and milk mixture. Turn the winter melon strips in the sauce until evenly covered. Leave the contents to simmer together for 1 minute and serve in a large deep-sided dish. Another excellent dish to eat with rice.

Serves 6–8.

Lotus Nut Soup
(Adapted from the Mo U Tsai Kitchen, Shanghai.)

225 g ($\frac{1}{2}$ lb) dried lotus nuts
225 g ($\frac{1}{2}$ lb) candied lotus nuts
60 ml (4 tablespoons) mixed glacé fruit
45 ml (3 tablespoons) sugar
45–60 ml (3–4 tablespoons) cream
30 ml (2 tablespoons) cornflour blended in 125 ml ($\frac{1}{4}$ pint) milk

Parboil the dried lotus nuts for 20 minutes. Drain, remove the skins, and grind them in a blender.

Add 625 ml (1$\frac{1}{4}$ pints) water to the ground lotus nuts, and bring them to a gentle boil in a heavy saucepan. Simmer gently for 30 minutes with an asbestos sheet inserted underneath the pan. Stir with a wooden spoon every few seconds. Add the candied lotus nuts, glacé fruit and sugar. Simmer for a further 10 minutes. Add the cream and the cornflour and milk mixture. Stir and simmer for 4 minutes, when the soup should have become quite thick. Serve in small individual bowls. This sweet dessert acts as a welcome change from the usual long series of savoury dishes in a Chinese meal.

Serves 6–8.

Braised Tou Fu (Bean Curd) with Tomatoes
(Adapted from the City Catering Co, Soochow.)

6–8 medium firm tomatoes
2 cakes bean curd
37 ml (2½ tablespoons) vegetable oil
2.5 ml (½ teaspoon) salt

5 ml (1 teaspoon) sugar
30 ml (2 tablespoons) soya
   sauce
60 ml (4 tablespoons) stock (b)
15 ml (1 tablespoon) lard

Blanch the tomatoes and remove the skins. Cut each into 4 slices.
Cut each bean curd cake into a dozen pieces.

Heat the oil in a large frying pan over a medium heat. Spread
the tomatoes and pieces of bean curd cake over the pan. Sprinkle
them with the salt, sugar, soya sauce and stock. Turn the ingredients
over 3–4 times in a couple of minutes. Add the lard, and cook for
a further 2 minutes. This is very much a 'dish of the people',
excellent with rice and other savoury dishes.
Serves 4–6.

Green Pepper and Dried Bean Curd Salad
(Adapted from the City Catering Co, Shanghai.)

3 medium green peppers
3 cakes dried bean curd
5 ml (1 teaspoon) salt
7 ml (½ tablespoon) sugar

7 ml (½ tablespoon) soya sauce
15 ml (1 tablespoon) stock (b)
15 ml (1 tablespoon) sesame oil

Cut the peppers into large double-matchstick-thick shreds (removing
the seeds). Cut the dried bean curd into similar-sized shreds. Place
them separately in large bowls or basins. Pour boiling water over
them. Leave the peppers to soak for 2 minutes, and the bean curd
to soak for 15 minutes. Drain them thoroughly.

Place the shredded peppers and bean curd pieces in a large deep-
sided dish. Sprinkle them with salt and sugar. Mix the soya sauce,
stock and sesame oil in a small bowl. Pour the mixture evenly over
the salad and toss just before eating. Although a simple dish, it is
much beloved by the locals.
Serves 5–6.

Rice, Noodles and Pasta

Shanghai Chicken Rice-Gruel

(This was originally an item of food cooked and served from street-stalls—now adapted from the Ling Foo Chai Restaurant, Shanghai.)

1 medium chicken (about 1.2–1.35 kg/2½–3 lb)
15 ml (3 teaspoons) salt
15 ml (1 tablespoon) sesame oil
22 ml (1½ tablespoons) lard

225 g (½ lb) rice
2 litres (4 pints) chicken stock (boil and simmer 1 chicken carcase for 1 hour, adding 2 chicken stock cubes)

Sauce

30 ml (2 tablespoons) chopped spring onions
30 ml (2 tablespoons) sliced and chopped root ginger
45 ml (3 tablespoons) soya sauce

30 ml (2 tablespoons) dry sherry or Chinese yellow wine
45 ml (3 tablespoons) sesame oil

Clean the chicken and plunge it into boiling water for 5 minutes; remove it from the water and drain. Allow the chicken to cool slightly, then rub it with the salt and sesame oil, and leave to season for 1 hour. Parboil the giblets (liver, kidney and heart) for 10 minutes, drain and cut them into thin slices.

Place the chicken in a large heavy pot or casserole. Add the lard, rice, chicken stock and giblets. Bring it to the boil. Insert an asbestos sheet under the pan and simmer gently for 1½ hours.

Chop the chicken through the bone into bite-sized pieces. Divide them among 6–8 saucers or small dishes. Mix the sauce ingredients in a bowl, and pour the mixture over the chicken pieces in the dishes. Each diner is served with a bowl of rice-gruel from the casserole, which he eats with his portion of chicken. The strength of the sauce makes the plain cooked chicken particularly palatable, and the copious amount of rice-gruel, half eaten and half drunk, is warming and refreshing.

Serves 6–8.

Vegetable Rice

(Another 'dish of the people' from the Mei Wei Ch'ai or Home of
Good Flavours Restaurant, Shanghai.)

450 g (1 lb) long grain rice   30 ml (2 tablespoons) lard
550 g (1¼ lb) spring greens or 12 ml (2½ teaspoons) salt
green cabbage

Soak the rice in water for 1 hour and drain it. Remove all the discoloured leaves from the cabbage, or spring greens, and cut away
the tough roots. Cut the leaves into 2.5 cm (1 in) slices.

Heat the lard in a large heavy pot or casserole. Add the cabbage,
or greens, and the salt. Turn the leaves in the hot oil for about 3
minutes until well covered. Pour in the rice, and add 500 ml (1 pint)
water. Bring contents to the boil. Reduce the heat to low and
simmer for 10–12 minutes. Turn the heat off and allow the contents
to continue cooking in the remaining heat, tightly covered, for the
next 10–12 minutes. Serve like ordinary rice at a Chinese meal as an
accompaniment to two or more other dishes, some stir-fried, others
stewed.
Serves 6.

Shrimp Soup Noodles

(Also known as the Three Shrimp Noodles; adapted from the
Chuan Lan-Ting Pavilion Restaurant, Shanghai.)

675 g (1½ lb) shrimps (fresh or   30 ml (2 tablespoons) soya
frozen)   sauce
750 ml (1½ pints) stock (b)   30 ml (2 tablespoons) dry
3 slices root ginger   sherry
7 ml (½ tablespoon) salt   675 g (1½ lb) Chinese noodles
30 ml (2 tablespoons) dried   (freshly made if available,
shrimps   otherwise use egg-noodles or
2 stalks spring onion   spaghetti)
30 ml (2 tablespoons) lard

Wash the shrimps, remove and retain the heads, and shell the bodies.
Add the heads to the stock to simmer together with the ginger and
salt for 30 minutes for the shrimp soup. Strain off and discard
the ginger and shrimp heads. Soak the dried shrimps in water for 2
hours to soften them. Coarsely chop the spring onions.

Heat the lard in a frying pan. Drain the dried shrimps, add them
to the hot fat and stir-fry for 1½ minutes. Add the chopped spring
onion and continue to stir-fry over a medium heat for 2 minutes.

Add the fresh shrimps, soya sauce and sherry. Mix and stir the contents together for 3 minutes, and remove from the heat.

Put the noodles in a large pan of boiling water to boil for 4–5 minutes and drain them (15 minutes for spaghetti).

Divide the noodles among 4–5 bowls. Heat the shrimp soup, bringing it quickly to the boil, and pour it into the bowls of noodles, leaving some noodles to rise above the soup. Return the frying pan over the heat; as the contents start to sizzle, pour an appropriate amount of them over the noodles and soup in the bowls. *Serves 4–5.*

Noodles with Braised Eel and Shrimps
(Adapted from the Chwan Yuan Restaurant, Hangchow.)

90 ml (6 tablespoons) shelled shrimps (fresh or frozen)
5 ml (1 teaspoon) salt
15 ml (1 tablespoon) cornflour
250 ml (½ pint) chicken stock (a)
1 medium eel (about 675 g/1½ lb)
2 slices root ginger, chopped
10 ml (2 teaspoons) salt
1 medium onion
oil for deep-frying

5 ml (1 teaspoon) sugar
30 ml (2 tablespoons) dry sherry
37 ml (2½ tablespoons) soya sauce
675 g (1½ lb) Chinese noodles (freshly made if available, otherwise use egg-noodles or spaghetti)
1 chicken stock cube
15 ml (1 tablespoon) lard

Rub the shrimps with 5 ml (1 teaspoon) salt and the cornflour, and leave to season for 15 minutes. Heat 250 ml (½ pint) water. When it boils add the shrimps. As soon as the water reboils, remove two thirds of the shrimps with a perforated spoon. Pour the stock into the pan and simmer the contents together for 20 minutes.

Rub the eel with the chopped ginger and 10 ml (2 teaspooons) salt. Leave to season for 1 hour. Chop the eel into six sections, and cut the flesh from the bones into medium-sized thick strips. Cut the onion into thin slices.

Place the eel pieces in a wire basket, deep-fry them in hot oil for 3 minutes and drain them. Heat 30 ml (2 tablespoons) oil in a frying pan. Add the onion, and stir-fry over a high heat for 1½ minutes. Add the eel pieces and sprinkle them with the sugar, sherry and soya sauce. Turn them around a few times, and leave to braise over a low heat for 2–3 minutes.

Meanwhile, having boiled the noodles for 2 minutes, drain them, and add them to heat in a smaller saucepan with the shrimp stock, stock cube and lard for 3 minutes.

Divide the noodles-in-stock equally among 4–5 bowls. Sprinkle with plain boiled shrimps and arrange pieces of eel in the centre. Pour the juices from the frying pan over each portion. The appeal of this dish is the contrast between the freshness of the plain boiled shrimps, and the rich brown strips of eel.
Serves 5–6.

Cold Tossed Noodles

(Adapted from the Ssi Rou Choong or Spring-Like Noodles Shop, Shanghai.)
This is essentially a noodle salad with a vegetable base, but it may be garnished with meat and seafood savouries.

450 g (1 lb) noodles (or spa-
    ghetti)

22 ml (1½ tablespoons) veg-
    etable oil

Garnish

60 ml (4 tablespoons) fresh,
    shelled shrimps

6 large Chinese dried mushrooms
225 (½ lb) small-cut spare-ribs

For Braising Spare-ribs

52 ml (3½ tablespoons) veg-
    etable oil
2.5 ml (½ teaspoon) salt
30 ml (2 tablespoons) soya
    sauce

5 ml (1 teaspoon) chilli sauce
4 ml (¾ teaspoon) hoisin sauce
7 ml (½ tablespoon) sugar
15 ml (1 tablespoon) tomato
    purée

For Tossing with the Noodles

6 slices root ginger (cut diag-
    onally across the roots)
5 ml (1 teaspoon) sugar
10 ml (2 teaspoons) sesame oil
225 g (½ lb) bean sprouts
30 ml (2 tablespoons) soya
    sauce
5 ml (1 teaspoon) sugar

45 ml (3 tablespoons) water
30 ml (2 tablespoons) sesame
    paste
22 ml (1½ tablespoons) sesame
    oil
22 ml (1½ tablespoons) best
    vinegar

Plunge the noodles into a large pan of boiling water to loosen and boil for 5 minutes (10 minutes for spaghetti). Drain, and plunge them into cold water to wash away any starch and thus prevent the noodles from sticking together. Drain and plunge them again into boiling water to boil for a further 3–4 minutes (7–8 for spaghetti). Drain, separate the strands and sprinkle them with vegetable oil to keep them separate as they cool.

Cut the ginger slices into long matchstick-thick shreds. Rub with the sugar and sesame oil, and leave to season for 30 minutes. Plunge the bean sprouts into boiling water for 3 seconds. Drain and plunge them into cold water. Drain again thoroughly.

Heat the soya sauce, sugar and water. Stir once or twice as soon as the mixture boils. Remove from the heat. Mix the sesame oil with sesame paste. When the soya sauce and sugar mixture has cooled a little, add it to the sesame oil and paste and blend well.

Soak the mushrooms in water for 20 minutes. Remove the stalks, and cut the caps in half. Boil the shrimp meat in water for 2 minutes and drain them. Chop the spare-ribs into small sections, and heat the vegetable oil in a frying pan. Add the small-cut spare-ribs, sprinkle with the salt, and stir-fry over a high heat for 2 minutes. Add the soya sauce, chilli sauce, hoisin sauce, sugar and tomato purée, and continue to stir-fry over a high heat for 3 minutes. Remove from the pan, and place in a bowl to cool. Meanwhile add 15 ml (1 tablespoon) vegetable oil and 15 ml (1 tablespoon) soya sauce to the pan. Stir them together over a medium heat. Add the mushrooms to braise and fry over a medium heat for 4 minutes, turning the caps over once. Remove and place on a dish to cool.

Spread the noodles on a well-heated, large, deep-sided dish. Sprinkle them evenly with the vinegar and shredded ginger. Arrange the poached bean sprouts all round the sides, and pour the soya and sesame paste mixture into the centre. Decorate the top of the sprouts and noodles with the shrimps, small-cut spare-ribs and mushrooms.

When the dish is brought to the table, the host or the diners themselves mix and toss all the ingredients together, and place them in separate bowls to eat. A good dish for the summer or to start a multi-course meal.
Serves 4–5.

Braised Noodles with Chicken and Heart of Cabbage
(Adapted from the Lu Yang Hsiang Restaurant, Shanghai.)

350 g (¾ lb) fine noodles or vermicelli

100 g (¼ lb) cooked breast of chicken

225 g (½ lb) tender heart of cabbage (or celery)

30 ml (2 tablespoons) vegetable oil

5 ml (1 teaspoon) salt

375 ml (¾ pint) stock (b)

7 ml (½ tablespoon) lard

30 ml (2 tablespoons) soya sauce

Boil the noodles or vermicelli for 3–5 minutes, rinse them under running water and drain. Cut the chicken into thin slices. Cut the heart of the cabbage into 1.8 cm (¾ in) pieces.

Heat the lard in a deep frying pan. Add the cabbage, sprinkle it with the salt, and stir-fry it over a high heat for 1½ minutes. Pour in the stock; when the contents reboil, add the noodles or vermicelli. On the second reboiling add 7 ml (½ tablespoon) lard and the soya sauce and chicken. Reduce the heat, cover the pan and leave to simmer for 3 minutes. Serve either from a large tureen or in individual bowls.

Serves 3–4.

Steamed Buns Stuffed with Crab-Egg Fillings, or Hsia Huang Paotzu
(Adapted from the Fu-Choon Tea House, Yangchow.)

Dough Casing

12 g (½ oz) dried yeast or brewer's yeast

15 ml (1 tablespoon) sugar

375 ml (¾ pint) lukewarm water

450 g (1 lb) plain flour

Filling

1–2 slices root ginger

22 ml (1½ tablespoons) lard

45 ml (3 tablespoons) crab eggs (the clusters of red or orange substances under the shells)

60 ml (4 tablespoons) crab meat

125 ml (¼ pint) stock (b)

1 ml (¼ teaspoon) salt

25 g (1 oz) pork rind

50 g (2 oz) lean and fat pork

22 ml (1½ tablespoons) vegetable oil

2.5 ml (½ teaspoon) sugar

15 ml (1 tablespoon) soya sauce

15 ml (1 tablespoon) dry sherry

To prepare the filling, shred and chop the ginger. Heat the lard in a small frying pan. Add the ginger and stir-fry for 1 minute. Add the crab eggs and crab meat, sprinkle with the salt, and stir-fry them together for 2 minutes. Remove from the heat.

Heat the stock in a small saucepan. Chop the pork rind into small pieces and add it to the stock. Simmer gently until the liquid in the pan has been reduced to a quarter of its original volume.

Chop the pork into small pieces. Heat the oil in a small saucepan. Add the pork and stir-fry for 1½ minutes over a high heat. Add the sugar, soya sauce and sherry. Continue to stir-fry for 1½ minutes. Pour the reduced stock and pork rind mixture into the pan, stir and cook over a high heat for 2 minutes. Remove from the heat.

Mix the contents of all three pans together in a bowl, and leave to cool in a fridge. When cold it should become a firm gelatinous mixture, ready for use as filling.

Place a dough disc on the palm of your left hand. Add 10 ml (2 teaspoons) filling mixture and place in the centre of the dough. Gather up the sides of the dough gently, wrapping them over the filling (the uncooked 'bun' should be a squat cone shape, some-what fatter than it is tall). Place the buns, a little apart, on a tray or heatproof dish lined with greaseproof paper. Put the tray into a steamer, and steam vigorously for 15 minutes.

These Steamed Buns or Paotzu should be eaten as a snack. For further flavouring, a dish or two of good quality Chinese aromatic vinegar should be placed on the table for the consumer to wet the bun with after the first bite.

Makes 18.

Paotzu with Pork, Bamboo Shoots and Snow Pickle Filling
(Adapted from the Fu-Choon Tea House, Yangchow.)

Dough Casing
Use the same ingredients and method as on page 188.

Filling

225 g (½ lb) lean and fat pork
100 g (¼ lb) bamboo shoots
22 ml (1½ tablespoons) snow pickle

30 ml (2 tablespoons) lard
22 ml (1½ tablespoons) soya sauce
5 ml (1 teaspoon) sugar

Chop the pork into very small cubes, and trim the bamboo shoots into similar-sized cubes. Chop the snow pickle into small pieces.

Heat the lard in a small frying pan. Add the pork to stir-fry over a high heat for 2 minutes. Add the soya sauce and sugar, and continue to stir-fry for 1 minute. Add the pickles and bamboo shoots, and stir-fry for 2 minutes.

Make the dough casing using the same ingredients, method, and measurements as in the recipe on page 188. Wrap in the same manner, and steam the buns for 15 minutes as before. Serve as a snack to be eaten hot or cold.
Makes 18.

Soup-Filled Steamed Buns with Pickle and Salt Pork

Dough Casing

Use the same ingredients and method as in the recipe on page 188, except for adding 22 ml (1½ tablespoons) lard when preparing the casing.

Filling

225 g (½ lb) salt pork	*7 ml (½ tablespoon) soya sauce*
100 g (¼ lb) pork skin	*5 ml (1 teaspoon) sugar*
250 ml (½ pint) water	*30 ml (2 tablespoons) snow*
2 young leeks	*pickle*
30 ml (2 tablespoons) lard	

Cut the pork into very small cubes. Cut the pork skin into small squares. Heat them together in the water, and simmer gently for 45 minutes or until the liquid has been reduced to a quarter of its original volume. Remove the pieces of rind with a pair of chopsticks or tongs. Clean the leeks and cut them into small slices. Add the lard, soya sauce, sugar and leeks to the pan. Increase the heat, stir-fry for 2 minutes, add the snow pickle and continue to stir-fry 1 minute. Pour the contents into a bowl with the pork and pork soup and leave to cool and solidify into a jelly in the refrigerator. When the liquid in the dish has jelled, the filling is ready for stuffing into the dough casing.

Wrap the filling in the same manner as in the previous recipe, using a dessertspoon to scoop up the meat-and-jelly filling. Place the stuffed buns in a steamer, and steam vigorously for 12 minutes (3 minutes shorter than in the previous recipes).

Serve as a snack or starter. As the buns are full of soup, it is advisable to have a bowl ready to catch the drips when biting into the buns!
Makes 12.

Fish Soup Noodles from Chingkiang

675 g (1½ lb) filleted fish (bass, mullet, bream, cod, carp, trout, salmon, whiting, halibut, sole, etc)
100 g (¼ lb) bamboo shoots
100 g (¼ lb) heart of cabbage
6–8 medium Chinese dried mushrooms
450 g (1 lb) noodles or spaghetti

45 ml (3 tablespoons) vegetable oil
22 ml (1½ tablespoons) soya sauce
30 ml (2 tablespoons) dry sherry
5 ml (1 teaspoon) sugar
7 ml (½ tablespoon) cornflour blended in 45 ml (3 tablespoons) water

Stock

1 large fish head (675–900 g/ 1½–2 lb)
1 fish tail (225 g/½ lb)
37 ml (2½ tablespoons) lard

3 slices root ginger
1 medium onion, sliced
10 ml (2 teaspoons) salt

Chop the filleted fish finely (be sure to remove all bones and membranes). Cut the bamboo shoots into medium-sized thin slices. Cut heart of cabbage into medium-sized pieces, removing the stalk and any discoloured leaves. Soak the mushrooms for 20 minutes and remove the stalks. Parboil the noodles for 4–5 minutes (or the spaghetti for 12 minutes), drain and rinse them under running water.

Prepare the stock by frying the fish head and tail in lard with the ginger and onion for 8–10 minutes over a medium heat until quite brown. Add 1½–2 litres (3–4 pints) water. Bring to the boil and simmer gently for 20 minutes. Add the salt and simmer for a further 5 minutes. Strain through a filter and a cheesecloth and retain the stock.

Add the cabbage and noodles to the stock in a large saucepan. Bring to the boil and simmer them gently together for 5 minutes.

Heat the oil in a frying pan. Add the mushrooms and bamboo shoots. Stir-fry them for 1½ minutes, drain and put aside. Add the chopped fish. Stir it to mix with the hot oil for 1½ minutes; add the soya sauce, sherry and sugar and continue to stir for 2 minutes.

Add the cornflour mixture to the fish. Leave it to cook over a gentle heat for 3–4 minutes.

Divide the noodles and cabbage among 4–5 bowls, and pour the soup (reheated for 30 seconds) over them. Top with chopped fish, bamboo shoots and mushrooms. This is a favourite dish in Chingkiang during the late spring.

Serves 5–6.

Szechuan and West-China Cooking

Szechuan and West-China Cooking

Szechuan is the great heartland of China, a uniquely self-contained geographical region with a history, unity and flavour unlike any other. Here in the Upper Yangtze is a landlocked basin, surrounded by mountain ranges, towards the east end of which the great river pours downstream out through its famous Yangtze Gorges. In this region of vast fertile plains and humid climate dwell over a hundred million people—this is probably the most populous upper river region in the world. Even the Mississippi and the Amazon, the Nile and the Ganges, can hardly compare with this, whether in terms of sheer size of population or the intensity of agricultural cultivation.

In its eastward flow to the sea, the Yangtze can be roughly divided into four regions. Its watershed is in the high-altitude marshy plateau of Chinghai; as the snows melt and the river gathers volume, it flows into the basin of Szechuan; there it bursts out through the Gorges into its Middle Reaches, which is the region of the Great Lakes, among them Tung Ting Hu, Pao Yang Hu and Tai Hu (Hu denotes lake), and which is also known as the 'Rice Bowl' of China (the province of Hunan, where Chairman Mao was born, is a part of this region). Finally, further to the east the Yangtze pushes towards its delta, which is marked near its point of entry into the sea by the city-port of Shanghai, one of the biggest metropolises in the world. Indeed, the banks of the Yangtze as it flows eastward are dotted at regular intervals with bustling river-ports and populous cities, such as Yangchow (famous for its cuisine), Nanking (a former capital), Chingkian (well-known for its vinegar), the other busy river-port of Kiukiang, Wuhan (the industrial complex and communication centre of China) and, further up the river, Chungking. Chungking became the capital of China for a period during the Second World War, but it is only an ordinary, bustling riverside town compared with Szechuan's best-loved and historically best-known city, Chengtu.

Chengtu first came into prominence during the period of the

G*

Three Kingdoms, soon after the time of Christ, when one of the most famous prime ministers of Chinese history, Kung Ming (also known as Chu-ke-lian) planned his last vain attempt to restore the glories of the Han Dynasty. There, in his epistles to his king, he described the wealth and resources of Szechuan and the myriad talents of its people which he had gathered behind him. Ever since then, Szechuan in the Chinese mind not only denotes a geographical unity but also holds strong historical associations. Many consider the city of Chengtu a second Peking. Behind its ancient walls and atmosphere of cultivated tranquillity, great dreams were hatched, and the achievements of empires initiated.

Szechuan is over a thousand miles from the sea, and until recently the Yangtze was its only means of contact with the outside world. Before Liberation the province was ruled by a succession of warlords, and the social stratification of the province was strictly feudal, consisting in the main of peasants and landlords, with an overlay of ruling mandarins (landlord magistrates and governors with pretensions to scholarship). Without a substantial middle class to provide elements of mobility and liberalism, Szechuan's relationship with the rest of China and the outside world was heavily dependent on the capital, Peking. Hence a strong Peking or 'official' influence is detectable in the cookery, especially in the extravagant formal dishes for special occasions. In the past, the most lavish dinners, called Kwang Yien, were prepared for inter-mandarin entertainments and receptions and on such occasions the chefs could be as extravagant as they pleased; the licence gave them a chance to indulge in their creative fancies, though within the limits of tradition. On the other hand, apart from these banquet dishes, all the other culinary products of the province can be termed 'native dishes', and were derived from the peasantry. These recipes were evolved or created by the ordinary people for themselves, with what material resources they had at hand, and from the traditions they had inherited.

Because of the region's distance from sea-traders, and the humidity of its climate, the preservation of food became an essential consideration, not only in the storage of ingredients but also in their preparation. Before the advent of freezing, food was kept by salting, drying, spicing, pickling and smoking. These methods of preservation impart a strong flavour to the food. Hence, in Szechuan, preserved products are also widely used as flavouring agents.

In addition to the distinctive tastes of these preserved foods, the Szechuan palate has become attuned to the more pungently flavoured vegetables, such as onions, spring onions, garlic, ginger, pepper, chilli (or Szechuan fagara), as well as some of the aromatic, nutty ones—peanuts, sesame seeds, oil and sesame butter. When these are used in conjunction with the salty soya-bean products— soya sauce, soya paste, bean-curd cheese and fermented salted black beans—they produce a piquant spiciness which is characteristic of many Szechuan dishes. It may be that this hot, spicy cooking, which is often capable of bringing a sweat to the brow of the consumer, is essential to healthy living in clammy Szechuan. Perhaps one could even add that the hot, strong, salty flavours of Szechuan cooking not only preserve the food but also help to preserve the man!

One of the characteristics of Szechuan cuisine is its awareness of the aromatic. Aromatic vinegar is often used, and the expression 'ma la' indicates the use of chilli in conjunction with nutty products such as toasted ground rice, peanuts, sesame seeds, sesame paste or butter, or sesame oil. When chilli is used in conjunction with aromatic vinegar the former becomes even more potent. Aromatic ground rice and sesame seeds are often used in coating meat which is to be deep-fried or stir-fried; sesame paste or butter is frequently the principal ingredient in sauces. In these latter instances, when chilli is added along with soya sauce or soya paste under the nutty aromatic covering, the effect of 'ma la', so typical of Szechuan food, is produced.

Because the bulk of Szechuan's population are peasants who derive their livelihood directly from the land, a wide variety of herbs and plants are naturally incorporated into the cooking, apart from the conventional Five Spices which are used throughout China. This closeness to the Good Earth is reflected in the frequent use of mushrooms, both wild and cultivated, and Wood Ears (tree fungi). Throughout Szechuan, bamboos of all types grow in great pro-fusion (after all, western Szechuan is 'panda country'). Bamboo shoots are selected with greater discrimination, and cooked with greater care and refinement, here than anywhere else in the country.

Anyone who has developed a taste for Szechuan cuisine will have noticed that many Szechuan dishes have a more chewy texture than those from elsewhere in China. This texture is often achieved by frying or stir-frying foods until quite dry, or even crusty, before the flavouring sauces and ingredients are added for a last turn and toss together over strong heat. Another method of cooking dis-tinctive of Szechuan is to give finely chopped or thinly sliced pieces of meat or vegetables a short period of rapid boiling in a limited amount of stock or water. When the liquid in the pan has almost disappeared, a small amount of sesame oil is added along with Chilli oil or chilli pepper and sometimes one or two other strong seasonings, for a last minute of quick cooking together over a high flame. The process produces a dish which is very tasty and chewy in texture, and which I often describe as having been 'stir-fried in stock' (or water), an unusual process by normal Chinese standards.

A similar process of cooking meat in Szechuan might be described as 'sautéing in stock or water'. Here the sliced meat (usually pork) is first seasoned with salt and pepper, and coated with cornflour and egg-white. The pieces are then lowered into boiling water for 3–4 minutes of rapid boiling. The meat is now drained and placed in a marinade consisting of a mixture of soya sauce, sugar, chilli, ground peppercorns and vegetable oil, to marinate for 15 minutes. The marinated meat is transferred to a frying pan or wok for another 15 minutes of steady frying, or 'sautéing', after which it is left to cool. It is treated to a further few minutes of renewed sautéing just before being served. This process produces a dish which is firm and chewy, yet smooth and of course full of flavour.

One of the best-known pork dishes of Szechuan is the Double-cooked Pork which is a slight variation on the genre of cooking just described. This has become so well known partly, I imagine, because of the ease with which it can be prepared, and partly because it is so characteristically Szechuan. A piece of lean-and-fat pork is simply boiled rapidly in water for a couple of minutes, and allowed to simmer gently for the next 20–25 minutes. The pork is then drained and left to cool, when it is sliced across lean-and-fat into thin slices. These are fried in a couple of tablespoons of oil with a sauce consisting of a mixture of mashed salted black beans, soya-bean paste, soya sauce, sugar, chilli, garlic, ginger, wine and chopped spring onion, a process which immediately turns the pork into a highly flavoured dish. The soya and chilli (a small amount of tomato purée may be added) quickly turn the meat brownish red, and with the freshly chopped spring onions added right at the end of the stir-frying, the dish becomes a succulent and spicy blend of red with a sparkling garnish of bright green.

Steaming seems to be a favourite form of slow cooking among the Szechuan peasantry. The Three Steamed and Nine Turned-out Dishes, with which the country people of the province entertain one another on family or village occasions are a notable combination. The 'steamed dishes' here denote open steaming, whereby food is cooked in a strong blast of steam for a comparatively short time

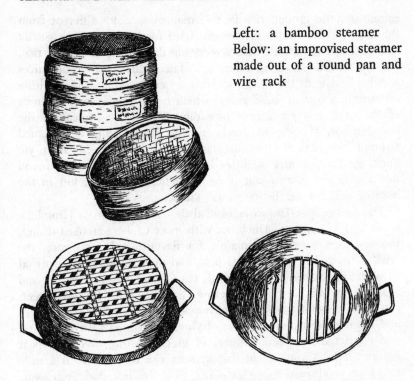

Left: a bamboo steamer
Below: an improvised steamer
made out of a round pan and
wire rack

(10–15 minutes). The 'turned-out' dishes are the meat or savoury puddings, in which the ingredients are packed—often in layers—in a heatproof bowl or basin and subjected to several hours of long, slow steaming. When ready for eating they are turned out on to serving dishes and brought to the table like puddings (most Chinese 'puddings' are savouries). It is frequently the practice among the peasantry, when cooking by steaming, to prepare a whole series of dishes at the same time, in several layers of 'basket steamers', with the dishes which require the hottest and shortest cooking placed in the bottom basket nearest to the boiling water, and the dishes for slower and longer cooking in the upper baskets.

Steaming is also the method of cooking employed in dishes where food (usually meat) is coated with ground rice. In Fen Tseng or steamed ground rice dishes the coarsely ground rice is first made aromatic by being roasted or dry-fried in a griddle or frying pan. Pieces of meat are then generously coated with the ground rice before being subjected to a long period of steaming. The effect of using aromatic ground rice in this manner is quite different from the use of breadcrumbs in Western fried food. The meat is usually seasoned and marinated before receiving its coating of ground rice, and prolonged steaming releases a fair amount of meat juices which blend with the aromatic ground-rice covering. The resulting mixture is a sort of 'solid gravy' which helps to reduce the fatness of the pork and provides a new dimension of enjoyment in the consumption of rice. In Szechuan this Feng Cheng or Steamed Ground Rice Pork is often marinated first in soya cheese, or fu-yu. Such are the gourmet qualities in Szechuan cooking, to be found not among the extravagant dishes of official banquets, but in the humble delights of the peasants' kitchens.

Among the best-known smoked dishes of Szechuan is Camphor-wood and Tea-smoked Duck. As with most Chinese smoked dishes, the smoking is employed mainly for flavouring. In this case, the duck is roasted or soya-braised first, and then subjected to a period of smoking above a mixture of tea, camphor-wood leaves and sawdust sprinkled over smouldering charcoal. After this treatment, the meat or poultry is sliced or chopped into large bite-sized pieces and given a short period of deep-frying, or brushed with sesame oil and subjected to a few minutes of quick-roasting over high heat before serving. Smoking in this manner can be applied to a wide range of food materials—including fish, shellfish and even some vegetables—with characteristic and delectable effect.

Szechuan cooking is one of the major schools of cooking in China on account of its distinctive character as well as the size of its repertoire. One cannot say the same of Hunan cuisine, in spite of its high billing in New York! Hunan is, after all, a much smaller area and its cooking methods are a peripheral part of that of Szechuan rather than a separate school. Like the food in Szechuan, Hunan dishes are hot and highly spiced. To achieve this end, cooks often employ the process of rapid reduction to thicken their sauces or gravies, rather than using cornflour, which is a more common practice in Canton (the capital of the adjacent province, immediately further south).

Although Szechuan cuisine has an earthy, satisfying appeal akin to English specialities like bread and butter pudding or steak and kidney pie, there is no suggestion of anything wild or frontier about it—characteristics which are strongly hinted at with some Peking dishes which have a Mongolian or Manchurian background. There are for instance very few of the mutton or lamb dishes, so characteristic of Peking. It is likely that the mountain ranges north of the city of Chengtu are thick enough to act as an impassable barrier, enclosing the province from influences from further north, which flowed along the route from north China along the 'Kansu Corridor', westward to Sinkiang, and along the Silk Route to Central Asia and points west. The dishes of Szechuan all seem very earth-bound and inward-looking to its own heavily populated hills, rivers, and vast plains. The only outside influence it admits is that from Peking, and that only 'officially', in its mandarin dishes served on special occasions.

Before embarking on the recipes let me mention a word or two about the cooking of Yunnan. The Chinese words for Yunnan mean 'South of the Clouds', which hints at the distance of the province: it is in fact much further south-west, and more remote than Szechuan; any further south and west would bring one into Burma and Tibet. This region is almost completely cut off from central and coastal China by the ranges of Traverse Mountains, which run from north to south in contrast to most of the great Chinese mountain ranges which run from west to east. Not so long ago the only way to reach Yunnan by modern methods of travel, without reverting to hundreds of miles of foot-slogging, was by going south by boat to Haiphong and Hanoi, and returning north by rail into China via Vietnam—it was as if in the United States, the only way of getting to Arizona or New Mexico was by going first of all to Mexico City! Being so secluded, mountainous and remote, the area naturally developed a distinctive cuisine of its own. Several of its cities, such as Kunming, are high-altitude cities where the climate is ideal, often evoking idyllic memories.

For people from central and coastal China the best-known culinary product from Yunnan is the Yunnan ham, which many Chinese consider the best in the world. Being both famous and plentiful, the ham is naturally served frequently, either on its own or as an ingredient in many recipes. Because Yunnan is an underpopulated and mountainous area various sorts of game, including venison, and items such as snails, sparrows, and even bear's paws, appear frequently on the table. A famous regional speciality is Distilled Chicken, which has to be cooked slowly in a special earthenware pot. Walnuts, pine nuts, chestnuts and peanuts are frequently incorporated into meat cookery, and a number of local herbs and fungi not easily obtainable elsewhere are included as cooking ingredients.

Pickles are widely used in Yunnan cookery; many dishes include a large measure of pickles and are described as 'sour and salty'. Perhaps as a contrast to these 'sour and salty' dishes and the saltiness of the ham, a number of dishes incorporate a generous amount of sugar or honey, often in the form of a sweet sauce to pour over the salty dish—such as over the ham itself. And in general contrast to these salty, nutty or highly spiced dishes, there is also a good range of dishes where food is simply steamed 'pure', the aim being to bring out the original flavour of the main ingredient itself, without the addition of heavy seasoning. A typical case is Distilled Chicken.

Soups

The soups of Szechuan are mostly 'soups of the people', good basic recipes created for everyday domestic eating from readily available local products.

Meat-Cake Soup with Winter Pickles

2 slices root ginger
225 g ($\frac{1}{2}$ lb) minced pork
60–75 ml (4–5 tablespoons) rice-flour
1 egg
15 ml (1 tablespoon) chopped chives (or spring onion)

7 ml ($\frac{1}{2}$ tablespoon) salt
pepper to taste
2–3 lettuce leaves
45 ml (3 tablespoons) Winter Pickles or Tung Ts'ai
875 ml ($1\frac{3}{4}$ pints) chicken stock (b)

Chop the ginger finely and mix it with the minced pork, flour, beaten egg, chives (or spring onion), salt and pepper until well blended. Form this into 5–6 round meat cakes. Place the pickles at the bottom of a casserole. Arrange the meat cakes on top. Pour in the stock; bring to a gentle boil; reduce the heat to very low, and simmer gently for 45 minutes.

Tear the lettuce leaves into small pieces and sprinkle into the soup. Adjust the seasoning. Continue to heat for 3–4 minutes, and serve in the casserole for diners to help themselves.
Serves 4–5.

Tripe and Green Pea Soup with Dried Squid

225–350 g ($\frac{1}{2}$–$\frac{3}{4}$ lb) pork or
beef tripe
2 slices root ginger
7 ml ($\frac{1}{2}$ tablespoon) salt
100 g ($\frac{1}{4}$ lb) dried squid
225 g ($\frac{1}{2}$ lb) Chinese dried green
beans, or 450 g (1 lb) green
peas

22 ml (1$\frac{1}{2}$ tablespoons) cornflour
750 ml (1$\frac{1}{4}$ pints) chicken stock
(a)
1 chicken stock cube
salt and pepper

Boil the tripe in 750 ml (1$\frac{1}{2}$ pints) water with ginger and salt for 20 minutes and simmer gently for 2 hours. Strain, and cut the tripe into double-matchstick-thick strips. Soak the squid in water for 3 hours and cut it into similar strips. Soak the dried beans or peas overnight then drain the peas and blend in a liquidizer for 3 minutes at medium speed. (If fresh or frozen peas are used, they can be liquidized without previous soaking.) Blend the cornflour in 60–75 ml (4–5 tablespoons) water. Heat the squid in 250 ml ($\frac{1}{2}$ pint) of water. Simmer until the liquid has been reduced to half. Add the tripe and the chicken stock. Bring to boil, and simmer very gently for 30 minutes. Add the green bean or pea purée, and the stock cube. Heat and stir gently for 15 minutes. Add the cornflour mixture and adjust for seasoning. Stir and mix well and heat gently for another 5 minutes.
Serves 4–5.

Beef and Turnip Soup with Watercress

Turnips are much more frequently used in soups in China than in the West. They are most often used in conjunction with a strong-tasting meat such as beef. I suspect that the beef in Szechuan is more suitable for long-cooking than quick stir-frying, being mostly meat from old oxen which once hauled salt in the salt mines.

450–675 g (1–1$\frac{1}{2}$ lb) beef (for
stewing or braising)
225 g ($\frac{1}{2}$ lb) turnips
1 bunch watercress
3 slices root ginger

1 litre (2 pints) water
pepper to taste
10 ml (2 teaspoons) salt
1 beef or chicken stock cube

Cut the beef into small cubes and the turnips into similar-sized triangular wedges. Clean the watercress thoroughly and remove the roots.

204

Place the beef and ginger in 500 ml (1 pint) of water in a saucepan. Bring to the boil and simmer until the liquid has been reduced to half (about 45 minutes). Skim off any impurities, and discard the ginger. Add the turnips, salt and pepper and the remaining water. Bring to the boil, and simmer gently together for 1½ hours. Add the stock cube and watercress. Stir and continue to heat for 5 minutes.

Serves 4–5.

Szechuan Oxtail Soup

1.5 *litres (3 pints) water*
1.35–1.8 *kg (3–4 lb) oxtail*
½ *chicken*
15 *ml (3 teaspoons) salt*
5–6 *slices root ginger*
7 *ml (½ tablespoon) peppercorns (lightly crushed)*

1 *chicken stock cube*
7 *ml (½ tablespoon) lard*
7 *ml (½ tablespoon) chopped chives or spring onion*
good quality soya sauce

Heat the water in a large heavy cooking pot or saucepan. Add the oxtail, chicken and 10 ml (2 teaspoons) salt. Bring to the boil, and simmer gently for 1 hour. Skim for impurities and add the ginger and peppercorns tied in a muslin bag for easy removal. Continue to simmer for 3 more hours, checking every hour to see that the soup in the pan has not been reduced by more than a quarter (if so, replenish to the original volume with water), and that the meats are well immersed.

Place the salt and the lard at the bottom of a very large tureen. Pour the contents of the pan into the tureen. Sprinkle with chopped chives and serve. Three or four small saucer-sized dishes of soya sauce should be placed in strategic positions on the table; the diners dip pieces of meat pulled off the oxtail or chicken in these before eating them with chopsticks.

Serves 6–8.

Szechuan Pickle Soup with Asparagus and Bamboo Shoots

1 *large piece of Szechuan pickle —about 50 g (2 oz)*
100 *g (¼ lb) lean-and-fat pork*
225 *g (½ lb) bamboo shoots*
1 *bundle of asparagus*

500 *ml (1 pint) water*
750 *ml (1½ pints) meat or chicken stock (a)*
7 *ml (½ tablespoon) sesame oil*
15 *ml (1 tablespoon) soya sauce*

Cut the pickle, pork and bamboo shoots into double or triple matchstick-thick slivers. Clean and remove roots from asparagus.

Place the pickle, pork, bamboo shoots and asparagus in a pan and pour in 500 ml (1 pint) water. Bring to the boil, reduce the heat and simmer gently for 30 minutes. Add the stock, and continue to simmer gently for 20 minutes. Adjust seasoning. Sprinkle with sesame oil and soya sauce. Simmer for a further 4–5 minutes, and serve in individual bowls or a large tureen from which diners may help themselves.

Serves 4–6.

Wild Mushroom and Tree Fungus Soup with Sliced Chicken

(If Chinese or wild grass mushrooms are not easily available use 2–3 types of fresh or tinned mushrooms.)

45–60 ml (3–4 tablespoons) wood ears or Chinese tree fungus
75–100 g (3–4 oz) Chinese dried black mushrooms
100 g (¼ lb) fresh mushrooms
100 g (¼ lb) button mushrooms
1 breast of chicken
5 ml (1 teaspoon) salt
10 ml (2 teaspoons) cornflour
1 egg-white
750 ml (1½ pints) chicken stock (a)
salt and pepper to taste
30 ml (2 tablespoons) soya sauce
7 ml (½ tablespoon) sesame oil

Clean and soak the wood ears in water for 30 minutes, then rinse and drain away the water. Soak the dried mushrooms in 250 ml (½ pint) warm water. Retain the water, remove the stalks from the mushrooms, and cut the larger in half. Clean the fresh mushrooms thoroughly. Remove and retain the stalks, and cut the larger mushrooms into halves or quarters.

Cut the chicken meat into small slices. Rub with salt and cornflour, and wet with egg-white.

Place the dried mushrooms in a saucepan with the mushroom water. Bring this to the boil and simmer gently for 10 minutes. Add the chicken stock, wood ears and all the fresh mushrooms. Bring this to the boil and simmer gently for 15 minutes. Adjust seasoning. Add the sliced chicken pieces, spreading them evenly into the soup. Simmer for a further 5 minutes. Sprinkle the top of the soup with soya sauce and sesame oil. Stir and serve. This dish is eaten throughout the meal. The chicken slices should appear

very white against the blackness of the liquid, which should taste very mushroomy.
Serves 4–6.

Vinegar and Pepper Soup with Sliced Fish

This soup is common to both Szechuan and Peking cooking, the Szechuan version being slightly more peppery.

225–350 g ($\frac{1}{2}$–$\frac{3}{4}$ lb) fillet of fish (sole, turbot, cod, carp, bream, halibut, etc)
7 ml ($\frac{1}{2}$ tablespoon) salt
15 ml (1 tablespoon) cornflour
1 egg-white
3 stalks spring onion
1 litre (1$\frac{3}{4}$–2 pints) chicken stock (b)

3 slices root ginger
10 ml (2 teaspoons) salt
2 ml ($\frac{1}{2}$ teaspoon) white pepper
22 ml (1$\frac{1}{2}$ tablespoons) soya sauce
75 ml (5 tablespoons) vinegar

Cut the fish into thin pieces and rub with salt and cornflour. Wet with egg-white. Leave to season for 30 minutes. Cut the spring onion into small segments.

Heat the stock and ginger in a large saucepan. Bring this to the boil and simmer for 4–5 minutes. Add the fish slices and chopped spring onions to the stock. Sprinkle with salt, pepper, soya sauce and vinegar. Simmer for a further 4–5 minutes.
Serves 4–5.

Hot and Sour Soup

This could be called a 'junk soup', to which almost anything can be added; but it must retain its essential character, which is that it must be thick (unusual among Chinese soups), dark and strongly flavoured. Indeed, the presence of pieces of bean curd, which is practically tasteless, act as a foil to this strong taste; while the lily-buds suspended in the soup act as colour-contrast to the general dark colour of the liquid.

100 g ($\frac{1}{4}$ lb) lean pork (or breast of chicken)
1–2 medium onions
8 medium Chinese dried mushrooms

2–3 stalks golden needles (lily buds: optional)
1–2 cakes bean curd
2–3 leeks

1 egg

30 ml (2 tablespoons) soya sauce

60–75 ml (4–5 tablespoons) vinegar

5 ml (1 teaspoon) black pepper

15 ml (1 tablespoon) sesame oil

30 ml (2 tablespoons) cornflour (blended in 90 ml (6 tablespoons) water)

15 ml (1 tablespoon) lard

750 ml (1½ pints) chicken or meat stock (b)

22 ml (1½ tablespoons) Chinese dried shrimps

30–45 ml (2–3 tablespoons) frozen or fresh green peas

45 ml (3 tablespoons) shelled shrimps (frozen or fresh)

1 chicken stock cube

7 ml (½ tablespoon) salt

Cut the pork (or chicken) into matchstick-sized shreds. Cut the onion into thin slices. Soak the dried mushrooms in 160 ml (⅓ pint) hot water for 30 minutes. Retain water. Remove the stalks and cut the mushrooms into quarters. Cut the lily buds into segments, and the bean curd into small cubes. Clean the leeks and cut them into very short segments. Beat the egg for 10 seconds with a fork. Blend the soya sauce, vinegar, pepper and sesame oil with the cornflour mixture.

Heat the lard in a saucepan. Add the pork and onion, and stir-fry together over a medium heat for 4–5 minutes. Pour in the stock. Bring to the boil and add the dried shrimps, lily buds, mushrooms and mushroom water. Bring to the boil again and simmer for 15 minutes. Add the leeks, peas, bean curd, fresh (or frozen) shrimps, stock cube and salt. Simmer for a further 10 minutes. Add the cornflour/soya/pepper mixture and stir well. Drip and trail the beaten egg along the prongs of a fork over the surface of the soup. This is a hot, savoury and substantial soup, useful to consume with plain rice when there is no great abundance of savoury dishes on the table.

Serves 5–6.

At the Chengtu Dining Rooms, the largest high-class catering establishment in the city of Chengtu in Szechuan, a more refined version of the above soup is made by adding crispy pork or beef croûtons to the soup just before serving. These meat croûtons are made by coating very thin slices of meat with batter made from a mixture of cornflour and egg-white. The slices of meat in batter are deep-fried for 4–5 minutes, drained and again cut into small squares or cubes. They are then deep-fried a second time for 2 minutes and drained before being sprinkled over the soup.

Chicken

Szechuan Barbecued Chicken

(From the Road of the Nationalities Dining Room, Chungking, the largest catering establishment in the city; the team of chefs is headed by Lau Ching Ting, who is a specialist in barbecues and roasts.)

1.35–1.8 kg (3–4 lb) chicken   sherry or yellow rice wine
30 ml (2 tablespoons) dry   15 ml (1 tablespoon) salt

Stuffing

75–100 g (3–4 oz) lean-and-fat   30 ml (2 tablespoons) lard
   pork   100 g (4 oz) bean sprouts
1 red pepper   2 ml (½ teaspoon) salt
1 green pepper   22 ml (1½ tablespoons) soya
2 dried chilli peppers   sauce
4–5 slices root ginger   7 ml (½ tablespoon) malt sugar
1 large onion   15 ml (1 tablespoon) sesame oil

Clean the chicken and rub it thoroughly with sherry or wine and salt, both inside and out. Hang up to dry for 2 hours.

Cut the pork into double-matchstick-sized shreds. Cut the peppers, chilli peppers (eliminate pips) and ginger into similar shreds. Cut onion into thin slices.

Heat the lard in a frying pan. Add the onion and pork and stir-fry over a high heat for 3 minutes. Add the pepper, chilli, ginger and bean sprouts. Sprinkle the mixture with salt and soya sauce and continue to stir-fry for 4–5 minutes. When these ingredients have cooled slightly, stuff chicken with them. Skewer or sew the chicken firmly to secure the stuffing.

Suspend the chicken in a large strainer or colander over a large pan of boiling water. Pour a dozen ladlefuls of the boiling water steadily over all the parts of the chicken. While the chicken is still warm, wipe dry, rub with malt sugar and hang it up to dry for 4 hours (or in winter, overnight).

Place the chicken on a spit under a large grill to grill steadily for 45 minutes or until the skin is well browned and crispy and the chicken cooked through; alternatively roast in the oven for 50 minutes at 190°C (375°F)/Gas 5. Remove the chicken from the grill and brush the skin with sesame oil.

Remove the stuffing from the chicken and arrange in the centre of a large oval serving dish. Cut off the crispy skin of the chicken, slice the breast and chop wings and legs into bite-sized pieces. Spread chicken pieces on top of the stuffings, surrounded by the pieces of skin. The chicken is best consumed with Steamed Buns (page 63) accompanied by dips of plum sauce, hoisin sauce and sweetened soya paste sauce. A party dish for 6 or more, to be eaten along with other dishes.

Braised Chicken Wings

6 medium Chinese dried mushrooms
1 medium onion
8–10 pairs of chicken wings
5 ml (1 teaspoon) salt
45 ml (3 tablespoons) lard
4 slices root ginger

27 ml (1¾ tablespoons) soya
sauce
250 ml (½ pint) chicken stock
(a)
10 ml (2 teaspoons) cornflour
30 ml (2 tablespoons) sherry
7 ml (½ tablespoon) sesame oil

Soak the dried mushrooms in water for 30 minutes. Cut the caps into halves or quarters (discarding the stalks), and the onion into thin slices. Poach the chicken wings in boiling water for 3 minutes. Drain and rub with salt. Chop each wing into 2 segments (eliminating the wing-tips).

Heat the lard in a frying pan with a lid. Add the onion and ginger and sauté over medium heat for 3 minutes. Add the chicken wings, and mushrooms, sprinkle with soya sauce, and turn them over several times with the other ingredients in the pan for 4–5 minutes. Pour in the chicken stock. Bring the contents to the boil. Reduce the heat, and leave to simmer gently for 1 hour, covered.

Discard the onion and ginger. Arrange the wings and mushrooms on a serving dish, increase the heat to high under the frying pan. Allow the liquid to reduce by a quarter. Add the cornflour (blended in 45 ml (3 tablespoons) water). Sprinkle the contents of the pan with the sherry and sesame oil, stir and pour the sauce over the chicken wings and mushrooms in the dish. Put this out, for the diners to help themselves, as an early course at a party, meal or banquet.
Serves 6–8.

Strange-Flavoured Chicken

5 pairs of chicken legs

2 large onions

Sauce

45 ml (3 tablespoons) sesame
  seeds
15 ml (1 tablespoon) sugar
10 ml (2 teaspoons) chilli sauce
15 ml (1 tablespoon) sherry
30 ml (2 tablespoons) sesame
  paste

37 ml (2½ tablespoons) vinegar
  (Chinese aromatic, if available)
2 ml (½ teaspoon) black pepper
45 ml (3 tablespoons) soya
  sauce

Place the chicken legs in a large pan of water. Bring to the boil, and
simmer gently for 25 minutes. Chop the onions and spread them
evenly as bed over a large serving dish.

Drain and remove the bones from chicken legs with a sharp knife,
minimizing the incision. Cut the meat slantwise into thin circular
pieces, and arrange them on top of the onion.

Heat the sesame seeds on a small dry frying pan over a low
heat. Stir for 3–4 minutes, until they have turned brown and
aromatic but not scorched. Mix half the sesame seeds in with
the other ingredients for the sauce and blend well. Pour the sauce
evenly over the chicken pieces and sprinkle them with the remainder of the toasted seeds. To be eaten with other dishes at a
party.
Serves 6–8.

Stir-Fried Shredded Chicken with Ginger and Onion

225 g (½ lb) chicken breast
5–6 slices root ginger
1 large onion
3 stalks spring onion
37 ml (2½ tablespoons) vegetable oil
2 ml (½ teaspoon) salt
22 ml (1½ tablespoons) soya
  sauce
30 ml (2 tablespoons) chicken
  stock (a)

15 ml (3 tablespoons) chicken
  fat
15 ml (1 tablespoon) vinegar
7 ml (½ tablespoon) chilli oil
5 ml (1 teaspoon) sugar
10 ml (2 teaspoons) cornflour
  blended in 30 ml (2 tablespoons) water

Cut the chicken and ginger into double-matchstick-sized shreds, the
onion into very thin slices and the spring onions into short segments.
Heat the oil in a large frying pan. Add the onion and ginger and
stir-fry quickly over a high heat for 1½ minutes. Add the shredded

chicken. Sprinkle the mixture with salt, soya sauce and stock. Continue to stir-fry quickly for 1½ minutes. Reduce the heat and allow the ingredients to simmer for 2½ minutes.

Add the chicken fat, vinegar, sherry, chilli oil, sugar, and finally the spring onion and blended cornflour. Turn the heat up to high, and stir-fry quickly for 1½ minutes.

Serve on a well-heated dish to be eaten immediately. Heat is as important to this dish as any of the ingredients.

Serves 4–5.

Tangerine-Peel Chicken

(Adapted from the Chengtu Dining Rooms, Chengtu.)

1 medium-sized chicken, about 1.35–1.5 kg (3–3½ lb)
2 medium onions
4 slices root ginger
10 ml (2 teaspoons) salt

22 ml (1½ tablespoons) soya sauce
30 ml (2 tablespoons) sherry
oil for deep- or semi-deep-frying

Sauce

1 red pepper
2–3 dried chilli peppers
30 ml (2 tablespoons) dried tangerine peel
30 ml (2 tablespoons) vinegar
30 ml (2 tablespoons) vegetable oil
45 ml (3 tablespoons) chicken stock (a)

15 ml (1 tablespoon) sugar
5 ml (1 teaspoon) peppercorns, lightly crushed
22 ml (1½ tablespoons) soya sauce
15 ml (1 tablespoon) cornflour blended in 75 ml (5 tablespoons) water

Clean and chop the chicken, cutting through the bone, into bite-sized pieces. Cut the onion into slices, and the ginger into shreds. Add them to the chicken together with the salt, soya sauce and sherry. Rub them together, and leave the chicken to season for 1 hour.

Cut the pepper and chilli pepper into shreds (discard the pips). Break the dried tangerine peel into small pieces.

Shake the chicken pieces free of onion and ginger. Deep-fry or semi-deep-fry them in sufficient oil (if semi-deep-frying, turn the chicken in 250 ml (½ pint) hot oil with a perforated spoon) for about 5 minutes, until chicken pieces are quite brown. Drain and put aside.

Heat 30 ml (2 tablespoons) oil in a large frying pan. Add the sweet pepper, chilli pepper and tangerine peel and stir-fry them together for 1½ minutes over medium heat. Add the remaining ingredients for the sauce and stir quickly. The sauce is ready when the liquid thickens.

Return the chicken pieces to the pan. Mix and turn them with the sauce over medium heat for 2 minutes.

Serves 6–8.

Stir-Fried Chicken with Ground Peanuts
(From the Yee Tze Ssi Dining Rooms, Chengtu.)

225 g (½ lb) breast of chicken
7 ml (½ tablespoon) salt
15 ml (1 tablespoon) cornflour
1 egg-white

100 g (¼ lb) peanuts
60–75 ml (4–5 tablespoons) vegetable oil

Sauce

2 stalks spring onion
2 chilli peppers
30 ml (2 tablespoons) lard
30 ml (2 tablespoons) vinegar
30 ml (2 tablespoons) chicken stock (a)

15 ml (1 tablespoon) soya sauce
15 ml (1 tablespoon) cornflour blended in 45 ml (3 tablespoons) water

Cut the chicken breast into triple-matchstick-sized slivers, rub these with salt and cornflour, and fold into beaten egg-white.

Roast or fry the peanuts over a low heat until slightly brown, and crush or grind coarsely. Cut the spring onions into short segments, and the pepper into shreds (discarding the pips). Mix the liquid ingredients for the sauce thoroughly.

Heat the oil in a large frying pan. Add the chicken slivers and turn them in the hot oil for 1 minute. Drain away any excess oil.

Heat the lard in a separate pan. Add the chopped peppers and spring onions to fry for 1½ minutes. Pour in the liquid ingredients for the sauce. Stir quickly to mix. When the liquid thickens return the chicken to the pan. Turn and stir the chicken in the sauce.

Sprinkle the peanuts over the chicken. Turn it over quickly a few times, and serve immediately in a well-heated serving dish. The roasted peanuts add an aromatic flavour to this chicken dish.

Serves 4–6.

White Flower of Chicken

(From the Ching Chen Yuan, one of the oldest restaurants in Chengtu.)

4 egg-whites
100 g (¼ lb) breast of chicken
30 ml (2 tablespoons) cornflour
7 ml (½ tablespoon) salt
375 ml (¾ pint) chicken stock
  (a)

salt and pepper
4 large lettuce leaves
30 ml (2 tablespoons) minced
  smoked ham

Beat the egg-whites with a rotary beater for 30–40 seconds. Mince the chicken and add it to the egg-whites along with the cornflour, salt, and 60 ml (4 tablespoons) stock. Beat for another 30 seconds.

Heat the stock in a saucepan and adjust the seasoning. Add the semi-stiff egg-white and chicken mixture to the stock. Bring to a gentle boil.

Place the lettuce leaves at the bottom of a deep dish, allowing the edges of the leaves to show over the top of the sides of the dish. Pour the chicken mixture into the centre of the dish and sprinkle the top with minced ham.

Serves 4–6.

The Family Quick-Fry of Chicken Slivers with Bamboo Shoots and Celery

(From the Yuen Chuan Restaurant, Chungking.)

225 g (½ lb) chicken flesh from
  breast and leg
7 ml (½ tablespoon) salt
15 ml (1 tablespoon) cornflour
45 ml (3 tablespoons) oil
3 stalks celery
225 g (½ lb) bamboo shoots
3 stalks spring onion

2 chilli peppers
3 cloves garlic
30 ml (2 tablespoons) lard
7 ml (½ tablespoon) soya bean
  paste
15 ml (1 tablespoon) hoisin
  sauce

Sauce

15 ml (1 tablespoon) soya
  sauce
7 ml (½ tablespoon) sugar
15 ml (1 tablespoon) vinegar

30 ml (2 tablespoons) dry sherry
12 ml (¾ tablespoon) cornflour
  blended with 45 ml (3 tablespoons) water

Cut the chicken into chopstick-thick slivers 3.75 cm (1½ in) long. Rub them with salt, cornflour and 7 ml (½ tablespoon) oil. Cut the celery, bamboo shoots and spring onions into similar-sized pieces. Shred the peppers (discarding the pips). Crush and chop the garlic. Mix the ingredients for the sauce together until well blended.

Heat the rest of the oil in a frying pan. Add the chicken, stir-fry quickly over a high heat for 1 minute and remove it from pan. Heat the lard in the pan. Add the celery, bamboo shoots, spring onion, pepper and garlic. Stir-fry quickly for 1½ minutes over a high heat. Add the soya paste and hoisin sauce, and continue to stir-fry for 1 minute.

Pour in the sauce mixture. Stir and turn a few times. Return the chicken to the pan and stir with the other ingredients for 1 minute. Serve immediately in a well-heated dish.
Serves 4–6.

La Tzu Chi Ting or Hot Quick-Fried Diced Chicken
(Adapted from the Silver Dragon Restaurant, West Chengtu.)

225 g (½ lb) breast of chicken	2 slices root ginger
5 ml (1 teaspoon) salt	3 cloves garlic
15 ml (1 tablespoon) cornflour	3 red chilli peppers
1 egg-white	2 stalks spring onion

Sauce

22 ml (1½ tablespoons) soya sauce	12 ml (¾ tablespoon) cornflour blended in 45 ml (3 tablespoons) water
22 ml (1½ tablespoons) dry sherry	15 ml (1 tablespoon) lard
30 ml (2 tablespoons) chicken stock (a)	7 ml (½ tablespoon) vinegar

Dice the chicken into small cubes. Rub these with the salt and cornflour, and wet them with the egg-white. Cut the ginger into shreds, crush and chop the garlic, and chop the pepper finely (discarding the pips). Cut the spring onions into short segments. Mix the sauce ingredients (except the lard) until well blended.

Heat the oil in a frying pan. Add the chicken and turn it quickly in the oil over a high heat for 40 seconds. Remove the chicken from the pan. Add the lard to the pan together with the ginger, garlic and

spring onion. Stir them around a few times. Meanwhile sprinkle the finely chopped chilli pepper over the chicken cubes. Mix them together, and return the chicken to the pan to stir-fry with the other ingredients for 1 minute over a high heat (the pepper turns the chicken pink). Pour the sauce over the mixture. Stir and turn for 30 seconds until the sauce thickens. Serve immediately on a well-heated dish.
Serves 6–8.

Sliced Chicken in Vinegar Sauce
(Adapted from the Dining Rooms of the Nationalities, Chungking.)

225 g (½ lb) breast of chicken
5 ml (1 teaspoon) salt
15 ml (1 tablespoon) cornflour
1 egg-white
225 g (½ lb) bamboo shoots

1 chilli pepper
3 slices root ginger
3 cloves garlic
30 ml (2 tablespoons) vegetable oil

Sauce

22 ml (1½ tablespoons) lard
5 ml (1 teaspoon) sugar
37 ml (2½ tablespoons) best vinegar (aromatic if possible)
15 ml (1 tablespoon) cornflour blended in 30 ml (2 tablespoons) water

1 medium onion
22 ml (1½ tablespoons) soya sauce
45 ml (3 tablespoons) chicken stock (a)

Cut the chicken into small, thin slices. Rub these with salt and cornflour and wet them with the egg-white. Cut the bamboo shoots into similar-sized pieces. Shred the pepper (discarding the pips) and ginger; crush and coarsely chop the garlic. Cut the onion into thin slices. Mix the sauce ingredients except the onion and lard in a bowl.

Heat the oil in a frying pan. Add the chicken pieces and turn them in the hot oil. Quick-fry rapidly for 1 minute and remove them to drain. Place the lard, bamboo shoots, ginger, garlic and onion in the pan. Stir-fry them over a high heat for 1½ minutes. Return the chicken pieces to the pan. Turn and stir with the other ingredients. Pour in the blended sauce mixture from the bowl. Stir-fry quickly for 30 seconds and serve on a well-heated dish, to be eaten immediately.
Serves 4–6.

Fire-Cracker Chicken

350 g (¾ lb) lean-and-fat pork   7 ml (½ tablespoon) salt
225 g (½ lb) breast of chicken   15 ml (1 tablespoon) chicken
100 g (¼ lb) smoked ham   stock (a)
3–4 stalks spring onion   2 eggs
5–6 golden needles (tiger lily   soya sauce
    buds)   45 ml (3 tablespoons) cornflour
3 cloves garlic   5 ml (1 teaspoon) sugar
3 slices root ginger   oil for deep-frying
1 medium onion

Boil and simmer the pork for 20 minutes; allow to cool and cut into thin slices. Cut the chicken likewise into slightly smaller thin slices, the ham into triple-matchstick-sized strips 5 cm (2 in) long; and the spring onions into longish segments. Soak the tiger lilies in water for 20 minutes and cut them into longish segments. Chop and mince the garlic, ginger and onion. Mix these with the salt, chicken stock, a quarter of the beaten egg and some soya sauce. Mix the rest of the egg with the cornflour into a batter.

Place the slices of pork on a large plate or chopping board. Spread 7 ml (½ tablespoon) of the onion, garlic, sugar, salt, soya sauce, egg and stock mixture over them. Place a slice of chicken over the mixture on top of each slice of pork, and a segment of spring onion and a strip of ham on top of the chicken. Roll up each pork-chicken 'sandwich' and tie the roll firmly with a strip of tiger lily. Turn each of the rolls in the egg and cornflour batter until they are evenly covered.

Deep-fry the pork-and-chicken rolls for 4½–5 minutes. Drain on absorbent paper. Arrange on a well-heated serving dish, and serve immediately. The recipe, which comes from Kweichow, a neighbouring province to Szechuan, is so called because of the resemblance in shape and size of the pork and chicken rolls to Chinese fire-crackers. The crisp outside should make an interesting contrast to the soft inside. *Serves 6–8.*

Distilled Chicken

This is essentially a Yunnan dish which frequently appears on Szechuan tables. It has to be cooked in a special earthenware pot, nowadays available from some Chinese foodstores abroad. The pot is devised for steaming. The centre of the bottom of the pot rises to a point in the form of a small spout aiming immediately below the centre of the pottery lid which covers the pot closely. When the pot is placed over boiling water or a rising blast of vigorous steam, a jet of steam will be shot inside the pot through the aperture of the spout, and will condense against the lid and drip down on to the chicken in the pot in the form of condensed distilled water. The Chinese regard the dish as a particularly 'pure' form of chicken.

75 g (3 oz) bamboo shoots
4–6 medium Chinese dried mushrooms
1.35–1.8 kg (3–4 lb) chicken (plus head and feet)

2 slices root ginger
6 slices Yunnan ham (or any smoked ham)
salt and pepper

Cut the bamboo shoots into 8–10 thin pieces and soak them with the mushrooms for 30 minutes and remove the stalks. Dip the chicken in a pan of boiling water for 2 minutes to help to eliminate impurities. Remove the head and claws. Cut the chicken in half. Cut both the legs and wings into 2–3 pieces, and the body into 8 pieces. Place the head and feet of the chicken, together with the ginger, at the bottom of the pot. Arrange the other pieces neatly on top, interspersing them with bamboo shoots and mushrooms, placing the ham on top.

Place the pot on top of a saucepan which is half or three-quarters filled with water. Bring the water to a vigorous boil and keep this vigorous boil for 3 hours. (Top up the saucepan with boiling water every 20 minutes.) When ready, open the lid and sprinkle contents with salt and pepper. Replace the lid.

Bring the pot to the table, and remove the lid in front of the assembled diners, for them to consume as a 'semi-soup' dish through-out the meal. A range of soya-based dips (eg. soya chilli, soya chopped chives, soya shredded ginger with aromatic vinegar) should be placed on the table for the diners to dip the chicken in before consuming.

A party dish for 8 people.

Duck

Szechuan Double-Cooked Roast Duck

1.35–1.8 kg (3–4 lb) duck
15 ml (1 tablespoon) salt
3 slices root ginger

3 chilli peppers
750 ml (1½ pints) water
15 ml (1 tablespoon) sugar

1 *chicken stock cube*   45 *ml (3 tablespoons) soya*
2 *ml (½ teaspoon) five-spice*   *paste*
  powder   45 *ml (3 tablespoons) soya*
                                          sauce

Clean the duck, rub it with salt, and leave it to season for 1 hour. Shred the ginger and pepper (discarding the pips), and bring them to boil in a large saucepan with the water, sugar, stock cube, five-spice powder, soya paste and soya sauce, and simmer them together for 10 minutes. Immerse the seasoned duck in this cooking sauce, and simmer for 30 minutes, turning it over every 10 minutes. Leave the bird to cool in the sauce for another 30 minutes, turning it over once.

Drain and dry the duck (retain the liquid), and put it on a wire rack into a preheated oven at 200°C (400°F)/Gas 6, to roast for 45 minutes, placing a roasting pan underneath to catch the drips.

The duck can be served in the Western style, or chopped through the bones into large bite-sized pieces in the Chinese style, using the contents of the drip-pan to make a sauce by adding 5 ml (1 teaspoon) of slightly crushed peppercorn, ½ chicken stock cube, 125 ml (¼ pint) cooking sauce and 12 ml (¾ tablespoon) cornflour (blended in 60 ml (4 tablespoons) water). Placing the pan over a medium heat, stir for 3–4 minutes and pour this sauce over the duck, or duck pieces.
Serves 8–10.

Szechuan Double-Cooked Aromatic and Crispy Duck
(Adapted from the Dining Rooms of the Nationalities, Chungking.)

Repeat the procedure and ingredients of the previous recipe, but braise the duck in the cooking sauce over medium heat for 1¾ hours instead of ½ hour, turning the bird over every 15 minutes. Drain the duck, and hang it up to cool for at least 1 hour, shaking it free of all liquid. Now, instead of roasting the duck, deep-fry it in ample oil for 8–10 minutes, until very brown and crispy. Lift the duck out to drain thoroughly, and serve whole.

The meat of the duck should be sufficiently tender and should loosen from the body to be easily scraped from the carcass with a fork. This crisp and tender duck meat is consumed wrapped in pancakes. At least 15–20 pancakes (similar to the traditional 'doilies' for Peking Duck made without the use of eggs) should be placed on the table along with shredded cucumber, spring onion segments,

and saucers of plum sauce, hoisin sauce, and a sweet soya-paste sauce made of 45–60 ml (3–4 tablespoons) of soya paste blended with 22 ml (1½ tablespoons) sugar and 15 ml (1 tablespoon) sesame oil. The diner spreads each pancake lightly with one of the sauces (use them like jam), cucumber shreds, spring onion segments and pieces or shreds of duck meat, and rolls it up before eating.
Serves 5–6.

Pepper and Salt Ginger Roast Duck

4 slices root ginger
12 ml (¾ tablespoon) peppercorns

1.8–2.2 kg (4–5 lb) duck
15 ml (1 tablespoon) sea salt
30 ml (2 tablespoons) lard

Shred and chop the ginger. Roast the peppercorns in a dry roasting pan for 10 minutes in a moderate oven; crush and pound them lightly in a mortar.

Rub the duck inside and out with half the salt, ginger and pepper. Leave to dry and season overnight. Mix the remaining seasoning with lard until well blended. Rub the mixture on the duck inside and out.

Place the duck on a wire rack in a preheated moderate oven at about 200°C (400°F)/Gas 5 (put a drip-pan underneath) and roast for 1 hour 15 minutes.

The duck can be served either carved in the Western way, or chopped through the bone into 15–20 large bite-sized pieces in the Chinese style for diners to eat along with other dishes. A good dish to go with drinks before a dinner party.
Serves 6–8.

Szechuan Camphor-Wood and Tea-Smoked Duck

(Adapted from a recipe from the Chengtu Dining Rooms, Chengtu.)

Repeat the ingredients and procedure of the previous recipe, but reduce the peppercorn by 1.5 ml (⅓ teaspoon), and the roasting time by 10 minutes.

Fuel for Smoking

60–75 ml (4–5 tablespoons)
   dried tea
30 ml (2 tablespoons) sugar
a bundle of camphor-wood twigs

(or 60–75 ml (4–5 table-
spoons) camphor-wood saw-
dust)
some smouldering charcoal

H

Equipment

wire rack; inverted kerosene tin (thoroughly cleaned) or inverted metal dustbin

Light the charcoal fire. When the charcoal is glowing red but not blazing, sprinkle half the tea, sugar and camphor wood (twigs or sawdust) over the fire. Place the duck on a wire rack and suspend it about a couple of inches above the now smoking charcoal fire. Close it in by inverting the tin or bin over both fire and duck. Leave the latter to smoke for 10 minutes. Repeat, turning the duck over for a further 10 minutes' smoking by sprinkling the remainder of the tea-and-sawdust mixture over the charcoal after poking and stirring it. By now the duck should have been sufficiently smoked. Brush it with 30 ml (2 tablespoons) sesame oil and put it in a moderate oven for a further 15 minutes' roasting.

Serve by chopping through the bones into 15–20 large bite-sized pieces. An excellent accompaniment to wine at the start of a multi-course dinner party or banquet.

Serves 6–8.

Double-Cooked Steamed and Roast Duck in Black-Bean Sauce
(Adapted from a recipe from the Dining Rooms of the Nationalities, Chungking.)

1.5–2.2 kg duck
2 ml (½ teaspoon) black pepper
30 ml (2 tablespoons) soya sauce

15 ml (3 teaspoons) salt
4–5 slices root ginger

Sauce

1 medium onion
1 red pepper
2 chilli peppers
30 ml (2 tablespoons) salted black beans
45 ml (3 tablespoons) sherry

7 ml (1½ teaspoons) sugar
7 ml (1½ teaspoons) cornflour blended in 45 ml (3 tablespoons) water
½ chicken stock cube
30 ml (2 tablespoons) lard

Clean and rub the duck inside and out with salt, pepper, chopped ginger and soya sauce. Leave to season for 2 hours.

Cut the onion, pepper, chilli pepper (discarding the pips) into thin slices. Soak the black beans in water for 20 minutes and drain, discarding the water.

Place the duck on a wire rack in a steamer, with a drip-pan under the duck, for 1 hour 15 minutes.

Transfer the duck on its wire rack with drip-pan below into a preheated oven at 200°C (400°F)/Gas 6 to roast for 45 minutes. Move the duck to a well-heated serving dish, and keep hot.

Meanwhile, heat the lard in a frying pan. Add the onion and stir-fry over a high heat for 1 minute. Add the pepper, chilli pepper and black beans and continue to stir-fry for 4 minutes. Skim away the excess fat from the contents of the drip-pan and add to the frying pan, along with the sugar, sherry and crushed stock cube. Stir and heat together for 4 minutes. Pour in the cornflour mixture. Turn and stir for a further minute.

Pour the sauce from the pan evenly over the duck in the serving dish and bring it to the table for the diners to help themselves. The duck should be tender enough for the diners to pick to pieces with chopsticks. An excellent dish to consume with rice.
Serves 5–6.

Quick Soft-Fried Sliced Duck's Liver
(From the Chengtu Dining Rooms, Chengtu.)

225–350 g ($\frac{1}{2}$–$\frac{3}{4}$ lb) ducks' liver	2 chilli peppers
7 ml ($\frac{1}{2}$ tablespoon) salt	3 slices root ginger
15 ml (1 tablespoon) cornflour	45 ml (3 tablespoons) lard
1 egg-white	30 ml (2 tablespoons) vinegar
30 ml (2 tablespoons) dry sherry	45 ml (3 tablespoons) stock (b)
45 ml (3 tablespoons) dried wood ears or tree fungi	7 ml ($\frac{1}{2}$ tablespoon) cornflour blended in 30 ml (2 tablespoons) water
6 dried Chinese mushrooms	30 ml (2 tablespoons) soya sauce
3 stalks spring onion	
100 g ($\frac{1}{4}$ lb) bamboo shoots	10 ml (2 teaspoons) sugar
3 cloves garlic	$\frac{1}{2}$ chicken stock cube (crushed)

Clean and cut the duck livers into very small thin slices. Sprinkle and rub with salt. Blend the cornflour with the egg-white and sherry into a batter. Coat the liver with the batter.

Clean and soak the wood ears in water for 30 minutes and then drain them. Soak the dried mushrooms in water for 30 minutes, drain and remove the stalks.

Cut the spring onions and bamboo shoots into short segments, the garlic into thin slices, and the chilli peppers into shreds (discarding the pips). Mix the soya sauce, vinegar, stock, sugar, crushed stock cube, and blended cornflour in a bowl.

Heat the lard in a large frying pan. When hot add the liver slices, spread them out over the pan and stir-fry for 1 minute. Add the ginger, garlic, spring onion, mushrooms and wood ears. Stir-fry them together over a high heat for 2 minutes. Pour the sauce mixture in the bowl evenly over the ingredients in the pan. Continue to stir-fry quickly for ½ minute, and serve at once on a well-heated serving dish, to be eaten immediately.

Serves 5–6.

Quick-Fried Shredded Smoked Duck with Ginger and Celery
(Adapted from the Tee Tzi Ssi Dining Rooms, Chungking.)

175–225 g (6–8 oz) smoked duck meat	22 ml (1½ tablespoons) soya sauce
8 slices root ginger	22 ml (1½ tablespoons) stock (b)
3 stalks celery	
6 stalks spring onion	5 ml (1 teaspoon) sugar
3 chilli peppers	22 ml (1½ tablespoons) vinegar
52 ml (3½ tablespoons) lard	2 ml (½ teaspoon) sesame oil
22 ml (1½ tablespoons) soya paste	

Cut the duck meat into triple-matchstick-sized strips and the ginger and celery similarly. Cut the spring onions into short segments, and the chilli peppers into shreds (discarding the pips).

Heat the lard in a large frying pan. Add the duck meat and soya paste. Stir-fry quickly over a high heat for ½ minute. Add the ginger, celery, pepper and spring onion. Sprinkle with soya sauce and stock. Continue to stir-fry the ingredients together for 2 minutes. Sprinkle the contents with the sugar, vinegar and sesame oil. Stir-fry quickly for a further ½ minute over a high heat and serve immediately on a well-heated dish.

Serves 5–6.

Pork

Szechuan Spare-Ribs with Crispy Skin

(In Szechuan called Ko Soo Fang or Barbecued Crispy Squares.)

5.4–6.6 kg (12–15 lb) piece of   22 ml (1½ tablespoons) malt
belly of pork rib-cage (with   sugar
skin attached)   45 ml (3 tablespoons) soya
15 ml (1 tablespoon) salt   sauce

Cut the pork into two sheets of equal size. Use the sharp end of the skewer to stab holes in the meat between the rib-bones, but not deep enough to puncture the skin. Mix the sugar with the soya sauce until well blended.

Heat a large cauldron of water. When the water boils, add the sheets of belly of pork, skin-side down. Bring to the boil, and simmer gently for 2 minutes. Remove the pork, drain and wipe it dry. When the pork is cooked, rub the skin with salt, and leave to dry and season overnight.

Place the pieces of pork under a large grill, and grill for 12–14 minutes (5–6 minutes rib-side up, 7–8 minutes skin-side up) until the skin becomes brown and starts to bubble. Cut the skin from the ribs and then cut the skin into 24 pieces. Cut the sheets of spare-ribs into individual ribs. Brush each piece of skin and each rib with the blended soya-sugar mixture.

Arrange the ribs in a roasting pan and put this into a preheated oven at 220°C (425°F)/Gas 7 for 10–12 minutes. Now arrange the pieces of skin on a wire rack and roast them at the top of the oven for 7–8 minutes. Remove the ribs and skin from the oven at the same time (after the ribs have been roasted for 20 minutes.)

Serve separately on two large, well-heated serving dishes, accompanied by steamed Lotus Buns, spring onion segments, plum sauce or sweet soya-paste sauce (blend 2 units of soya paste with 1 unit of sugar, and ½ unit sesame oil).

Spare-ribs with Crispy Skin are often served together with Spare-rib Soup. The soup can be prepared to go with the above recipe.

Spare-Rib Soup

1.35–1.8 kg (3–4 lb) additional   4 stalks coarsely chopped spring
spare-ribs   onion
4 slices root ginger   30 ml (2 teaspoons) salt

15 ml (1 teaspoon) pepper-   2 chicken stock cubes
corns

Boil the spare-ribs and simmer gently in 1.75 litres (3½ pints) of
water for 1¼ hours with the salt and peppercorns. Leave to cool.
When cold, skim away the fat and impurities. Add the stock cubes,
bring the soup and spare-ribs again to the boil, and simmer for 2
minutes. Place a pinch of chopped spring onion at the bottom of
10–12 soup-bowls or ordinary Chinese rice-bowls. Divide the soup
and spare-ribs into the bowls and serve hot, with the dishes described above. An excellent starter for a dinner party or banquet.
Serves 10–12.

Big Szechuan Casserole
(Adapted from the Chengtu Dining Rooms, Chengtu.)

225 g (½ lb) bêche de mer *(sea*   900 g (2 lb) pork bones
cucumber—optional)   1 pair pig's trotters
12 large Chinese dried mush-   60 ml (4 tablespoons) lard
rooms   2 large onions, chopped
½ duck (about 900 g/2 lb)   6 slices root ginger
½ chicken (about 900 g/2 lb)   10 ml (2 teaspoons) salt
450 g (1 lb) smoked ham   15 ml (1 tablespoon) rock or
675 g (1½ lb) stewing beef   granulated sugar
6 stalks golden needles (tiger   105 ml (7 tablespoons) soya
lily buds)   sauce
100 g (¼ lb) dried squid   750 ml (1½ pints) yellow wine
450 g (1 lb) bamboo shoots   or dry sherry
6–8 eggs   750 ml (1½ pints) boiling water
1.35–1.8 kg (3–4 lb) knuckle of
pork

Soak the *bêche de mer* in water overnight, and cut it into 10 pieces.
Soak the dried mushrooms for ½ hour, and remove the stalks. Chop
the duck and chicken through the bone into 2 pieces each. Cut the
ham and beef each into 8–10 pieces. Soak the golden needles in
water for 20 minutes and cut into 5 cm (2 in) segments. Soak the
dried squid in water for 1 hour, and cut it into 6 pieces. Cut the
bamboo shoots in triangular wedged-shaped pieces. Hard-boil the
eggs, shell them, and put them aside.
Bring a large cauldron of water to the boil. Add all the meat
ingredients, including the knuckle of pork, pork bones, trotters, duck,

chicken, beef, ham, *bêche de mer* and squid, to boil in the water for 6–7 minutes. Drain away all the water and impurities.

Heat the lard in a giant casserole. When the fat is hot, give the knuckle of pork, trotters, duck, chicken and beef each a turn in the fat for 2–3 minutes, over a high heat.

Remove the casserole from the heat, and arrange the ingredients in it with the knuckle of pork in the middle and the pork bones around the sides. Distribute the duck, chicken, ham, beef and squid pieces evenly around the knuckle, along with the mushrooms, bamboo shoots, golden needles, onion, ginger and eggs.

Sprinkle the contents with salt, sugar and soya sauce and pour in the wine or sherry and water. Bring the contents to a gentle boil on top of the cooker for 30 minutes. Transfer the casserole into the lower half of a preheated oven at 170°C (325°F)/Gas 3 for 6 hours.

Put the casserole in the middle of the table for diners to help themselves. The dish is sufficient for a complete self-contained dinner, served with boiled rice or Steamed Buns (see page 63), and one dish of quick-fried vegetables. The meat should be tender enough to be taken to pieces with a pair of chopsticks. In Szechuan the dish is not generally cooked in an oven, but buried in the ground with smouldering charcoal and sawdust. Although somewhat rustic, the dish is considered a 'party piece'.
Serves 8–10.

Sweet and Aromatic Pork
(An unusual dish from the Jade Dragon Restaurant, West Chengtu.)

450–550 g (1–1¼ lb) belly of pork
2 eggs
30 ml (2 tablespoons) cornflour
30 ml (2 tablespoons) sesame seeds
37 ml (2½ tablespoons) brown sugar (blended in 90 ml (6 tablespoons) water)
vegetable oil for semi-deep-frying (about 125 ml/¼ pint)

Bring the pork to the boil in a large panful of water, and simmer gently for 1 hour. Drain the meat and cut it into very thin medium-sized slices. Beat the egg and cornflour together into a batter and coat the pork slices with it. Stir the sesame seeds in a dry frying pan over medium heat until brown and aromatic. Remove from the heat.

Heat the oil in a large frying pan. Lower the pork slices, piece by

piece, to 'shallow-fry' (frying without stirring) for 3 minutes on
either side over medium heat. Drain away all the oil, and sprinkle
the pork with sugar water.

Remove and arrange the pork slices on a well-heated serving dish.
Sprinkle them with roasted sesame seeds. To be eaten hot.
Serves 5–6.

Quick Water-Fried Sliced Pork
(From the Jade Dragon Restaurant, West Chengtu.)

'Water-frying is a typical Szechuan cooking process where the meat,
cut into thin slices, is cooked instantly in a small amount of water in
a frying pan, instead of conventionally in oil.

350–450 g (¾–1 lb) fillet of
pork
10 ml (2 teaspoons) salt
1 egg-white
22 ml (1½ tablespoons) dry
sherry
30 ml (2 tablespoons) cornflour
350 g (¾ lb) Chinese celery/
cabbage
4 stalks spring onion
2 slices root ginger
3 dried chilli peppers
7 ml (1½ teaspoons) peppercorns

30 ml (2 tablespoons) vegetable oil
22 ml (1½ tablespoons) soya
sauce
15 ml (1 tablespoon) hoisin
sauce
15 ml (1 tablespoon) sherry
125 ml (¼ pint) stock (b)
½ chicken stock cube
30 ml (2 tablespoons) vegetable
oil

Cut the pork into medium-sized thin slices and rub them with salt.
Mix the egg-white, sherry and cornflour into a batter and coat the
pork slices with the mixture. Cut the cabbage into pieces the same
size as the pork; chop the spring onion into longish segments, and
the ginger into shreds. Shred the chilli peppers (discarding the pips)
coarsely, and grind the peppercorns.

Heat the oil in a large frying pan. Add the cabbage, ginger and
spring onion and stir-fry quickly over a high heat for 1 minute. Add
the soya sauce, hoisin sauce, sherry, and crushed stock cube. Continue to stir-fry for 2 minutes over a high heat. Remove the cabbage
and spring onion with a perforated spoon, and spread them over
the bottom of a serving dish as a bed.

Heat the remaining liquid in the pan over a high heat. Add water and bring to a full boil. Lower the slices of pork in batter into it piece by piece, spreading them over the pan in a single layer. After 2 minutes, turn the pork slices over and cook them for 1 more minute. Remove the pork with a perforated spoon, and arrange the slices on top of the cabbage in the serving dish.

Heat the oil in a small frying pan. Add the pepper and the chilli pepper and stir over a medium heat for 2–3 minutes, until the 'hotness' of the ingredients permeates the oil. Sprinkle the oil over the pieces of pork.

Serves 6.

Pork Sweetbread in Chicken Fu-Yung
(From the Ching Chen Garden Restaurant, Chengtu—well known for Szechuan dishes.)

The use of Fu-yung—beaten egg-white with minced chicken or fish—in Szechuan cooking seems to bear the influence of Peking, where it is also often eaten.

225 g (½ lb) breast of chicken
2 egg-whites
30 ml (2 tablespoons) corn-
flour
250 ml (½ pint) stock (b)
2 slices root ginger
small chicken stock cube

60 ml (4 tablespoons) dry
sherry
225 g (½ lb) pork sweetbreads
45 ml (3 tablespoons) lard
60 ml (2 tablespoons) minced
ham

Chop and finely mince the chicken. Beat the egg-whites with the cornflour, 30 ml (2 tablespoons) stock and the salt, using a rotary beater, until almost stiff.

Heat the stock with the ginger, stock cube and sherry, and leave it to simmer for 5 minutes. Add the sweetbreads, and leave to cook for 8 minutes. Remove the sweetbreads, and cut them into longish julienned strips, about as thick as a chopstick.

Heat 30 ml (2 tablespoons) lard in a large frying pan. Add the beaten chicken Fu-yung, and turn it in the hot fat over a medium heat for 2–3 minutes. Scoop out half the Fu-yung and place it at the bottom of a deep-sided serving dish. Add the remaining lard and sweetbread to mix with the Fu-yung in the pan. Turn and stir for a couple of minutes. Spread the sweetbread, together with the balance of the Fu-yung, on top of that already in the serving dish. Sprinkle the top of the dish with minced ham.

Serves 6–8.

H*

Sliced Pork Fu-Yung
(From the Ching Chen Garden Restaurant, Chengtu.)

350 g (¾ lb) fillet of pork
salt and pepper to taste
30 ml (2 tablespoons) cornflour
1 egg-white
2 slices root ginger
1 medium onion
2 cloves garlic

60 ml (4 tablespoons) lard
15 ml (1 tablespoon) soya sauce
2 ml (½ teaspoon) sugar
½ chicken stock cube (crushed)
30 ml (2 tablespoons) dry
  sherry

Fu-Yung

2 egg-whites
30 ml (2 tablespoons) minced
  chicken breast

2 ml (½ teaspoon) salt
30 ml (2 tablespoons) cold
  stock (a)

Cut the pork into small, thin slices. Season with salt and pepper, rub with cornflour and wet with egg-white. Leave to season for 30 minutes.

Cut the ginger and onion into thin slices, and then into shreds. Crush and chop the garlic.

Prepare the Fu-yung by beating the remaining two egg-whites with a rotary beater for 15 seconds. Add the minced chicken, salt and stock, and beat until nearly stiff. Put the mixture in a bowl and then into a steamer and steam gently for 10 minutes.

Heat the lard in a large frying pan. When hot, lay the pork slices into the hot fat evenly spread out over the pan. Fry gently over a medium heat for 2 minutes. Push the pieces of pork to one side of the pan, pouring away any excess fat, and placing the opposite side of the pan over the heat.

Add the ginger, garlic and onion on this side of the pan. After stirring and turning a few times add the soya sauce, sugar, stock cube (crushed) and sherry. Turn the heat up high, and stir-fry these ingredients together for 15 seconds. Bring the pork slices over and stir them all together for 30 seconds.

Add a quarter of the Fu-yung to the pork in the pan. Turn the mixture over a few times, and transfer to a well-heated, deep-sided serving dish. Ladle the remainder of the Fu-yung evenly on top of the pork. The dish of pork is served buried under the 'white snow' of Fu-yung.

Serves 6–8.

Szechuan Double-Cooked Pork
(A dish for a family meal, adapted from the Ching Chen
Garden Restaurant, Chengtu.)

675–900 g (1½–2 lb) belly of   30 ml (2 tablespoons) lard
pork

Sauce

15 ml (1 tablespoon) salted   15 ml (1 tablespoon) dry sherry
  black beans   22 ml (1½ tablespoons) sweet
3 cloves garlic   bean paste
3 stalks young leeks   15 ml (1 tablespoon) tomato
45 ml (3 tablespoons) lard   purée
5 ml (1 teaspoon) sugar   7 ml (½ tablespoon) chilli sauce
22 ml (1½ tablespoons) soya
  sauce

Boil the pork in a large pan of water for 30 minutes. Drain and
leave to cool for 30 minutes, then cut into medium-sized thick
slices. Soak the black beans in water for 30 minutes, then drain
and mash them.

Heat the lard in a large flat frying pan. Lay the slices of pork
evenly over the pan and fry them gently over a medium heat for 1–2
minutes: then turn the slices over and fry for another 2 minutes.
Remove the pork from the pan with a perforated spoon or fish-
slice.

Now add the garlic and leeks and turn them in the hot fat a few
times. Add all the remaining ingredients. Turn and mix the contents together over a high heat for 1 minute. Return the pork to the
pan, mix with the other ingredients for 2 minutes, and serve on a
well-heated dish. This sweet, spicy recipe is excellent with rice.
Serves 6–8.

Szechuan Ground-Rice Steamed Pork Pudding with Soya Cheese
(Adapted from Mass-Strength Dining Room, Chengtu.)

900 g (2 lb) belly of pork   30 ml (2 tablespoons) soya
2 chilli peppers   sauce
2 medium onions   15 ml (1 tablespoon) red
3 slices root ginger   southern soya cheese

15 ml (1 tablespoon) brown
  sugar
15 ml (1 tablespoon) sherry
2.2–2.65 kg (5–6 lb) ground
  rice (coarsely ground, and

made aromatic by roasting or
  frying in a dry pan until
  brown)
60–90 ml (4–6 tablespoons)
  green peas

Cut the pork into medium-sized thick slices. Shred the pepper (discarding the pips). Cut the onion and ginger into shreds. Add them with the pepper to the pork in a bowl with the soya sauce, soya cheese, sugar and sherry. Turn and mix them thoroughly. Leave them to season and marinate for 30 minutes. Finally sprinkle the pork slices evenly with the ground rice, and mix them into the marinade.

Place the pork, covered with the marinade and ground rice, in a heatproof bowl, fat and skin-side down, with the leaner pieces at the top so that when the dish is turned out for serving the succulent skin and fat, much appreciated by the Chinese, is facing up. Sprinkle the peas on top of the lean pork. Cover the bowl with tin-foil, put it in a steamer and steam steadily for 3–3½ hours.

Invert the bowl and turn the pork pudding on to a serving dish. This is a delicacy for the rice-eaters of China, who relish the hot jellied savoury pork (skin, fat and all) with copious quantities of rice. Serves 6–8.

Szechuan Red Ground-Rice Steamed Pork Pudding with Pickles

This recipe incorporates the same ingredients as the one on page 229, except that the soya cheese is replaced by 75 ml (5 tablespoons) salted pickles (say, 30 ml (2 tablespoons) chopped Winter Pickle, 30 ml (2 tablespoons) Snow Pickle, and 15 ml (1 tablespoon) chopped Szechuan Cha Tsai Pickle), to mix with the pork along with 15 ml (3 teaspoons) red rice (ground rice coloured bright red—available from Chinese foodstores), 30 ml (2 tablespoons) extra sherry and 15 ml (1 tablespoon) brandy. This is quite a wine-flavoured dish. If red rice is not available, simply mix 1 ml (¼ teaspoon) cochineal or red colouring and 15–30 ml (1–2 tablespoons) extra tomato purée with the pork before cooking.

Quick-Fried Fish-Flavoured Pork Liver

There is a range of Szechuan dishes curiously known as Fish-flavoured dishes. According to natives of Szechuan, they are so-called not because they carry the flavour of fish, but because they are cooked with ingredients normally associated with the cooking of fish: ginger, garlic, onion, dried, salted black beans, chilli pepper, wine and vinegar. This dish of pork liver is one example.

450 g (1 lb) pig's liver
7 ml (½ tablespoon) salt
22 ml (1½ tablespoons) cornflour
30 ml (2 tablespoons) sherry
15 ml (1 tablespoon) vegetable
  oil

3 slices root ginger
3 cloves garlic
2 chilli peppers
3 stalks spring onion
52 ml (3½ tablespoons) lard
15 ml (1 tablespoon) salted
  black beans

Sauce

30 ml (2 tablespoons) soya
  sauce
22 ml (1½ tablespoons) aromatic vinegar

45 ml (3 tablespoons) stock (b)
30 ml (2 tablespoons) cornflour

Cut the liver into medium-sized thin slices. Rub these with the mixed salt, cornflour, sherry and oil. Leave to season for 30 minutes. Shred the ginger, crush and coarsely chop the garlic and shred the chilli (discarding the pips). Cut the spring onions into medium-sized segments. Mix the sauce ingredients in a bowl, and blend well.

Heat 37 ml (2½ tablespoons) lard in a large frying pan. Add the liver and stir-fry over a high heat for 30 seconds and then push it to one side of the pan. Add the remaining lard, ginger, garlic, black beans, chilli pepper, and spring onion to other side of the pan. Stir-fry quickly over a high heat for 30 seconds. Bring the liver over and stir-fry it with the other ingredients in the pan, still over a high heat, for 1 minute.

Pour the sauce mixture evenly over the contents of the pan, reduce the heat to medium, and stir-fry everything together for 1 minute. Serve immediately on a well-heated dish.
Serves 6–8.

Stir-Fried Fish-Flavoured Shredded Pork with Shredded Bamboo Shoots

350 g (¾ lb) leg of pork
5 ml (1 teaspoon) salt
7 ml (½ tablespoon) cornflour

7 ml (½ tablespoon) vegetable oil
6 medium Chinese dried mushrooms

225 g (½ lb) bamboo shoots
7 ml (½ tablespoon) salted black
  beans
52 ml (3½ tablespoons) lard

3 slices root ginger
3 cloves garlic
3 stalks spring onion
2 chilli peppers

Sauce

22 ml (1½ tablespoons) soya
  sauce
5 ml (1 teaspoon) sugar
30 ml (2 tablespoons) dry
  sherry

22 ml (1½ tablespoons) vinegar
  (Chinese aromatic, if available)

Cut the pork into slices, and then into double-matchstick-thick shreds. Rub these with the salt, cornflour, and oil. Leave them to season for 30 minutes. Soak the mushrooms in water for 30 minutes, discard the stalks and chop the caps and bamboo shoots into similar-sized shreds. Soak the black beans in water for 30 minutes; drain and discard the water.

Heat 30 ml (2 tablespoons) lard in a large frying pan. Add the pork and stir-fry it over a high heat for 30 seconds, then push it to one side of the pan. Add the remaining lard to the other side of the pan together with the ginger, garlic, spring onion, chilli pepper, black beans, bamboo shoots and mushrooms. Stir-fry them together with the other ingredients over a high heat for 2 minutes. Pour the sauce mixture evenly over the contents, and stir-fry them all together, still over a high heat, for 45 seconds. Serve immediately on a well-heated dish.
Serves 6–8.

Beef

Beef seems to be more commonly used in Szechuan cuisine than is usual in southern (Canton) cooking, or that of the Lower Yangtze (Shanghai). This is probably chiefly due to the fact that cows and oxen are widely used for haulage in Szechuan, particularly in the vast salt-mines of Kung Si County. Since the cattle are bred for transport rather than for the table the meat is liable to be tough, and in some Szechuan dishes where the beef is cut small or shredded and often 'dry-fried', the result is meant to be chewy rather than tender. But more often than not the meat is slowly cooked for several hours so that it becomes tender and full of flavour through the sheer length of cooking time.

Dry-Fried Hot-Spiced Beef Shreds

(Adapted from the Dining Rooms of the Nationalities, Chungking, the largest catering establishment in the city. The kitchen is headed by Chef Liao Ching Ting, who has had over forty years' experience in the kitchen, and is well known for his innovations, especially his roasts and braised dishes.)

350 g (¾ lb) fillet of beef
7 ml (½ tablespoon) salt
15 ml (1 tablespoon) cornflour
75–90 ml (5–6 tablespoons)

vegetable oil
175 g (6½ oz) celery
175 g (6½ oz) carrots
4 slices root ginger

Sauce

15 ml (1 tablespoon) soya paste
22 ml (1½ tablespoons) soya sauce
15 ml (1 tablespoon) hoisin sauce

22 ml (1½ tablespoons) sugar
7 ml (½ tablespoon) chilli sauce
22 ml (1½ tablespoons) sherry
pepper to taste

Cut the beef into long double-matchstick-thick strips. Rub these with the salt, cornflour and 7 ml (½ tablespoon) oil. Cut the carrots and celery into similar-sized strips. Mix the sauce ingredients together until well blended.

Heat the oil in a large frying pan. Add the beef, spread it over the surface of the pan and stir-fry it over a medium heat for 5–6 minutes until the meat begins to turn dark brown. Drain away any excess oil, and add the carrot, celery and ginger. Stir-fry the vegetables together with the beef for 4 minutes, making sure that they are evenly mixed. Sprinkle the mixed sauce evenly over the contents. Continue to stir-fry for 1½ minutes, over a high heat. Serve on a well-heated dish. Beef cooked by this method is very chewy and is considered an excellent accompaniment to wine.

Serves 5–6.

Nutty and Hot Quick-Fried Shredded Beef
(Adapted from the recipes of the Old Szechuan Restaurant, Chungking.)

900 g (2 lb) leg of beef
15 ml (1 tablespoon) salt
4 slices root ginger
7 ml (½ tablespoon) chilli powder
2 ml (½ teaspoon) black pepper
10 ml (2 teaspoons) caster sugar
pinch five-spice powder

22 ml (1½ tablespoons) soya sauce
15 ml (1 tablespoon) hoisin sauce
15 ml (1 tablespoon) dry sherry
7 ml (½ tablespoon) sesame oil
15 ml (1 tablespoon) sesame paste (or peanut butter)
oil for deep-frying

Cut the beef into very thin slices. Rub these with the salt, and leave to dry for 3 hours. Shred the ginger, and mix together the chilli powder, pepper, sugar and five-spice powder. Mix the soya sauce, hoisin sauce, sherry, sesame paste and sesame oil until well blended.

Place the beef slices on a wire rack, and cook them in a pre-heated oven at 80°C (350°F)/Gas 4 for 15 minutes. Transfer them to a steamer and steam for 1¼ hours. Remove to cool. When the meat is cold, cut along the fibre, chopping it into long matchstick-sized shreds. Sprinkle these with the mixed dry ingredients and rub this in thoroughly. Leave to season for 30 minutes. Add the sauce mixture of soya sauce, etc, and rub this into the seasoned beef. Leave to marinate for 2–3 hours. When quite dry, spread the slices out in a fine-meshed wire basket and deep-fry over a moderate heat for 3–4 minutes; remove and drain thoroughly.

This dish, which can be served hot or cold, is usually placed in small dishes on occasional tables, to be nibbled as an appetizer before or between meals; although it is sometimes offered as a starter at a dinner, accompanied by wine.
Serves 6–8.

Cold Tossed Boiled Beef
(Adapted from the Hsing Ling Hsiang Moslem Restaurant, Chungking.)

There seem to be Moslem eating establishments in most large Chinese cities. I suspect that the elements of Moslem cooking in Szechuan must have drifted into the province from Peking, rather than having travelled directly over the mountain ranges separating

Szechuan from the 'Kansu Corridor' and the territories of Sinkiang and Mongolia, where Chinese Moslems are most numerous.

900 g (2 lb) topside or rump of beef

Dressing

30 ml (2 tablespoons) soya sauce
10 ml (2 teaspoons) chilli sauce
a pinch freshly ground pepper
22 ml (1½ tablespoons) vinegar (Chinese aromatic, if available)

7 ml (½ tablespoon) sugar
12 ml (¾ tablespoon) sesame oil
3 cloves garlic
4–5 large crisp lettuce leaves

Bring 3–4 pints of water to the boil in a saucepan. Add the beef, bring to the boil, and simmer gently for 45 minutes. Remove the meat from the pan to cool. When the beef is cold, cut it with a sharp knife into medium-sized thin slices. Meanwhile, crush and finely chop the garlic, and mix this with the other ingredients for the dressing.

Spread the lettuce leaves as a bed over a large serving dish. Arrange the beef slices neatly on top. Pour the 'dressing' evenly over the beef.

Serves 6–8.

Pure Long-Simmered Steamed Beef
(Adapted from Yeu Chung Hsiang Restaurant, Pao An Road, Chungking, well known for beef dishes.)

1.35 kg (3 lb) leg or brisket of beef
½ chicken
6 slices root ginger
450 g (1 lb) turnips

225 g (½ lb) carrots
10 ml (2 teaspoons) salt
1½ chicken stock cubes
5–6 large crisp lettuce leaves

Dip

22 ml (1½ tablespoons) salt

7 ml (1½ teaspoons) black pepper

Plunge the beef and chicken into a pan of boiling water and boil vigorously for 10 minutes. Remove and drain. Cut the beef into 6 pieces and the chicken into 4 pieces. Arrange them in a casserole or

heatproof dish. Add 1 litre (2 pints) water, and the ginger.
Cut the turnip and carrots slantwise into medium-sized triangular wedges.

If you are using a heatproof dish, put this in a steamer and steam for 3 hours; if using a casserole, put it in the middle of a preheated oven at 170°C (325°F)/Gas 3 for 2½ hours.

Remove the beef and cut into large bite-sized pieces. Place these in a deep-sided heatproof dish, in a steamer, and steam for 30 minutes.

Skim away any grease from the soup in the original casserole or heatproof dish and pour it into a saucepan. Add the turnips and carrots, together with the salt and stock cubes. Bring this to the boil and simmer gently for 40 minutes.

Serve by bringing the heatproof dish containing the beef direct from the steamer to the table. Mix the salt and pepper and divide between 2 small saucer-sized dishes as dips for the beef. Pour the soup in the casserole or heatproof dish into a large tureen or bowl lined with lettuce leaves to consume with the beef. 'Pure', plainly cooked dishes like this are generally served together with a couple of stir-fried dishes at a Chinese dinner.

Serves 6–8.

Lotus-Leaf Wrapped Long-Steamed Beef in Aromatic Ground Rice

1.35 kg (3 lb) beef (topside or silverside)
225 g (½ lb) beef fat
2 slices root ginger
30 ml (2 tablespoons) soya sauce
15 ml (1 tablespoon) hoisin sauce
15 ml (3 teaspoons) salt
2.5 ml (½ tablespoon) red soya-bean curd cheese

10 ml (2 teaspoons) chilli sauce
1 ml (¼ teaspoon) pepper
7 ml (½ tablespoon) sugar
90–105 ml (6–7 tablespoons) ground rice (made aromatic by being first fried in a dry pan for 2–3 minutes and then ground)
1–2 sheets of dried lotus leaf

Cut the beef into 12–16 large slices. Cut the beef fat into half the number of slices of beef. Shred the ginger and mix it with the soya sauce, hoisin sauce, salt, soya-bean curd cheese, chilli sauce, pepper rice and sugar until well blended. Rub the mixture into both sides of the beef.

Soak the lotus leaf in water until malleable. Cut it into 8–10 pieces. Wrap 2 pieces of beef and one piece of beef fat in each sheet of lotus leaf, sandwiching the beef fat between the pieces of beef. Use wooden cocktail sticks, if necessary, to secure the wrapping.

Pile the lotus-leaf-wrapped beef (6–8 parcels) in a heatproof dish, put the dish into a steamer, and steam vigorously for $3\frac{1}{2}$–4 hours. Serve in the heatproof dish. The diners open the lotus-leaf-wrapped packages with their chopsticks to eat the meat, which should by then be tender, succulent and full of flavour. An excellent dish to eat with rice.

Serves 6–8.

Long-Cooked Beef Pudding

575 g (1¼ lb) brisket of beef
5 ml (1 teaspoon) salt
37 ml (2½ tablespoons) soya sauce
15 ml (1 tablespoon) hoisin sauce
10 ml (2 teaspoons) soya bean-curd cheese
pepper to taste
30 ml (2 tablespoons) sherry
15 ml (1 tablespoon) vegetable oil
2 slices root ginger

2 chilli peppers
2 medium onions
30 ml (2 tablespoons) Chinese winter pickle
30 ml (2 tablespoons) Chinese snow pickle
30 ml (2 tablespoons) Szechuan Cha Tsai pickle (hot)
675 g (1½ lb) potato or yam
350 g (¾ lb) glutinous rice (pudding rice)
5 ml (1 teaspoon) sugar

Cut the beef into large bite-sized pieces. Add the salt, soya sauce, hoisin sauce, soya bean-curd cheese, pepper, sherry and oil. Shred the ginger and chilli peppers (discarding the pips), and add them to the beef; cut the onions into thin slices and add half of them to the beef. Mix the rest of the onion with the pickles. Turn and toss the various ingredients, now mixed with the beef, until they are thoroughly mixed, and leave this to season for 15 minutes. (Retain any excess of marinade.)

Peel and cut the potato or yam into small, thin pieces. Add the three types of pickles to them and mix well. Boil the rice for 7–8 minutes; drain, and add the onion and the remainder of the marinade mixture from the beef, mixing thoroughly.

Pack the marinated beef together with the marinade at the bottom of a deep heatproof dish. On top of this put the yam or potato mixed with pickles. Finally, spread the rice and onion over the pieces of potato or yam. Cover the top firmly with tinfoil. Place

238 CHINESE PROVINCIAL COOKING

the dish in a steamer, and steam steadily for 3–3½ hours.

Turn the contents out on to a serving dish, as you would a boiled pudding. In this case the beef will cap the 'pudding', its gravy oozing down into the potato and rice. The diners should help themselves to this quite substantial domestic dish.
Serves 6–8.

Stock or Water-Fried Beef
(Adapted from the Dining Rooms of the Nationalities, Chungking.)

10 ml (2 teaspoons) salted black beans
550 g (1¼ lb) fillet of beef or rump steak
10 ml (2 teaspoons) salt
1 egg
22 ml (1½ tablespoons) corn-flour
5 ml (1 teaspoon) peppercorns
4 stalks young leeks
3 slices root ginger

4 stalks asparagus tips
3 cloves garlic
2 dried chilli peppers
22 ml (1½ tablespoons) lard
125 ml (¼ pint) stock
22 ml (1½ tablespoons) soya sauce
30 ml (2 tablespoons) dry sherry
30 ml (2 tablespoons) sesame oil

Soak the black beans for 30 minutes and then drain them. Cut the beef into very thin medium-sized slices. Rub these with the salt, and coat them with batter made from the beaten egg and cornflour. Lightly crush the peppercorns. Cut the leeks slantwise into 2.5 cm (1 in) sections. Shred the ginger. Cut each asparagus tip into halves.

Crush the garlic, and shred the chilli pepper (discarding the pips).

Heat the lard in a large frying pan over a high heat. Add the black beans, peppercorns and ginger and stir in the lard for 30 seconds. Add the stock, asparagus, soya sauce, sherry and leeks. Bring the contents to a vigorous boil for 1½ minutes. Push the solid contents to the sides of the pan. Spread the slices of beef in batter in the centre of the pan. Stir these with the boiling stock for 1½ minutes, when they should be cooked. Remove the beef with a perforated spoon and place it in the centre of a deep-sided serving dish. Return the leeks and asparagus to the centre of the pan. Continue to stir over a high heat until the liquid in the pan has been reduced to less than half. Ladle out the leeks and asparagus, arrange them around the beef in the serving dish, and pour the gravy in the pan over them.

Place the heated sesame oil in a small frying pan and add the shredded dried chilli pepper. Stir in the hot oil over a medium heat

for 1 minute. Add the garlic and stir again for 30 seconds. Pour the mixture over the beef, and serve. This is a spicy dish of tender beef full of Szechuan flavour.
Serves 6.

Braised Beef Tripe with Coriander

675–900 g (1½–2 lb) beef tripe
3–4 slices root ginger
15 ml (1 tablespoon) salt
1 medium green pepper
2 red chilli peppers
1 large onion
15 ml (1 tablespoon) black beans
75 ml (5 tablespoons) transparent pea-starch noodles
45 ml (3 tablespoons) lard
125 ml (¼ pint) stock (b)

45 ml (3 tablespoons) dry sherry
45 ml (3 tablespoons) soya sauce
15 ml (1 tablespoon) hoisin sauce
15 ml (1 tablespoon) sesame oil
30 ml (2 tablespoons) coriander leaves
7 ml (½ tablespoon) sugar
12 ml (¾ tablespoon) vinegar (aromatic, if available)

Boil the tripe in 1 litre (2 pints) water with the ginger and salt for 1 hour. Drain and cut into chopstick-thick longish slivers. Cut the green pepper into similar thin slivers, shred the chilli peppers (discarding the pips) and chop the onion into thin slices. Soak the black beans for 30 minutes and the noodles for 10 minutes, and drain.

Heat the lard in a heavy saucepan. Add the black beans, onion, green pepper and chilli pepper, and stir them in the hot fat for 2 minutes. Add the tripe and turn and stir-fry this together with the other ingredients for 3 minutes over a high heat. Add the noodles, stock, sherry, soya sauce and hoisin sauce. Reduce the heat and leave this to simmer gently, under cover, for the next 45 minutes. Add the sesame oil, half the coriander leaves and the sugar and simmer for a further 5 minutes. Sprinkle this mixture with the remainder of the coriander leaves and the vinegar and serve, accompanied by rice.
Serves 6.

Long-Cooked Calf's Foot and Oxtail Stew

1.8–2.2 kg (4–5 lb) oxtail
1.2–1.35 kg (2½–3 lb) calf's foot

7 ml (½ tablespoon) peppercorns
250 ml (½ pint) water

250 ml (½ pint) stock (b)
4 slices root ginger
*90 ml (6 tablespoons) soya
sauce*
*30 ml (2 tablespoons) soya paste
(or hoisin sauce)*

*75–90 ml (5–6 tablespoons) dry
sherry*
10 ml (2 teaspoons) sugar
10 ml (2 teaspoons) salt
*22 ml (1½ tablespoons) cori-
ander leaves*

Boil the oxtail and calf's foot in a large pan of boiling water for 20
minutes and drain completely. Lightly crush the peppercorns in a
mortar.

Distribute the oxtail pieces and calf's foot evenly in a large
casserole. Add the water, stock, ginger, soya sauce, peppercorns and
soya paste. Stir and turn a few times until well mixed. Bring the
contents to the boil and put the casserole into a steamer, or into
the middle of a low–moderate oven at 170°C (325°F)/Gas 3 for 4
hours, stirring once every hour. Add the sherry, sugar, salt and
half the coriander. Continue to cook for 30 minutes at the same
temperature.

Serve from the casserole at the table. The meat on the bones
should now be very tender, and delicious served with a sprinkle of
coriander on boiled rice or plain boiled noodles, with fresh or
quickly cooked vegetables.
Serves 7–8.

Calf's Foot and Oxtail in Aspic

The ingredients of the previous recipe (page 239) can be set and
served in aspic simply by cooking them in the same manner, and
leaving the cooled dish in the refrigerator for a couple of hours.
Scrape off the meat from the oxtail and cut each piece of calf's
foot into 6 pieces (discarding bones and any impurities). Return
the meat to the stock, add 60 ml (4 tablespoons) sherry, and reheat
the ingredients. Pour the contents into a suitable deep-sided
dish, and allow to cool and set in the refrigerator a second
time.

When the mixture is well chilled and set, turn it out on a flat
serving dish on a bed of fresh lettuce leaves. Decorate the top of the
jellied meat with a few sprays of coriander leaves or parsley. Another
excellent dish to eat with hot boiled rice.
Serves 6–8.

Quick-Fried Ox Kidney with Wood Ears

350 g (¾ lb) ox kidney
7 ml (½ tablespoon) salt
52 ml (3½ tablespoons) vegetable oil

60–75 ml (4–5 tablespoons) dried wood ears (tree fungi)
2 slices root ginger
1 medium onion

Sauce

15 ml (1 tablespoon) brown sugar
22 ml (1½ tablespoons) dry sherry
15 ml (1 tablespoon) cornflour (blended in 75 ml (5 tablespoons) water)

22 ml (1½ tablespoons) vinegar (Chinese aromatic if available)
22 ml (1½ tablespoons) soya sauce

Trim the kidney and cut it into long, thin strips. Rub these with the salt and 7 ml (½ tablespoon) oil. Soak the wood ears in water for 15 minutes and then wash them in 2 changes of water. Shred the ginger, and cut the onion into thin slices. Mix the sauce ingredients together until well blended.

Heat 45 ml (3 tablespoons) oil in a frying pan. Add the onion and ginger and stir-fry over a high heat for 1 minute. Add the kidney and wood ears; stir and turn them over a high heat for 1¾ minutes. Pour the sauce mixture evenly over the contents. Continue to stir-fry over a high heat for ¾ minute and serve immediately. Serves 5–6.

Fish and Shellfish

Because Szechuan is so far inland, it is natural that most seafood used in its cuisine is dried: dried squid, bêche de mer, dried prawns, shark's fin, fish lips, etc. Those crustaceans and fish which are served fresh are all fresh-water products—eel, carp, pike, perch, and so on. The fish is often simmered in a clear liquid as a contrast to the many spicy dishes on the table, or served in a thick, strong-tasting sauce. This is intended to enhance the freshness of the fish, which is often fried, sautéed or clear-simmered for a very short time to preserve the fresh juiciness just under the skin.

Fried Fish in Clear Ginger Sauce

1.2–1.35 kg (2½–3 lb) fish
(carp, perch, etc)
15 ml (1 tablespoon) salt
5–6 slices root ginger
3 stalks spring onion
1 clove garlic

oil for deep- or semi-deep-frying
500 ml (1 pint) clear stock (b)
45 ml (3 tablespoons) dry
    sherry or white wine
15 ml (1 tablespoon) vinegar

Wash the fish thoroughly. Rub it inside and out with the salt, and leave for 30 minutes. Shred the ginger, and cut the spring onion into medium-sized lengths.

Heat the oil in a large frying pan or deep-fryer. Lower the fish into the hot oil to fry gently for 5 minutes (2½ minutes on either side if in a shallow pan—baste if necessary). Drain thoroughly.

Heat the stock in a large frying pan. Add the ginger and garlic and adjust the seasoning. Bring to the boil and simmer for 3 minutes. Lower the fish into the stock and leave it to simmer for 10 minutes, adding the wine, vinegar and spring onions 1 minute before dishing out.

Serve in an oval dish with the fish swimming in the hot stock, surrounded by the greenness of the spring onions. The diner ladles the fish 'consommé' from the communal dish over his own bowl of rice, along with pieces of fish (taken with chopsticks). The ginger-and-fish consommé is considered a delicacy by gourmets.

Serves 6–8.

Fried Fish in Hot Five Willow Sauce

1.2–1.35 kg (2½–3 lb) fish
(carp, perch, pike, etc)
2 slices root ginger
15 ml (1 tablespoon) salt

oil for deep- or semi-deep-frying
30 ml (2 tablespoons) cornflour
    (blended in 150 ml (10 table-
    spoons) water)

Sauce

3 stalks spring onion
3 stalks golden needles (tiger
    lily buds—optional)
1 small green pepper
1 small red pepper
2 chilli peppers
3 slices root ginger

2 rashers bacon
45 ml (3 tablespoons) lard
30 ml (2 tablespoons) Chinese
    winter pickle
45 ml (3 tablespoons) stock (b)
10 ml (2 teaspoons) sugar
30 ml (2 tablespoons) sherry

52 ml (3½ tablespoons) soya   22 ml (1½ tablespoons) sweet
  sauce   bean paste (or hoisin sauce)
15 ml (1 tablespoon) salted
  bean paste

Wash and clean the fish thoroughly. Finely chop the ginger and
mix it with the salt. Rub the fish inside and out with the mixture
and 15 ml (1 tablespoon) oil.

To prepare the sauce, cut the spring onion and golden needles
into medium-sized sections. Shred the red and green peppers, chilli
pepper (discarding the pips), ginger and bacon.

Deep- or semi-deep-fry the fish for 6 minutes (3 minutes on
either side if the pan is shallow), and drain thoroughly.

Heat the lard in a large frying pan. Add all the vegetables for
the sauce as well as the pickle and bacon and stir-fry over a high
heat for 2 minutes. Add the stock, sugar, sherry, soya sauce, both
salted and sweet soya paste and the cornflour. Stir and mix over a
high heat. Lower the fish into the sauce. Baste with the liquid and
vegetables for 1½ minutes. Turn the fish over and cook (meanwhile
basting) for another 2½ minutes over a medium heat. Reduce the
heat and leave the contents to cook slowly for 5 more minutes.

Transfer the fish to a warmed oval dish, and pour the now
thickened sauce from the pan over the length of the fish, dressing
it with the vegetables, pickle and bacon. The fish flesh should taste
very sweet and fresh, contrasting with the strong-tasting sauce.
Serves 6–8.

Quick-Fried Shredded Squid with Bamboo Shoots
(Adapted from the Chengtu Dining Rooms, Chengtu.)

75–100 g (3–4 oz) dried squid   7 ml (½ tablespoon) cornflour,
75–100 g (3–4 oz) belly of pork   blended in 45 ml (3 table-
  (or any fat and lean pork)   spoons) water
100 g (4 oz) bamboo shoots   22 ml (1½ tablespoons) soya
2 chilli peppers   sauce
45 ml (3 tablespoons) stock (a)   10 ml (2 teaspoons) sesame oil
7 ml (½ tablespoon) salt   52 ml (3½ tablespoons) lard
30 ml (2 tablespoons) sherry

Soak the squid in water for 1 hour. Cut it into strips as thick as a
chopstick. Cut the pork crossways through the lean and fat, and
the bamboo shoots, into similar chopstick-sized strips. Shred the
chilli peppers (discarding the pips).

Mix the stock, salt, and sherry in a bowl until well blended.

Heat the lard in a frying pan over a medium heat. Add the squid, stir-fry for 1 minute and leave to sauté for 3 minutes. Add the pork and pepper, stir-fry for 1 minute and leave to sauté for 3 minutes. Add the stock, sherry and salt mixture and the bamboo shoots. Turn and stir them together with the other contents of the pan, for 3 minutes. Pour in the soya-sauce mixture, turn and stir once more, and leave to cook for a further 2 minutes. Sprinkle with sesame oil and serve. This is a crunchy, chewy dish, very savoury, with a 'smoky' taste. An excellent dish to accompany wine.

Serves 6–8.

Quick Dry-Fried Shredded Eel
(Adapted from the Chengtu Dining Rooms, Chengtu.)

675 g (1½ lb) eel
4–5 sticks celery
3 stalks young leeks
4–5 slices root ginger
15 ml (1 tablespoon) salted black beans
60 ml (4 tablespoons) oil
5 ml (1 teaspoon) salt
30 ml (2 tablespoons) sherry

15 ml (1 tablespoon) hoisin sauce
22 ml (1½ tablespoons) soya sauce
22 ml (1½ tablespoons) vinegar (Chinese aromatic, if available)
2.5 ml (½ teaspoon) freshly ground pepper

Bone the eel and cut into medium-sized sections. Cut each section into chopstick-thick strips. Clean and cut the celery and leeks into similar strips, and the ginger into shreds. Soak the black beans for 20 minutes and drain them.

Heat the oil in a large frying pan. Add the strips of eel and shredded ginger and stir-fry, spreading the strips over the surface of the pan. Leave to fry for 3 minutes over a medium heat, stirring lightly now and then. Sprinkle with salt and sherry. Add the celery, leeks, hoisin sauce and soya sauce. Stir the contents together for 2 minutes, and cook over a low heat for 3 minutes more. Sprinkle with vinegar and pepper, and serve on a well-heated dish. This is a piquant, highly savoury and aromatic dish, very good with wine.

Serves 6–8.

Steamed Eel in Consommé
(Adapted from the Chengtu Dining Rooms, Chengtu.)

1.2–1.35 kg (2½–3 lb) eel
3 slices root ginger
15 ml (1 tablespoon) salt

4 rashers bacon
1 bundle watercress
2 egg-whites

Consommé

500 ml (1 pint) stock (b)
10 ml (2 teaspoons) salt
45 ml (3 tablespoons) dry sherry

freshly ground black pepper to taste

Clean the eel and chop it into 8 sections. Finely chop the ginger, and rub it, with the salt, over each section of the eel. Leave to season for 1 hour. Cut each rasher of bacon in half. Wrap or roll one piece of bacon over each section of eel (secure with a wooden cocktail stick if necessary). Remove the roots of the watercress. Beat the egg-whites until stiff, put the basin in a steamer and steam for 8–10 minutes. Prepare the consommé by bringing the stock to the boil and stirring in the salt, pepper and sherry.

Place the bacon-wrapped eel sections in a deep-sided heatproof bowl. Pour in a kettleful of boiling water, leave for 30 seconds and drain. Repeat quickly once more and drain.

Spread a bed of steamed beaten egg-white (Fu-yung) over a deep-sided heatproof or glass dish. Arrange the watercress over the egg-whites and put the eel sections on top. Pour in the consommé. Place the dish in a steamer and steam vigorously for 25 minutes.

Bring the original heatproof dish directly from the steamer to the table after sprinkling it with freshly ground pepper. This is what we call in China a main course soup, and a useful variation from the stir-fry dishes.
Serves 8–10.

Home-Cooked Fish in Soup
(Adapted from the Dining Rooms of the Nationalities, Avenue of the Nationalities, Chungking.)

675–900 g (1½–2 lb) carp
15 ml (1 tablespoon) salt
3 slices root ginger
3 stalks spring onion
2 small carrots

375 ml (¾ pint) stock (b)
1 chicken stock cube
30 ml (2 tablespoons) dry sherry
pepper to taste

Cut the fish into a dozen chunks. Rub the pieces with the salt and leave to season for 30 minutes. Shred the ginger and cut the spring onion into large sections and the carrots into strips of similar width and length.

Heat 250 ml (½ pint) oil for semi-deep-frying in a deep-sided frying pan. Put the fish into the hot oil piece by piece. Turn the chunks over a medium heat for 4–5 minutes until they begin to brown. Drain away all the oil.

Add the ginger, spring onion and carrots to the fish pieces in the frying pan. Pour in the stock, and add the stock cube. Bring to the boil, and simmer gently for 10 minutes. Sprinkle constantly with the sherry, and the pepper to taste.

Serve in a deep-sided china or glass dish. Pan Tang Yu, as it is called, is a satisfying dish for a family dinner, accompanied by stir-fried dishes.

Serves 6–8.

Szechuan Soya-Braised Shark's Fin with Pork and Chicken
(Adapted from the Chengtu Dining Rooms, Chengtu.)

Every region has its own version of this banqueting dish. The Szechuan version of shark's fin is less exotic and more down to earth than others, being only flavoured by pork and chicken. The chicken and pork used in the cooking can be eaten in other recipes. (In China shark's fins are eaten for their texture and flavour-composition rather than for themselves.)

450 g (1 lb) dried shark's fin
1.5 litres (3 pints) superior
   stock (see page 266)
4 slices root ginger
20 ml (4 teaspoons) salt
2 Chinese celery/cabbages of the
   best quality
2 medium onions
1.35 kg (3 lb) chicken

900 g (2 lb) piece of leg of
   pork
90 ml (6 tablespoons) soya
   sauce
45 ml (3 tablespoons) white
   wine
45 ml (3 tablespoons) lard (for
   frying the cabbage)

Soak the shark's fin in water for 3 hours. Drain off the water and boil and simmer the shark's fin in 500 ml (1 pint) stock with 3 slices root ginger and 10 ml (2 teaspoons) salt for 1 hour. Drain away the stock (it can be used for other purposes). Repeat the process with a second pint of stock. Cut off the outer leaves of the cabbages, retaining only the hearts. Cut the hearts vertically into 2 equal halves. Cut the onions into thin slices. Quarter the chicken and the pork.

Heat the oil in a large, deep frying pan. Add the pork and chicken pieces and turn them in the hot oil for 7–8 minutes, until they begin to turn brown. Drain them completely.

Place the fins, pork, chicken and onion in a casserole, or heavy cooking pot. Add the remaining stock 500 ml (1 pint) and the soya sauce. Bring to a gentle boil, reduce the heat to the minimum (put an asbestos sheet under the pot or casserole), and leave to simmer for 2½ hours, turning the contents over every ½ hour. Sprinkle the contents with the wine, and cook for a further 10 minutes.

Meanwhile, heat the lard in a large frying pan. When it has melted, turn the cabbage halves a few times in it, leaving them to sauté for 2 minutes on either side.

Add 45 ml (3 tablespoons) of the liquid from the chicken-pork-fin mixture to the frying pan. Turn over the cabbage hearts again and leave them to sauté for a further 3 minutes.

Spread out the pieces of cabbage on a fine china serving dish. Spoon the pieces of shark's fin from the pot and arrange them neatly on top of the cabbage. Ladle a few tablespoons of the rich gravy from the pot carefully over the fins, and serve.
Serves 10.

Quick-Fried Shrimps Set in Jade
(Adapted from the Chengtu Dining Rooms, Chengtu.)

450 g (1 lb) peeled shrimps
10 ml (2 teaspoons) salt
22 ml (1½ tablespoons) corn-flour
1 egg-white
15 ml (1 tablespoon) vegetable oil
37 ml (2½ tablespoons) lard
450 g (1 lb) green peas (fresh or frozen)
45 ml (3 tablespoons) small button mushrooms

45 ml (3 tablespoons) finely chopped smoked ham
30 ml (2 tablespoons) soya sauce
30 ml (2 tablespoons) dry sherry
5 ml (1 teaspoon) sugar
30 ml (2 tablespoons) stock (b)
pepper to taste

Rub the shrimps with the salt and cornflour. Wet them with the egg-white, add the oil and toss them together.

Heat the lard in a large frying pan. Add the shrimps and stir-fry over a high heat for 1 minute; remove and keep hot. Quickly add the peas and all the other ingredients into the pan. Stir-fry over a high heat for 2 minutes. Return the shrimps to the pan, and stir-fry them together for 1 minute. Serve immediately on a well-heated dish. This is a comparatively simple recipe, quick to cook, and almost invariably a success.

Serves 6–8.

Flambeed Drunken Shrimps in Red Bean-Curd Cheese

3 slices root ginger
7 ml (½ tablespoon) salt
450 g (1 lb) peeled shrimps (must be very fresh)
15 ml (1 tablespoon) southern bean-curd cheese
22 ml (1½ tablespoons) sesame oil
45 ml (3 tablespoons) dry sherry

30 ml (2 tablespoons) vegetable oil
45–60 ml (3–4 tablespoons) brandy or one of the strong Chinese spirits (Mow Tai, Kaoliang, Mei Kwei Lu, Pai Kang, etc)

Chop the ginger finely. Rub this and the salt on to the shrimps. Leave to season for 30 minutes. Mix the bean-curd cheese with the sesame oil and sherry and add to the shrimps. Leave to marinate for 30 minutes.

Heat the oil in a frying pan. Pour in the shrimp mixture and stir quickly over a high heat for 1½ minutes. Transfer to a well-heated dish.

Sprinkle the shrimps with brandy or one of the Chinese spirits. Light the liquor with a match, and bring the dish to the table. In Szechuan, when the shrimps are very fresh they are sometimes served and eaten raw. In this case, the dish is sprinkled with fresh lemon juice and chopped chives before serving, and the shrimps are simply flambeed and then doused with an additional 30 ml (2 tablespoons) of liquor without stir-frying. Alternatively, add 7 ml (½ tablespoon) extra salt and 22 ml (1½ tablespoons) selected liquor to the fresh raw shrimps, leave them to season for 30 minutes longer and eat them raw.

Serves 6–8.

Tossed Deep-Fried Shredded Fish with Quick-Fried Bean Sprouts and Celery in Hot Sauce

450 g (1 lb) carp
10 ml (2 teaspoons) salt
22 ml (1½ tablespoons) cornflour
1 egg-white
2–3 celery sticks

oil for deep- or semi-deep-frying
30 ml (2 tablespoons) lard
350 g (¾ lb) bean sprouts
30 ml (2 tablespoons) soya
sauce
5 ml (1 teaspoon) sugar

Sauce

2 slices root ginger
2 dried chilli peppers
3 cloves garlic

45 ml (3 tablespoons) vegetable
oil

Cut the fish into medium-size strips, as thick as a chopstick. Rub them with the salt and cornflour and wet them with the egg-white. Cut the celery into the same-sized strips as the fish. Shred the ginger and chilli peppers (discarding the pips). Crush and coarsely chop the garlic.

Heat the oil in the deep-fryer, or heat 250 ml (½ pint) oil in a frying pan. Add the fish a few pieces at a time, and fry for 4–5 minutes, until they are beginning to brown and crisp. Remove and drain.

Heat the lard in a frying pan. Add the celery and stir-fry for 10 minutes, then add the bean sprouts and sprinkle with soya sauce and sugar. Stir-fry them together for 1½ minutes. Add the fish and toss it with the other ingredients in the pan for 1½ minutes.

Heat 45 ml (3 tablespoons) oil in a small pan. Add the ginger and chilli, and cook over a medium heat for 2 minutes, stirring now and then. Add the garlic, and continue to heat and stir for 30 seconds.

Transfer the fish and vegetables to a well-heated serving dish. Sprinkle with the pink 'hot oil' from the smaller pan, and serve. The contrast between the crisp texture of the fish, and the crunchiness of the vegetables, sprinkled with hot oil, makes this an interesting combination.
Serves 6.

Vegetables and Bean Curd Dishes

Szechuan Hot Salted Cabbage

Salted cabbage is used extensively in domestic cooking in Szechuan, especially in winter. In the absence of the particular type of cabbage grown in Szechuan, the best type to use would be a hard variety such as Christmas Drumhead or Savoy.

3 medium cabbages (about 1.35 kg (3 lb) each)	12 dried chilli peppers 45 ml (3 tablespoons) salt

Wash the cabbage, and cut it vertically into quarters. Place in an airy spot to dry overnight. Shred the dried chilli peppers (discarding the pips). Sprinkle the cabbage with salt and chilli pepper and rub in the seasoning evenly and thoroughly. Pack the cabbage in a jar. Put a dish or lid inside the jar on top of the cabbage, and a weight of at least 2.2–2.65 kg (5–6 lb) on top to press down the cabbage. Leave to season for 5 days. The hot salted cabbage should then be ready for use.

Cabbage prepared in this way can be shredded and tossed with other vegetables in salads, combined with other ingredients in stir-fried, braised or stewed dishes, or used to flavour soups.

Stir-Fried Winter Bamboo Shoots with Salted Cabbage in Chicken Fat

(Adapted from the Jade Dragon Restaurant, West Chengtu.)

675 g (1½ lb) winter bamboo (this should be about the thickness of asparagus)	22 ml (1½ tablespoons) soya sauce
75 g (3 oz) hot salted cabbage (see above)	30 ml (2 tablespoons) dry sherry 22 ml (1½ tablespoons) chicken fat
37 ml (2½ tablespoons) lard 45 ml (3 tablespoons) chicken stock (b)	10 ml (2 teaspoons) cornflour (blended in 37 ml (2½ table-spoons) water)

After removing the tough outer layer of the bamboo shoots, cut them slantwise in long segments. Coarsely chop the hot salted cabbage.

Heat the lard in a frying pan. Add the bamboo shoots, stir-fry for 1 minute and continue to fry over a medium heat for 3 minutes more. Add the cabbage, stock, soya sauce and sherry. Stir-fry together for 1 minute and sauté over a low heat for 3 minutes. Turn the heat to high and add the chicken fat and cornflour mixture. Stir-fry for 30 seconds and serve.

This is a dish for the connoisseur who is able to appreciate the subtle flavour and crunchy texture of bamboo shoots, especially as the fresh taste of the vegetable contrasts with the richness of the sauce.
Serves 6–8.

Crunchy Pickled Cucumber or Cabbage

2 medium cucumbers or 1 large hard white cabbage	20 ml (4 teaspoons) salt
	45 ml (3 tablespoons) gin
4 dried chilli peppers	250 ml (1 pint) malt vinegar

Cut the cucumber or cabbage into thin slices. Shred the chilli peppers (discarding the pips). Sprinkle and rub the salt, pepper and gin over the vegetable. Leave to season for a couple of hours. Place the mixture in a jar, pour in the vinegar and mix the ingredients together; leave to stand for 3 days in winter or 2 days in summer (the marinade can be drained off or used again), turning or shaking once a day.

Cabbage or cucumber prepared in this way is drained and served in small dishes as an accompaniment to any rich meat, fish or seafood dishes, for the diners to pick up with their chopsticks as they please, in between mouthfuls of rich highly flavoured foods.

Szechuan Pickle Pot

1 medium broccoli	4 dried chilli peppers
1 medium cauliflower	6 cloves garlic
1 medium, hard cabbage	15 ml (1 tablespoon) pepper-corns
1 red pepper	
2 medium onions	6 slices root ginger
1 medium cucumber	30 ml (2 tablespoons) salt
1 medium turnip	500 ml (1 pint) water
6 radishes	

Clean and cut the broccoli, cauliflower and cabbage into thin slices, and the green and red peppers, onions, cucumber and turnip into even thinner slices. Cut each radish in half, shred the chilli peppers (discarding the pips), crush the garlic and peppercorns and chop

I

the ginger. Leave all the vegetables to dry in an airy place for 12 hours.

Mix all the vegetables together in a large jar. Dissolve the salt in the water, and pour the brine over all the assorted vegetables. Close the top of the jar firmly, and leave to stand for 10–14 days. Pour away the brine and the pickles are ready for use.

Plain Stir-Fried and Sauteed Winter Bamboo Shoots with Bean Sprouts
(From the Dining Room of the Nationalities, Chungking.)

900 g (2 lb) winter bamboo shoots
2 slices root ginger
3 stalks spring onion
3 cloves garlic
90 ml (6 tablespoons) lard
7 ml (½ tablespoon) salt
225 g (½ lb) bean sprouts
22 ml (1½ tablespoons) soya sauce
30 ml (2 tablespoons) stock (b)
45 ml (3 tablespoons) dry sherry
pepper to taste
12 ml (¾ tablespoon) sesame oil

Remove the tough outer leaves of the bamboo shoots, cut away any roots, and chop the tender insides slantwise into small segments. Shred the ginger, and finely chop the spring onions and garlic.

Heat the lard in a large frying pan. Add the bamboo shoots and stir-fry over a medium heat for 1 minute. Leave to fry for 5 minutes. Pour away any excess fat. Sprinkle the bamboo shoots with the salt, stir a few times and remove with a perforated spoon.

Put the ginger, garlic and spring onion in the pan. Turn the heat to high, and mix the ingredients around a few times. Add the bean sprouts. Sprinkle with the soya sauce, stock, sherry and pepper. Stir this over a high heat for 1 minute. Return the bamboo shoots to the pan, sprinkle with sesame oil, fry for 1 minute and stir-fry for 1 minute more.
Serves 6–8.

Braised Stuffed Mushrooms
(Adapted from the Hsing Hua Inn, Mule and Pony Market, Chengtu.)

15 large Chinese dried mushrooms
2 eggs
30 ml (2 tablespoons) cornflour
225 g (½ lb) chicken breast
50 g (2 oz) lean-and-fat pork
5 ml (1 teaspoon) salt
30 ml (2 tablespoons) vegetable oil
45 ml (3 tablespoons) lard

Sauce

45 ml (3 tablespoons) chicken stock (b)

30 ml (2 tablespoons) soya sauce

30 ml (2 tablespoons) dry sherry

2 slices root ginger

15 ml (1 tablespoon) chicken fat

7 ml (½ tablespoon) cornflour

(blended in 45 ml (3 tablespoons) water or stock)

15 ml (1 tablespoon) hoisin sauce

30–45 ml (2–3 tablespoons) coarsely chopped Yunnan ham

30 ml (2 tablespoons) coarsely chopped spring onion

10 ml (2 teaspoons) sesame oil

Choose the mushrooms carefully so that they are of even size and shape. Soak them for 30 minutes and remove the stalks. Beat the egg with the cornflour, rub half the mixture inside the mushroom caps.

Mince the chicken and pork finely and add the salt and the remaining half of the egg and cornflour mixture. Divide the chicken and pork mix into 15 portions, shape each portion into a small ball and press each ball to the inside of a mushroom. Press the stuffing flat, ensuring that the meat is well stuck to the mushrooms. Brush the top of the meat with oil.

Heat the lard and remaining oil in a large flat frying pan. Place the stuffed mushrooms, one by one, stuffed-side down in the hot fat of the pan. Sauté over a medium heat for 3 minutes. Using a fish slice, turn over the stuffed mushrooms. Continue to sauté over a low heat for 5 minutes.

Meanwhile, prepare the sauce in a smaller pan by heating the chicken fat over a medium heat, then add the ginger, stock, spring onion, soya sauce, hoisin sauce, sherry and ham. Stir over a high heat for 45 seconds. Add the cornflour mixture and stir until the sauce thickens. Sprinkle the sauce with sesame oil.

Transfer the stuffed mushrooms one by one on to a well-heated level dish. Pour the sauce from the pan over each of the mushrooms, and serve. It is an easier dish to prepare than it sounds, but it is always effective. The usual way of arranging the mushrooms on the dish is to arrange 5 mushrooms stuffed-side up, ringed by 10 mushrooms stuffed-side down.

Serves 6–8.

Plain Boiled Tou-Fu (Bean Curd) with Hot-Sauce Dressing

2 cakes bean curd

Dressing

30 ml (2 tablespoons) sesame paste (or peanut butter)
45 ml (3 tablespoons) best quality soya sauce
30 ml (2 tablespoons) stock (b)

10 ml (2 teaspoons) chilli sauce
15 ml (1 tablespoon) hoisin sauce
30 ml (2 tablespoons) sesame oil

Place the bean curd in boiling water in a pan, and simmer gently for 5–6 minutes. Drain completely, and cut each piece of bean curd into quarters.

Mix the ingredients for the dressing until well blended.

Arrange the pieces of hot bean curd on a serving dish and pour the cold dressing over them.

Serves 6–8.

Bean Curd in Hot Peppery Soup

2 cakes bean curd
vegetable oil for semi-deep-frying
1 breast of chicken
22 ml (1½ tablespoons) cornflour (blended in 90 ml (6 tablespoons) water)
6 crisp lettuce leaves (or Chinese cabbage)

750 ml (1½ pints) stock (b)
12 ml (2½ teaspoons) salt
2.5 ml (½ teaspoon) freshly ground white pepper to taste
22 ml (1½ tablespoons) vinegar (Chinese aromatic, if available)

Put one cake of bean curd into boiling water to simmer for 5–6 minutes; drain and cut it into 10–12 pieces. Cut the other bean curd into 10–12 pieces. Deep-fry these for 3½ minutes and then drain. Place in cold water to rinse.

Chop and finely mince the chicken and mix thoroughly with the blended cornflour. Cut each lettuce leaf slantwise into 4 pieces.

Heat the stock in a saucepan. Pour in the chicken and cornflour mixture and stir until it is well dispersed throughout the stock (if inclined, add a little milk to whiten the soup). Now add the lettuce leaves and the boiled and fried bean curd pieces. When the contents are simmering, add the salt, pepper and vinegar. Stir and simmer gently for 5–6 minutes.

Serve in a large soup bowl or tureen. The hot peppery soup, contrasting with the blandness of the bean curd, and the fresh green vegetables, makes an interesting 'semi-soup' dish.
Serves 6–8.

Ma Po Tou-fu

This nationally well-known dish was invented in the reign of Emperor Tung Chi (1862–75) of the Manchu Dynasty by the wife of one Chen Ling-fu, a well known chef in Chengtu. The lady had a badly pock-marked face; hence the name, Tou-fu of the Pock-Marked Wife.

3 cakes bean curd
30 ml (2 tablespoons) salted black beans
3 stalks spring onion
3 cloves garlic
4 chilli peppers
45 ml (3 tablespoons) vegetable oil
225 g (½ lb) minced beef

5 ml (1 teaspoon) salt
150 ml (10 tablespoons) strong stock (b)
15 ml (1 tablespoon) cornflour
22 ml (1½ tablespoons) soya sauce
2.5 ml (½ teaspoon) freshly ground pepper

Simmer the bean curd in boiling water for 3 minutes. Drain and cut each cake into a dozen pieces. Soak the black beans in water for 20 minutes, then drain them. Cut the spring onions into small segments, crush and coarsely chop the garlic, and shred the peppers (discarding the pips).

Heat the oil in a large frying pan. Add the beef, salt and black beans. Stir and mash the black beans with the beef for 3–4 minutes. Add the pepper, spring onions and garlic. Turn them together for 2 minutes over a medium heat. Add half the stock and the bean curd; mix this with the other ingredients in the pan and leave it to cook for 4–5 minutes over a medium heat.

Mix the remaining stock with the cornflour and soya sauce. Pour this over the ingredients in the pan. Turn the heat to high. Stir gently and turn the contents over a few times. Cook for 2–3 minutes. Sprinkle with pepper and serve with rice. To be authentic, the dish should be hot enough to bring beads of sweat to the brow even when consumed in winter!
Serves 6–8.

Noodles

Chungking Dan Dan Mein, or Plain-Tossed Economy Noodles

(From the Cheng Tung Dan Dan Mein Noodle Shop, Chungking.)

900 g–1.2 kg (2–2½ lb) noodles (spaghetti-shaped variety)

Sauce

90 ml (6 tablespoons) bean sprouts

15 ml (1 tablespoon) chilli sauce (or chilli oil)

30 ml (2 tablespoons) lard

30 ml (2 tablespoons) sesame oil

75 ml (5 tablespoons) good quality soya sauce

30 ml (2 tablespoons) stock (b)

45 ml (3 tablespoons) sesame paste (or peanut butter)

4 cloves garlic, crushed and finely chopped

60 ml (4 tablespoons) coarsely chopped spring onion

Boil the noodles for 5–6 minutes (or spaghetti for 15 minutes) and drain. Mix the sauce ingredients together thoroughly in a bowl.

Divide the sauce ingredients equally among 6 large bowls. Immediately after draining the noodles, put them in the bowls on top of the sauce. Sprinkle each bowl with chopped spring onions. Each diner tosses his own portion of noodles with its sauce and garnish. An economical but aromatic and highly satisfying dish.
Serves 6.

Sung's Sister-in-Law's Fish-Soup Noodles

According to legend this dish is so-called because when Emperor Chien-Lung of the Manchu Dynasty made his famous tour of the South, incognito, he was given a bowl of fish-soup noodles in a sampan. On enquiring who was the lady who cooked it, he was told the same was Sung. The term 'sister-in-law' is often employed in China to indicate kinship and domestic endearment. This recipe is from one Liu Fan-fa, chef of the Teacher and Friends Noodle Shop, Chengtu.

900 g (2 lb) carp

1.5 litres (3 pints) stock (b)

22 ml (1½ tablespoons) cornflour

1 egg

oil for deep- or semi-deep-frying (for the latter, 250 ml/½ pint)

900 g (2 lb) noodles (or spaghetti)

Soup

1.5 litres (3 pints) stock (b)
4 slices root ginger
10 ml (2 teaspoons) salt
225 g (½ lb) bamboo shoots
15 ml (1 tablespoon) dried
   shrimps

30 ml (2 tablespoons) soya
   sauce
2 chicken stock cubes
pepper to taste
15 ml (1 tablespoon) cornflour
   blended in 60 ml (4 tablespoons) water

For Tossing with Noodles

90 ml (6 tablespoons) coarsely
   chopped bean sprouts
60 ml (4 tablespoons) coarsely

chopped spring onion
45 ml (3 tablespoons) lard
45 ml (3 tablespoons) vinegar

Fillet the fish and retain the head, tail, skin and bones to boil in the stock with the ginger and 10 ml (2 teaspoons) salt for 45 minutes, for the soup. Remove solid ingredients with a perforated spoon. Cut the bamboo shoots into thin slices. Dice the fish fillets into small cubes. Rub these with salt and cornflour, and wet them with the beaten egg. Deep-fry the cubes for 75 seconds in hot oil and drain them.

Add the bamboo shoots, dried shrimps and soya sauce to the soup and simmer for 30 minutes. Finally add the stock cube, fish and pepper. Stir and simmer for 5 minutes more. Stir in the cornflour mixture. The soup is now ready.

Prepare the noodles in the usual way by boiling for 5–6 minutes for Chinese noodles or 12–15 minutes for spaghetti, and drain.

Divide the chopped bean sprouts and spring onion equally among 6 large Chinese rice or noodle bowls. Put the drained noodles on top, and pour in enough fish soup to cover.
Serves 6.

Three Yunnan Specialities

Simmered Pork with Soup

1.35 kg (3 lb) belly of pork

Sauce

15 ml (1 tablespoon) sesame oil
45 ml (3 tablespoons) good

quality soya sauce
7 ml (½ tablespoon) chilli sauce

Garlic-and-Ginger Oil (makes 30 ml/2 tablespoons)

2 slices root ginger   30 ml (2 tablespoons) vegetable
2 cloves garlic   oil

Soup

12 ml (¾ tablespoon) salt   30 ml (2 tablespoons) chopped
                                                      spring onion

Cook the pork in boiling water for 10 minutes. Drain and cut it
into chopstick-thick, longish slivers. Prepare the garlic-and-ginger
oil by heating the slices of ginger and adding the garlic (crushed)
in the vegetable oil. Blend this mixture with soya sauce, chilli sauce,
and sesame oil.

Heat 1.5 litres (3 pints) water in a large heavy saucepan. Add the
pork slivers and simmer gently for 1¼ hours, when the liquid in the
pan should be reduced by a quarter. Drain the pork. Skim the soup
for any excess fat.

While the pork is still hot, pour the sauce mixture over it and
serve. At the same time divide the salt and chopped spring onion
among 6–8 bowls. Pour the soup into the bowls and serve. A good
savoury-and-soup course to start a meal with.
Serves 6–8.

Quick-Fried Sliced Ham with Spring Onion

450 g (1 lb) Yunnan ham (or   225 g (½ lb) bamboo shoots
    York ham)   60 ml (4 tablespoons) lard
6 stalks large firm spring onions 7 ml (½ tablespoon) sugar

First cut the ham into medium-sized thick slices, and then cut each
piece lengthwise into matchstick-sized strips. Cut the spring onions
into longish segments, and the bamboo shoots into similar-sized
strips.

Heat the lard in a large frying pan. When hot add the ham and
bamboo shoots and stir over a high heat for 30 seconds, then add
the spring onion, and stir and turn for 20 seconds. Sprinkle the
contents with sugar, and stir and turn for a further 10 seconds.
Serve immediately on a well-heated dish. A simple, quick-to-cook
but effective recipe.
Serves 4–6.

Yunnan Escalope

(This recipe is over 100 years old, and is considered one of Yunnan's delicacies.)

1.2 kg (2½ lb) leg of pork
2 ml (½ teaspoon) salt
1 ml (¼ teaspoon) five-spice powder
37 ml (2½ tablespoons) soya sauce
30 ml (2 tablespoons) dry sherry
3 eggs

45 ml (3 tablespoons) flour
30 ml (2 tablespoons) cornflour
250 ml (½ pint) vegetable oil for semi-deep-frying
15 ml (3 teaspoons) sea salt
5 ml (1 teaspoon) black pepper
60 ml (4 tablespoons) stock (b)

Cut the pork into 4 pieces, and boil gently for 15 minutes. Drain and cut the meat into long, wide, thin strips. Place these in a bowl and add the salt, five-spice powder, soya sauce, and sherry to season and marinate for 20 minutes. Transfer the pork into a pan, heat gently for 20 minutes and turn over every 5 minutes. Remove the pork from the pan, drain and leave to cool.

Beat the egg with the flour and cornflour into a batter. Coat the pork with the mixture.

Heat the oil in a large frying pan. When hot—but not boiling hot—add the pork piece by piece to slow-fry over a medium heat for 6–7 minutes, turning it over twice. Remove the pork with a perforated spoon. After draining on absorbent paper, cut each piece of pork lengthways into 4 strips, and arrange them on a well-heated dish.

Heat the sea salt and pepper in a dry pan over a medium heat for 2 minutes and stir them into an aromatic 'salt and pepper mix'. Sprinkle this over the escalopes on the dish.

Serves 6–8.

Glossary of Chinese Ingredients

Abalone: a kind of shellfish with a highly savoury meat of distinct flavour. Used in soups, stews, or stir-fried dishes. Available dried or canned (in California fresh). If stir-fried it should only be cooked for a very short time otherwise the meat immediately becomes tough. Used more often as a flavourer than eaten by itself.

Aromatic Ground Rice: coarsely ground grains of rice which have been quickly roasted, or stir-fried on a dry pan until they become somewhat aromatic. It is used much as breadcrumbs are in the West.

Aromatic Vinegar: there are many brands of vinegar in China, mainly named after the localities in which they are produced. Some of them are distinctly aromatic.

Bamboo-Shoots: not to be confused with bean-sprouts. A bamboo shoot can have a diameter of several inches. The smallest are about the size of asparagus tips. They are used in Chinese cooking mainly for their crunchy texture. Their flavour is distinct but extremely subtle, and can be appreciated only by the connoisseur.

Bamboo-Shoots, Winter: bamboo-shoots which have sprouted in the winter—supposedly more tender, certainly in shorter supply and rarer than in the spring.

Bean Curd: bean curd is produced by boiling ground soya beans in water, and allowing the milk produced to settle into a curd by adding small amounts of catalysts. The curd is practically tasteless; it acquires flavour through cooking with other ingredients, or when sauces are added. It is a highly nutritious substance, and is used extensively in China in mixed dishes. Sold in small cakes (fresh) or canned.

Bean-Curd Cheese: fermented bean curd which has a strong cheesy flavour. Often used for flavouring, or eaten in small quantities with congee (rice-gruel) at breakfast time.

Bean-Curd Cheese, Red: similar to the Bean-curd Cheese except red on the outside.

Bean-Curd Skin: the skin of bean-curd milk corresponds to the skin of ordinary milk. It is usually supplied in dried form, when it is quite a hard substance, and needs to be soaked before being used for cooking. It is used for Chinese vegetarian cooking.

Bean Paste, Salted: ground salted black beans in paste form. Used often in the cooking of meats when a thicker sauce than soya sauce is required.

Bean Paste, Sweet: ground bean paste with sugar added, usually black in colour. Usually used for stuffing sweet pancakes or sweet dumplings.

Bean-Sprouts: fresh sprouts of mung beans, used as a vegetable.

Bêche de Mer: also called sea-cucumber, or sea slugs. A plant or animal, the shape of a small cucumber, which is found on the bottom of the sea. It is usually supplied dried, and needs to be soaked for at least 48 hours before it is used in cooking.

Black Beans: salted and partly fermented soya beans, black in colour. Used frequently in small amounts as a flavouring for both meat and fish dishes.

Brown Bean Paste: similar to salted bean paste, but brown in colour. Used in the same way as black bean paste.

Green Beans, Dried: small green beans which are mostly cooked with rice in sweet rice-gruels (or sweet congees).

Red Beans, Dried: a variety of small Chinese beans used in a very similar manner to green beans, usually as an ingredient when cooking with rice into sweet congees or sweet rice-gruels.

Cha Shao Pork: the Cantonese way of cooking pork by barbecue-roasting, ie, roasting marinated pork by hanging strips of it in the oven over a high heat for a short period of time. The cooking can also be done by barbecuing the strips of pork over an open charcoal fire.

Chilli Oil: hot-tasting oil, produced by frying chopped dried chilli pepper in a small amount of oil.

Chilli Sauce: this is the same thing as Tabasco, a hot-tasting sauce which may be bought bottled. Used in cooking or placed on the table in the form of a dip.

Chinese Cabbage: or Chinese Celery Cabbage—a variety which is grown and used extensively in north China and in appearance looks a cross between a celery and a cabbage. Can be used in cooking or for salads. It is very crunchy and slightly sweet in flavour.

Chrysanthemum Flowers: the petals of chrysanthemums are often scattered over cooked dishes or hotpots as a garnish.

Crab Eggs: the orange-red-coloured eggs which are usually found in clusters under the main shell of the crab. Used often as an ingredient when cooking vegetables and soups.

Duck, Smoked: smoked duck dishes are usually dishes where smoking forms part of the process of cooking, usually done over burning tea, sugar, camphor wood, etc, in a confined space for a period of 10–15 minutes. Afterwards the cooking is often continued by roasting or deep-frying.

Five-Spice Powder: a cocoa-coloured combination of ground dried anise, anise pepper, fennel, cloves and cinnamon. Very strong in flavour and must be sparingly used.

Five Spices, Mixed: the same ingredients as five-spice powder, but unground. Not as strong as the ground variety, normally used in stews.

Frogs: frogs are called 'field chickens' in China and are cooked in much the same manner as chicken.

Garlic and Ginger Oil: oil in which garlic and root-ginger have been fried. Usually prepared in the kitchen in small quantities by stir-frying a few teaspoons of ginger and garlic in a few tablespoons of oil for a short period of time.

Golden Needles: (or tiger lily buds) come in dried form as brown-yellow-coloured strips. They are used by the Chinese in stews or steamed dishes.

Hoisin Sauce: a thick dark brownish-red soya-based vegetable sauce into which some garlic, chilli and other spices have been added. Can be used in conjunction with soya sauce for cooking meats, fish or vegetables, or as a condiment (dip) on the table.

Lotus Nuts: the nuts of lotus flowers, about 1 cm ($\frac{1}{2}$ in) in diameter and white in colour. They are subtle in flavour, and used mostly in braised, steamed, or stewed dishes, or in soups.

Lotus Roots: the roots of the lotus, about $\frac{1}{2}$ metre (1–1$\frac{1}{2}$ ft) in length and 5 cm (2–3 in) in diameter, with several holes extending the length of the root. When cut in slices it is used in stewed dishes, or in vegetable dishes. When fresh it is used as an ingredient in sweet dishes.

Lotus Seeds, Candied: used in sweet dishes (eg, Eight-treasure-Rice).

Malt Sugar: it is like barley sugar, and is used in preference to ordinary sugar in marinades.

Mushrooms, Dried: the Chinese seldom use fresh mushrooms and the dried variety are used practically all the time. They need to be soaked for 20–30 minutes in water before using (the stalks are usually too tough for use even after soaking, and should be discarded). They have a much firmer texture than fresh mushrooms, and contain and impart much more flavour.

Oyster Sauce: a highly savoury sauce made from oysters, often used when cooking with beef, or for flavouring vegetables.

Pea-Starch Noodles: they are also often called transparent noodles. Their distinctive characteristic is that they do not become mushy even after prolonged cooking. They are generally used in soups, or cooked with meat in stews where they absorb all the meat gravy. Excellent with rice.

Pickles, Salted: Cantonese salted pickles are salted green vegetables often used in making Cantonese soups.

Pickles, Snow: are green salted pickles extensively used chopped and stir-fried with minced meats, and also for garnishing noodles, or any plain-cooked foods. Usually bought in cans.

Pickles, Szechuan: are called Cha Tsai. They are hot in flavour, and when shredded are often used with shredded meats to intensify the hotness in a dish.

Pickles, Winter: usually come in jars. Yellowish-brown in colour, they are very savoury and can be used as an ingredient in fish, meat and mixed-fried dishes.

Plum Sauce: a sweet sauce the colour and texture of apple sauce. Very useful as a dip for crispy food, or foods which have a high fat content.

Rice Flour: flour made from finely ground rice. Normally used for making rice-flour noodles.

Rice, Glutinous: this is normally used for making sweet rice dishes and puddings.

Rice, Red: a red-coloured powder, normally used as food-colouring.

Rice-Gruel: this is not a rice pudding, having a much larger proportion of water in it. It is used by the Chinese mainly as a breakfast food or when only a light meal is required, (eg midnight supper). Because it is very bland it is usually consumed with a small amount of salted or pickled food.

Root-Ginger, Fresh: this looks like a gnarled piece of root, a few inches long. It is used by cutting off thin slices which are cooked with other ingredients. It is cooked extensively with fish and sea-foods to reduce their fishy flavour, and will reduce rankness in game.

Sea Clams: thick-shelled seafood, normally first poached and then used with other foods.

Sesame Oil: a vegetable oil used extensively in China, often for giving a nutty flavour by simply adding a drop or two on top of soups etc. Seldom used in quantity, as it is an expensive substance.

Sesame Paste: a paste made from ground sesame seeds, which has much the taste and character of peanut butter. Often used in China for making sauces.

Sesame Seeds: a Middle East product used extensively in China for dusting cakes and buns to make them aromatic.

Shark's Fin: these are usually purchased dried and need several days' soaking in water, and many hours' simmering in stock, before being used in cooking. It is a very expensive substance these days. Dishes cooked with sharks' fins are generally regarded as special dishes and served only at banquets.

Shrimp Sauce: a sauce made with shrimps which give it a strong savoury flavour. It should be sparingly used, normally on noodles and in mixed vegetable dishes.

Shrimps, Dried: small dried shrimps which are often used as flavour-ing, particularly of soups. They have a strong salty flavour. Only a few need to be added to vary the flavour of bone or meat stock. They can also be fried in oil to produce a flavoured oil which can in turn be used to flavour other foods.

Soya Dips: small saucer-sized dishes of soya sauce placed on the table for use as condiments (or dips). It is the Chinese tradition to dip foods rather than pour sauces over food in diners' personal bowls or plates.

Soya Chilli-Dip: Soya-Shredded Ginger Dip: Soya-Vinegar Dip: Soya-Garlic-and-Chives Dip: various dips which use soya sauce as a base with other ingredients mixed into it.

Star Anise: a small, dry, brown seed or clove which has the shape of a starfish. Used in Chinese cooking for flavouring stews.

Sugar-Cane Juice: juice extracted from sugar-canes by crushing them in a press.

Swallow Skins: a dough-skin from the province of Fukien, which is made by pounding flour, cornflour and minced meat together. Used for wrapping small dumplings.

Water Chestnuts: the root of a round-shaped water-plant.

Winter Melon: large round melon, green and tough on the outside. Delicate and pulpy-white inside. Can be stir-fried as a vegetable, or used as an ingredient in a soup. At banquets soups are often served, steamed, inside a winter melon shell.

Wontun Skin: thin sheets of dough which are used for wrapping small wontun dumplings for soups.

Wood Ears: mushroom-type of fungi which grow like ears on trees. Used mostly in mixed-ingredient dishes to give variation in texture.

Yunnan Ham: like York ham, Chinese hams are often named after the locality where they are produced. Yunnan Ham is one of the two or three most famous brands of ham produced in China.

Spirits and Wines

Kaoliang: a grain wine produced and drunk mostly in north China. Similar in appearance to gin or vodka but stronger.

Mei Kwei Lu: or Rose Dew; a fragrant spirit. Although it sounds somewhat dainty and feminine, it is in fact very potent.

Mow Tai: a clear distillation from west China, which became famous after Premier Chou En-lai used it when entertaining President Nixon in 1972. Very potent.

Shao Hsing Wine: or Yellow Wine, made from rice, which is universally drunk in China.

Wine Lee: the sediment of wine which has settled at the bottom of a wine jar. Used in China as an ingredient for cooking (mostly in fish and seafood dishes).

Stocks

Chinese Stocks are produced largely in the same manner as Western stocks. Apart from boiling bones, carcases and meat together for a prolonged period of time, for the sake of variation in flavour the Chinese often add such items as shrimp-shells (including heads and tails) and for superior stocks, small amounts of ham or beef. One ingredient which is added to most Chinese stocks is a few slices of root-ginger; this has the effect of reducing fishiness, rankness, or any chemicalized taste there may be in seafood, game or battery-produced' poultry.

For the very best stock, used for high-quality soups and semi-soup dishes, stocks which have been produced by prolonged cooking will often have freshly chopped or minced chicken added. These are allowed to cook in the stock for just a few minutes, and then carefully strained away through muslin or a filter. This last addition of fresh meat is said to add a new life and freshness to the stock, making it somewhat sweeter when originally it had only the quality of richness.

In China stocks are divided roughly into three categories:

a) *Secondary Stock:* where only a chicken carcase and pork bones are used, simmered in water with a few slices of root-ginger for a time of 2 hours upwards. Salt only is used as a seasoning.

b) *Primary or Good Stock:* where, in addition to carcase and bones, a certain amount of lean pork is added (say 225 g ($\frac{1}{2}$ lb) to 1 litre (2 pints) water). Here a small amount of soya sauce is also added to season the stock (15–30 ml 1–2 tablespoons).

c) *Superior Stock:* here for 1.25 litres (2$\frac{1}{2}$ pints) Primary Stock 100–225 g ($\frac{1}{4}$–$\frac{1}{2}$ lb) finely minced chicken is added to the stock to simmer for 4–5 minutes before being filtered away, thus producing a finished stock which is not only rich, but sweet and fresh as well.

Specialist Suppliers

Aberdeen	Quality Food Products (Aberdeen) Limited Craigshaw Place West Tullos Industrial Estate Aberdeen
Birmingham	Wing Yip Supermarket 96 Coventry Street Birmingham
Bournemouth	The Delicatessen 162 Old Christchurch Road Bournemouth BJ1 1NU Dorset
	Taj Mahal Stores 216 Old Christchurch Road Bournemouth Dorset
Bradford	Quality Foods 794–796 Leeds Road Bradford Yorks
Bristol	Wah Hing Mini Market 148 Ashley Road Montpelier Bristol
Cardiff	Far East Emporium 62–64 Tudor Road Cardiff
Colchester	Golden Crown Oriental Supplies 37 Crouch Street Colchester Essex
Coventry	Alma Coventry Limited 89 Lower Precinct Coventry

Dover	John Mann Supermarket 45 High Street Dover Kent
Edinburgh	Edinburgh Chinese Company 26 Dublin Street Edinburgh EH3 6NN
Glasgow	Chung Ying Supermarket 63 Cambridge Street Glasgow G3
Grantham	Chong Kee 2–6 Manthorpe Road Grantham Lincs
Hull	Sui Hing Supermarket 22–23 Story Street Hull Humberside
Leeds	Hong Kong Stores 29 Lady Lane Leeds 2
Leicester	Sabat Bros 26–28 Cork Street Leicester 4E5 5AN
Liverpool	Ghung Wah Trading 31–32 Great George Square Liverpool L1
London West End	Loon Moon Supermarket Ltd 9A Gerrard Street London W1V 7LJ
	Great Wall Supermarket 31–37 Wardour Street London W1
	Loon Fung Chinese Supermarket 39 Gerrard Street London W1
	Chung Ying Supermarket 6 Lisle Street London WC2
	See Woo Hong 19 Lisle Street London WC2

Walton Cheong Leen Ltd
4–10 Tower Street
Cambridge Circus
London WC2H 9NR

London Suburbs   Lees Emporium
2F Dyne Road
Off Kilburn High Road
London NW6

Hoo Hing Catering Supplies
412 Green Street
Upton Park
London E13

Eastyle Ltd
11–12 Romford Shopping Hall
Market Place
Romford Essex

Good Companions Chinese Supermarket
230 High Street
Croydon Surrey

Patel Grocers
33 Fife Road
Kingston upon Thames
Surrey

Asian Food Centre
175–177 Staines Road
Hounslow Middx

Bargain Grocers
61 The Broadway Market
Tooting Broadway
Tooting SW17

Manchester   Woo Sang & Company
19–21 George Street
Manchester 1ML 4HW

Wing Yip Supermarket
45 Faulkner Street
Manchester M1 4EE

Wing Hing Loon Supermarket
46 Faulkner Street
Manchester M1

Newcastle	Wing Hing Loon Supermarket 87–89 Percy Street Newcastle upon Tyne 1
Northampton	Gill Bros & Company Limited Trading as—Continental Food Supply 166 Kettering Road Northampton
Nottingham	Wah Yan Company 77 Mansfield Road Nottingham
Oxford	Palms Delicatessen The Market Oxford
Plymouth	Continental Fruiterers 148 Cornwall Street Plymouth P11 1RQ Devon Wah Lung Supermarket 95 Mayflower Street Plymouth Devon
Portsmouth	Eastern Stores 214 Kingston Road Portsmouth
Sheffield	Kung Heng Co 169 London Road Sheffield
Southampton	Yau Food Store 62 Park Road Freemantle Southampton Taj Mahal 69 Derby Street Southampton

Index